New Paradigms For College Teaching

edited by

Wm. E. Campbell
University of Wisconsin at River Falls

Karl A. Smith
University of Minnesota

Interaction Book Company
7208 Cornelia Drive
Edina, Minnesota 55435
Phone: (612) 831-9500
Fax: (612) 831-9332

Address orders to:

Interaction Book Company
7208 Cornelia Drive
Edina, Minnesota 55435
Phone: (612) 831-9500
Fax: (612) 831-9332

Table of Contents

Introduction

William E. Campbell

Bill Campbell has taught philosophy and directed academic assistance and honors programs at University of Wisconsin-LaCrosse, Western Illinois University, and University of Minnesota, Morris. He is currently Director of Grants and Research at University of Wisconsin-River Falls. His E-mail address is <wm.e.campbell@uwrf.edu>.

Some years ago I asked Toby Fulwiler to lead a writing-across-the-curriculum workshop for the faculty of the college where I worked. I had participated in two Fulwiler workshops and we had become friends. A course I was teaching conflicted with Toby's first session, so after I helped him set up his overhead projector I excused myself. "I have to prepare a lecture for this afternoon's class," I said. Toby replied, with a smile, "are you still lecturing? I guess it's okay, if you don't care whether or not your students learn anything." I laughed (a little ruefully, I confess) and went off to write my lecture.

But his comment rankled, so I decided to try a writing-across-the-curriculum experiment. Instead of lecturing on the content of the chapter I had asked my students to read—my original plan—I asked them to write for five minutes on the three most important points in the chapter. Then they reported, one by one, on what they had written. Their lists were all somewhat different, but taken together with the discussion which followed, they neatly summarized the chapter. I asked a follow up question here and there, added some historical perspective and suggested a few additional connections, but the students did most of the work. They covered exactly the same material I would have covered, but they used their own examples, raised their own objections, and had a much livelier discussion than any we had previously enjoyed.

The net result was an excellent class, from everyone's perspective. I covered the material I wanted to cover that day. The students internalized a reasonable summary of that material. The two or three students who had not read the assignment were deeply embarrassed. I didn't get to show off quite as much as I like, but my pleasure in a good discussion and engaged students was recompense enough.

That day changed my teaching forever. Even though I had been a part of a couple of Toby's workshops before and had even incorporated some of the teaching-across-the-curriculum methods in my courses, I was teaching for the most part just as my instructors in graduate school had taught: standing in the front of the room and telling my students the truth. On that day I learned that, no matter how satisfying it is to tell my students the truth, it's not a very effective way to help them learn.

Karl Smith tells a similar story. He began his career teaching as he had been taught, through lectures. After a few years he realized that it wasn't working very well. As a conscientious faculty member, he cast about for alternatives. His breakthrough came through a workshop on cooperative learning led by David and Roger Johnson. He began using cooperative learning techniques in his classes and found that his students were more engaged, more interested, and learned more than if he did nothing but lecture. What's more, he was having more fun.

Since our first introductions to writing-across-the-curriculum and cooperative learning, we have both attended many workshops and learned a variety of exciting ways to teach. (We both enjoy more freedom to do that sort of thing than most faculty. I have been a full-time administrator for many years, with some faculty development responsibilities and a modest travel budget. I teach only occasionally, alas. Karl consults widely, leads workshops on cooperative learning and other topics, and has become an authority on teaching improvement.) Both of us wish that we had become acquainted with these ways of teaching much earlier in our teaching careers.

Hence this book. We hope that it will be read by college and university faculty within the first few years of their teaching careers.

We hope that it will introduce them to alternatives to the traditional lecture method of teaching. We hope that each chapter will introduce readers to a new way of teaching, a new paradigm, which is intriguing enough to warrant further investigation. To that end, each chapter concludes with a list of references for further reading. In addition, most of the contributing authors give workshops on their topics. We encourage readers to participate in them as their time and budgets allow.

Why do we need new paradigms for college teaching? Because the old one doesn't work very well any more. Perhaps it did once, when the professor was the only one who had access to the relevant books and the students hung on his (it was almost always a male) every word. But today our students have access to the same books and other resources that we have. And—let's face it—few of our students are that interested in what we have to say. Most of the students in most of our classes are there for some other reason than interest in the material: they need the course to meet some requirement (e.g. general education distribution requirements, graduation requirements, certification requirements); it meets at a convenient time; it requires no math; their parents insisted that they take it; it was the only course available when they registered.

Does that mean that they are disinterested? Not at all. They are very interested in completing the requirements and being credentialed. But most of them are not particularly interested in philosophy or math or English or chemistry for its own sake. Faculty lounges are thick with complaints about today's students: they don't read, they can't think, they're only interested in getting ready for a job. I am convinced that the root of most of these complaints is that our students are different from us. They have not fallen in love with an academic discipline the way we did when we were in school and we hold them responsible for it. "When I was their age," we say, "I took my professors seriously, I listened to their every word. Why just this morning a student said my lecture was bogus, do you believe it? These students today, they just don't want to learn, how soon can I retire?"

So what else is new? Professors have struggled with not-very-interested students for a very long time. When I went to college and first started teaching, it didn't matter. In the growth years of the sixties and seventies we acted as if there were an inexhaustible supply of students. Our attitude was, if they're not interested, they can go away; we're here to teach the ones who care about our subjects. As a result, as many as a third of the first year students at large public institutions would fail to register for a second year. We have learned, to our sorrow, that we do not have an inexhaustible supply of students. As the population of 18 year-olds rises and declines, so do our enrollments. Retention of the students who have already enrolled has become important to our department chairs and deans and presidents and legislators.

Consequently, we can no longer aim our teaching solely at the students who are interested in what we have to say. That makes teaching much harder. When students hang on our every word, we don't have to worry about keeping their attention, about being relevant, about being inclusive—they will be interested enough to learn in spite of anything we might do. But when students are taking our courses only to fill out a graduation requirement or to earn three (relatively) painless credits on the way to graduation and a job, we have to work harder to make sure that they learn something. And helping students learn something, after all, is the primary responsibility of a teacher.

Fortunately, the interests of our department chairs and deans and presidents and legislators are congruent with an interest most of us share, at least to a degree. Most of us would like our students to succeed in their chosen endeavors and would be willing to help them—if only we knew how. But all most of us know how to do is lecture.

Is lecturing always bad? Certainly not. Karl Smith and I both lecture occasionally and, I daresay, successfully. But neither of us is good enough to lecture successfully all of the time. Very few teachers are. (I can think of two, among my many teachers. And both of them would have helped us learn more and better if they had encouraged more active learning, more collaboration, more reflection on the process.) In my experience, lectures work the best when students are prepared (that is, they have read the assigned material and thought about it at least a little), when I'm prepared (that is, I have thought about the points I want to make well enough to draft a lecture), and we're all interested in the same issues. How often does that happen? Not very often.

In most class meetings, only a few students are thoroughly prepared (and if they show it, it annoys their less-prepared colleagues—

a genuine disincentive to either prepare or perform). I am almost always well-enough prepared, but I am seldom interested in the same issues as my students: what will be on the test, how does this material affect my life, do I need to know this stuff for my major? And so, when I used to lecture every day, I would tell a few jokes to get their attention, scare them with dire warnings about the upcoming exam, and occasionally throw a tantrum (surprisingly successful, if not overdone).

But now I use some of the techniques described in the following chapters. I ask my students to write a little about a given topic and share what they have written with each other or with the whole class. Since they know I am likely to ask them to write, they usually prepare better. And writing for a few minutes helps us all to think about the same issues (and yes, every now and then the topic is what should be on the exam or why this material is important). Sometimes I lecture for a bit after these writing exercises, sometimes I ask the students to talk. In either case, the class almost always works better than when I spend the entire hour lecturing. The students learn more about the material, I learn more about what they still need to learn, and we all have a much better time.

Then why doesn't everyone do it? Well, there are disadvantages. I remember describing this writing-across-the-curriculum method to a burned-out colleague from the history department. She'd been telling me how awful her classes were, the students weren't learning anything, she was bored and cranky, it was a disaster for everyone. She thought the write-a-little, speak-a-little routine I described was worth a try, so I helped her implement it in one introductory class. All semester she would tell me how much everyone liked it: the students were more involved (and so was she), they were learning at least a little more, and they seemed much more interested in the material. I was very pleased. Next semester, I asked her how her classes were going. "They're awful," she said. "The students aren't learning, they hate me, I'm bored stiff and I hate them." I was amazed: "The writing-across-the-curriculum routines aren't working anymore?" "I had to give it up," she said. "I couldn't cover the material."

That is a problem. If you adopt writing-across-the-curriculum or cooperative learning or other techniques described in this book, you probably will not be able to cover the same amount of material as when you do nothing but lecture. Is that bad? If your prime responsibility is to your department, then it may be very bad. Some departments structure their curricula such that the introductory course is prerequisite for more advanced courses; if students have not covered certain topics in the first course they are lost later on. Those are usually the departments which use the introductory course to weed out large numbers of students so that their enrollments in advanced courses are manageable. When only a few students earn A's in the introductory course, the instructor has been a successful gate-keeper.

But if your primary responsibility is to your students, covering the material is not so important. You may decide that what students actually learn is more important than how much material you cover; that helping the students develop the tools to manipulate the information they learn is more important than the material itself; that encouraging the students to draw connections with what they are learning in their other classes is as important as whatever they learn in yours.

How much does the amount of material we cover really matter? In philosophy—my original discipline—we can still design a curriculum which will be largely relevant 25 or 50 years from now. Philosophy students will always read Plato and Aristotle, Hume and Kant, Russell and Wittgenstein. But few disciplines are like that. In most, the information we present to our students is obsolete within a few years. In some (e.g. computer science or biotechnology) it is obsolete within months. And even if the material we cover had lasting value, how much of it will our students remember? Not very much—especially if the information only passed through their minds between a lecture and an exam. If it had lasting value and they could remember it, how many would? Career counselors say that we change careers an average of four and a half times during our lifetimes. The specific information we learned in our major fields is mostly irrelevant after the first career change.

How many of us consciously adopted lecturing as our primary mode of teaching? Not very many, I think. Most of us started lecturing on the first day of class because that's what all of our teachers have always done. Besides, that's what they pay us for: being the authority, the sage, the one who knows all and tells some. And it's very satisfying to put together a coherent, tidy lecture: main point, subordinate points, illustrative examples, counterargument, counter-counterargument, any questions? See you tomorrow.

So satisfying—but, as Toby pointed out to me that day, the students don't learn the material very well. Why not? Perhaps because lectures are a distancing mechanism, a way of telling the students that we are different from them and we know more than they do. Graduate students respond in that sort of setting because they are desperate to be like us. But most undergraduates have a different ambition. So they tolerate our lectures, glean what they need from them, and dismiss us as irrelevant to their lives. And we stomp into the faculty lounge, complaining.

Why do we want to distance ourselves from our students? Perhaps because we are so different from most of them. We've always been successful at school, the smartest in the class. Our class-mates were athletic heroes or social successes. We were the stars in the classroom. So we earned undergraduate and graduate degrees and found teaching jobs in colleges and universities. We stayed in school, the place where we shine. But when we began teaching, we discovered that our classes are just like the ones we were part of as children. Only a few of our students want to be the smartest in the class; most shine elsewhere. So we distance ourselves. We stand, they sit; we talk, they listen; we think, they take notes.

But at the same time, we're dissatisfied. We know that our jobs are not only to be the sage, but to help our students learn. Even though we feel that we are different from them, we want them to like and respect and admire us. Most of all, we want to help them succeed. But we don't know how. The chapters in this book are meant to show us.

Parker Palmer tells us that the most important thing is to connect with our students and help them connect with the material we are teaching. Nel Noddings encourages us to connect through the use of stories. Wendy Bishop and Toby Fulwiler demonstrate how the braiding of voices—students and faculty intertwined—can help us connect with one another and can help us all learn. Craig Nelson attacks various taboos which drive most college teachers. Terry Collins shows us how to draw students into a course through an inclusively-written syllabus. Ed Nuhfer describes a classroom man-agement procedure which can help us measure how well we are con-necting with our students and how well they are learning. Don

Dansereau and Dianna Newbern explain how knowledge maps can help us teach when words fail us, when we are describing relationships which are not amenable to linguistic description. Tom Creed tells us how electronic communication (E-mail and the World Wide Web) can liberate us from the temporal and spatial constraints of the typical classroom. Karl Smith and Alisha Waller describe both the principles and particulars of cooperative learning—techniques which undergird many of the chapters in this book. David and Roger Johnson, gurus of cooperative learning, explain the value of structured controversies in drawing students into the learning process. Valerie Bystrom presents a variety of learning communities, wherein students are encouraged to draw connections between different courses and ways of thinking. Smith and Waller conclude with an overview of the changing paradigms of college teaching.

These paradigms are not really new. Teachers have been practicing them since students first gathered. In recent years, as faculty started to become conscious of their roles as teachers as well as professors, they have been discussed at conferences and in workshops and described in articles and books. Ken Eble's *The Craft of Teaching* (Jossey-Bass, 1972); Bill McKeachie's *Teaching Tips: A Guidebook for the Beginning Teacher* (D.C. Heath, 1986); Joseph Katz' (ed.), *Improving Teaching Styles,* volume 1 of Jossey-Bass' admirable *New Directions in Teaching and Learning* series; the succeeding volumes of that series; and other books and articles have summarized and detailed some of these paradigms. But descriptions of them have not, to our knowledge, been collected in a readily accessible form in one volume until now.

We encourage you to sample them all, read the ones you find intriguing, and apply the bits and pieces of technique which you think hold promise for you, in your particular teaching situation. But please read Parker Palmer's chapter first. Parker is eloquent and persuasive, as always. He makes one point which all of us should heed: *don't get caught up in the techniques of teaching!* Teaching techniques are helpful, says Parker, but they are only techniques. The best teachers are the ones who connect with their students, form a community with them. Some teachers can do that through lectures, others through small group exercises, still others through learning communities or mind maps or cooperative learning. The technique is less important than making the connection. Please use this book in that spirit: as a set of paradigms which may help you connect with your students and thereby become a better teacher.

A final note: When editing a volume of essays, one must balance between making the essays look and sound the same or letting each author have his own voice. We have edited lightly, so that the format is more or less consistent but the distinctive voices of each author or set of authors comes through. And so there is quite a range in voice, from the scholarly (Johnson & Johnson, Dansereau & Newbern) to the impassioned (Nelson, Nuhfer) to the conversational (Creed, Collins, Nodding). One chapter (Bishop & Fulwiler) braids several voices into an integrated whole.

The authors welcome your comments; E-mail addresses of those who have them precede most chapters. I welcome your comments as well.

The Renewal of Community in Higher Education

Parker J. Palmer

Parker Palmer received a Ph.D. in sociology at Berkeley during the 60's where he absorbed an appreciation for community. Today he is a writer, teacher, and activist who works independently on issues in education, community, leadership, spirituality, and social change. His work spans a wide range of institutions—universities, public schools, community organizations, religious institutions, corporations, and foundations. He travels widely in this country and abroad giving workshops, lectures, and retreats, and has often been cited as a master teacher. His most recent book is *The Active Life* (HarperCollins); a second edition of *To Know as We Are Known* (HarperCollins) has recently been published. A new book, *The Courage to Teach,* is forthcoming.

In November, 1995, Palmer gave the keynote address at a conference of annual faculty development conference of The Collaboration for the Advancement of Teaching and Learning in Bloomington, MN. The following is the talk he gave, lightly edited.[1]

When I was first invited to speak at this conference, the Bush Foundation was still the sponsoring organization. At some point the sponsorship changed, and I remember clearly the call I got one day from someone who identified herself as so-and-so from "The Collaboration." I thought, "This is really

---

[1]Videotapes of Palmer's address are available from The Collaboration for the Advancement of Teaching and Learning, 401 Galtier Plaza, Box 40, 175 5th St. East, St. Paul, MN, 55101-2901; (612) 228-9061; <collab@mnprivco.org>.

cool—this is just like Berkeley in the sixties!" Back then you would answer the phone and someone would say, in a hushed voice, "This is Susan from The Conspiracy..." So I thought, "I'm really glad I signed up for this conference!"

Well, even though this is *not* the same as Berkeley in the sixties, it's a wonderful collaboration, and it builds on a movement that is happening all across this country—a movement toward the renewal of teaching and learning, a movement that cares about students, that cares about the world, a movement that cares about all the connections that this word "community" suggests to us. I want to spend a little time this morning trying to talk about some of those connections, trying to offer some images and frames of both the theoretical and the practical sort that might support the probes of those of you who are on the front lines of the struggle to reform higher education.

The world is always with us, and this week it's with me in an especially painful way because of the assassination of Yitzhak Rabin. I'm still in the process of mourning that. And in an effort to use my grief creatively, I turned to some literature that I think is so important for higher education in the 20th century. It's the literature about the complicity of higher education in the Third Reich, the complicity of learned people and institutions of teaching and learning in the great evil of Nazi Germany.

I read about a group that has always inspired me, a group that was known as the White Rose. The White Rose had a short life—from 1941 until 1944—but it was a group of students from the University of Munich, finally joined by one of their professors, who took on the life-threatening task of publishing a newsletter that called for resistance to the evils of Nazism. I want to read their names to you because we need to remember them: Hans and Sophia Scholl, Christl Probst, Alex Schmorell, Willi Graf, Jurgen Wittenstein, Traute Lafrenz, and Kurt Huber. Most of them were executed by the Nazis for their resistance, but they lived and died as people who had overcome the profound deformations of the classical German form of higher education—deformations that we live with to this day—in order to stand as free women and men of conscience in a society not unlike our own that was filled with shadows. They transcended their education and spoke a voice of truth.

In reading about the White Rose, in trying to remember this history, I came across this quote, and I want to offer it as a way of framing our entry into the work of this conference. The quote is from a book called *Hitler's Death Camps* by Konnilyn Feig:

We have identified certain "civilizing" aspects of the modern world: music, art, a sense of family, love, appreciation of beauty, intellect, education... [But] after Auschwitz we must realize that being a killer, a family man, and a lover of Beethoven are not contradictions. The killers did not belong to a gutter society of misfits, nor could they be dismissed as just a collection of rabble. They were scholars, artists, lawyers, theologians and aristocrats.

We cannot assume that a traditional higher education in the humanities and the sciences will consistently yield justice or even humanity. Too much is missing in such a course of studies—we have a fair amount of evidence that traditional higher education does not always work towards such noble ends.

In preparing for this gathering, I asked myself *what* is missing in traditional higher education that makes it *not* a contradiction to know the great books and yet still to do evil, and the answer I came up with involves this conference.

The missing elements in the form of education that helped fuel the Third Reich were *community, diversity,* and larger forms of *social accountability*—the three emphases of this conference. Community, diversity and the kind of social osmosis that Lesley talked about a moment ago between higher education and the rest of the society—these were not a part of the elitist, tradition-bound, hierarchical, and objectivist forms of higher education that deformed people into the habits of evil and complicity with evil. In the context of this particular week in 20th century history and its tragic events, I don't know any better way of saying how important are the concerns that you are exploring in these two days together.

Before I dig in more deeply, let me say a word about each of these three themes: community, diversity, and larger forms of social accountability. Community is a tricky one, because a good case can be made that the Third Reich was one of the most powerful forms of community that has ever been known. There are forms of community that are more of the shadow than of the light, so we should not be using the word in a romantic way. We should be using it with great critical discernment.

Community can be sexism and community can be racism as well as forms of liberal democracy that enlarge and enlighten people's lives. But most of the forms of community that I see rising in our society do not have the qualities of light. I think most of the forms that are arising in our time are forms of community that exploit the phenomenon of the empty self, of people who lack a sense of identity—not least because education involves such a culture of judgment that it takes identity away rather than giving identity to people.

People without identity, educated or not, are very susceptible to forms of community that come along and say, "You want to know who you are? We'll tell you who you are. Here's the script you follow; here's what you should think; here's what you should believe; here's what you should feel. If you go along, you are one of us, and if you don't, you're among the damned." So let us not use the word community in a romantic way. The reminder of the Third Reich itself should remind us that community can partake of deep darkness.

The word "diversity" names one of the things we need in order to open community to its richer, more complex and life-giving forms. Diversity is precisely the quality that fascist community lacks. It is precisely in this inability to embrace diversity, difference, variety, to find in variety light and challenge and growth and energy, that community becomes demonic instead of life-giving.

I want to say just a little more about diversity before I move along because I'm troubled sometimes about how that gets translated. Let me take an example from outside of higher education which it may be a little easier for us to hear. I do a lot of work with church groups around the country, usually churches on the liberal, activist side of the spectrum. And one of the commonest complaints I hear is about "the homogeneous white congregation." But I have come to the conclusion that there is no such thing as a homogeneous white congregation. There's only a group of white people working very hard to keep their differences under cover, expending an enormous amount of energy to avoid those points of conflict that are already in their midst where something new might happen, something that would be challenging and demanding and frightful, but something that would open the door into the possibility of true community. When a community of white people is characterized by a systematic evasion of the differences that are already among them internally, why would anyone who bears an external difference ever want to join them—when that community can't even cope with the diversity that is already there?

I think you can draw your own parallels to the situation in higher education where we have too often cheapened this issue of diversity by saying "Let's try to get some folks who don't look like us to come here," only to leave those folks isolated, alone, without resources, without context, without support. Perhaps our first task is to learn to deal creatively with the differences that are already within us and among us and to create a community that meets the real test—which is the capacity to embrace the conflict that diversity always brings in creative and life-giving ways.

Third, and finally, in these prefatory notes, the whole issue of larger forms of social accountability, of osmosis between the semipermeable boundaries of higher education and the rest of the society, is another crucial strand in this nexus of moral and educational concerns that I think we all share. I'm thinking here about the value of service learning, of engagement with folks outside the academy. This is something that I learned a lot about a two years ago when I spent a year as a visiting professor at Berea College in Kentucky.

Some of you may know this fascinating institution that has a mission to the young people of Appalachia. You can't go to Berea College if your family can afford to send you to college. And Berea charges no tuition because many kids who end up there don't have a cent in the world. Berea College has one of the most remarkable service learning programs that I have ever seen called "Students for Appalachia." I found that if I wanted to find on that campus students who were moving beyond fear, who were learning to be at home in their own skins and at home in a complex world, the traditional classroom was not the place to find them. I went instead to the meetings of Students for Appalachia where a rich mix of cognitive insight and engaged experience was happening—and that's where these particular young people were being freed from all that constrains a young woman or a young man who has grown up in a "holler" in the Appalachian mountains. That was where the vitality was happening.

I don't think community can exist without boundaries. I think when we say we're in community we're automatically saying something about "us" and "them." But I think the key issue in community is how does that community relate to the stranger who is outside the boundaries. Do we avoid the stranger because we're afraid of the stranger? Do we kill the stranger because our fear has grown so deep that we don't know how to live with that otherness? Or do we do something that's deep in our spiritual tradition and deep in the liberal humanism that informs higher education—offer hospitality to the stranger, not simply for the stranger's sake, but for the sake of the largeness of our own lives?

That's what was happening in the service learning programs at Berea. Community was being enhanced by teaching young people to walk across the communal boundary and come back with a deeper sense of identity that is enlarged by creative encounter with the other, with the stranger.

I hope I've established a context of meaning for this conference at the level that I feel it in this particular week of our particular time—and in the work that you're committed to—around the three themes we are here to consider: community, diversity, and the connections between higher education and the larger world.

I want to offer a concrete model for such an education in a moment. But before I do so, I want to say just one more word, again in the spirit of trying to make creative use of my own grief about the assassination of Yitzhak Rabin, a word about my own educational experience vis-a-vis the Third Reich. I was taught in high school and college and in graduate school the history of Nazism by some very fine professors, probably some of the best objective historians this country has to offer. But I was taught that history in such a way that for many years I somehow felt that all of that—the murder of six million Jews, of God knows how many gay and lesbian people, gypsies, persons with mental retardation or physical disability, anyone who didn't fit the mold—that all of that had happened on another planet to another species. I've never known how to say that because it was a perception or intuition that had nothing to do with the words that were said to me in those courses.

None of my professors ever said "other planet, other species." They were not revisionists. But the feeling level of the information I got, my personal relation to that knowledge, was one of immense emotional distance. There were two things I never learned that I should have learned, things that I think are relevant to this conference. I never learned that the community that I grew up in—Wilmette, Illinois, on the north shore of Chicago—practiced its own systemic form of fascism in the 50s and the 60s. If you were a Jew in that part of the world, you lived in Glencoe. You didn't live in Winnetka, Wilmette or Evanston. You lived in a gilded ghetto called Glencoe which was sustained by systemic real estate practices that we all in one way or another collaborated with. I never learned that the big story of Nazi Germany intersected the little story of my own life. And my understanding of the little story of my own life was shallow and false as a consequence of that.

The second thing I never learned was that I have within me a little Hitler, a shadowy force, that will, when the difference between you and me becomes great—when your otherness from me becomes too challenging to my sense of identity or worth—this shadow force within me will find some way to kill you off. I won't do it with a gun or gas chamber, but I will do it with a word, a category, a dismissal of some sort, a kind of spiritual Nazism that renders you lifeless to my universe. "Oh, you're just a fill-in-the-blank—Republican, administrator, romantic, deconstructionist, or whatever." We do that kind of thing a lot in the academic community, and our study of history should help us move beyond it.

To be an educated person is to understand how the big story of the Third Reich can illumine and check and correct the little story of your own life. I've thought a lot about how that failed to happen for me. It didn't happen because any teacher ever said directly, "This has nothing to do with you." It happened because the data that we were offered were almost always the abstract words and numbers that served the purposes of objectivism—which is precisely the commitment to distancing the knower from the known, distancing the student from the field, in the service of "objective" truth.

In those courses, as far as I can recall, we never saw the art produced by the children who died in those camps; we never read the poetry written by the survivors; we never saw the photographs of the bodies piled up like cordwood. And I think the reason we never looked at those things is that all such data are too subjective to be entertained within the puristic assumptions of traditional higher education—the very same assumptions that led German higher education into complicity with great evil.

I think that what we're talking about during these three days is terribly important. And I would suggest that these remarks, although they come from deep feeling in me, have not overpainted the picture. I think what we are reflecting on is no less about life-and-death than some of my images may suggest.

Now, how does one put wheels on these concerns? How do you implement a commitment to community in higher education? I've never felt that a lecture of this sort is the place for a "how-to-do-it." But I have found that telling true stories from the real world can at least encourage us to believe that if real people in real space and time are doing something like this somewhere else, maybe we, in our space and time, could do it too. And so I want to construct in our midst here a little paradigm, a little model, that comes from a real story of the real world in higher education. Then I want to walk around it awhile and see, in a period of dialogue before we have to end, where it is that you might like to go with it.

Several years ago I was on the west coast at a major research university. I had talked for a couple of days in workshops and other formats about community in higher education. A man came up to me at the end of the last day and said, "I'd like to take you out for a meal and tell you my own story about community in higher education. I'm the dean of the medical school," he said, "and I think that we have accomplished something here that might interest you." So we went to dinner and he told me the following tale.

Six or eight years earlier some faculty and administrators of this particular medical school had begun to get very discouraged with the outcomes that medical education was having. They had young women and men coming into medical school with very high levels of compassion for patients and for human suffering—that's why they were there. But they followed the same curve, the dean said, as all of the other research that we read around the country, which indicates that two, three and four years later those high levels of compassion are almost gone. The very movement of the heart that had brought these young women and men to medical school had been crushed in the process of medical education itself. Then, he said, we wonder why too many doctors learn to behave like mercenaries, like people interested in nothing other than their own economic survival.

The dean said they were also very concerned about the failure of ethics in their program and in the practice of medicine itself. This school, along with other medical schools, frequently had the experience of a professor assigning an article on reserve in the library, and by the time the fifth or sixth student went to get it, it had been razored out of the book so that the cutter would have a competitive edge over those yet to come. With that kind of deformation, the dean said, we shouldn't really wonder why there's a lack of ethical behavior in the later years of medical practice.

In addition to the loss of compassion and the failure of ethics, they were concerned that the traditional model of medical education simply was not preparing young men and women for the rapidly evolving nature of the disciplines that go into the practice of medicine, where the information they get today is simply not valid tomorrow, where the need is not simply to have today's information, but to know how to generate the new information, to check it, to critique it, to research it, to do all of those things that a practicing scholar of a field has to know how to do.

And so, the dean told me, on the basis of those concerns they struggled for a couple of years to institute a new curricular and pedagogical model. He told me that the model had been invented at McMaster University in Canada, and then come down to Harvard, and then hop-scotched across the country to several places ending up at this particular west coast university.

To describe this model to you, the dean said, I want first to give you an image of traditional medical education. The image—which is an oversimplification but nonetheless has truth in it—is that through the first couple of years of med school, we kept those young people seated in rows in auditoriums while someone with a pointer in his hand standing on stage next to a skeleton hanging from a rack went through the bones and asked those students to memorize the connections. "The foot bone connected to the ankle bone, the ankle bone connected to the shin bone, the shin bone connected to the knee bone..." (I asked him if they ever got to, "...now hear the word of the Lord...," but he was not acquainted with the phrase so we moved quickly on!)

The dean said that for two years, these young women and men who came to medical school with a passion to know and to help whole persons, found those whole persons stripped down to the objectified skeletal form hanging from that rack—and then we wondered why two years later when they had their first clinical experience they tended to treat their patients as objects! Obviously their whole formation, or deformation, for two years had been the objectification of the patient herself or himself.

Now, he said, in this new model of medical education, which we adopted from McMaster, from day one the students are seated in small circles around a living patient with a real problem. They're trying to discern what's going on with this patient. They're trying to come up with a diagnosis, and ultimately with a prescription. There's a mentor seated in that circle to make sure that they don't do grievous harm to the patient in question. But the students themselves are learning to talk to this person, they're learning to discern what's going on with this person, they're learning to pick up clues from the patient, from their own hunches, and from each other, and the mentor is guiding them in that process.

From that central hub of the wheel, as it were, there are spokes in this curriculum that move outward so that students can go from that hub to a lecture hall where they get some information that's necessary to go back to the circle the next day and be more precise about their diagnosis; they move along another spoke to a laboratory; they move along another one to an independent research project or library study; along another one to a consultancy or a seminar. But always, at the core of their education, they are being asked to do the very thing that brought them to school in the first place—to be a doctor, even before they have the "book learning" for it, and that core experience drives them out into a whole variety of places where the knowledge and information necessary to function well at the core might be gained.

The dean said a very interesting thing about the students: "Of course, on one level, they don't know much. They may have had a pre-medical curriculum, but they've never been in a clinical situation. On that level they're really groping in the dark when they attempt to understand this patient at the center of the circle. But on another level they know a lot. They know a lot simply because they are human beings with bodies. They have had illness themselves, or they know people who have had illness. And they remember things, and they pick up things, and they intuit things. They know things in a bodily way, an experiential way, that prove to be very, very relevant in performing the task that's at the core of their medical education from day one."

The dean told me that when they first instituted this curriculum, it passed by the narrowest of margins. He said that the dissenting faculty made a prediction once the new curriculum had passed. They said that, yes, compassion levels would stay steady and maybe even go up because there's a real person at the heart of this way of learning to be a doctor. They predicted that ethical behavior would probably increase because that person at the center of the circle is a focus of accountability. You don't razor the article out of the book on reserve when you know that the reason that somebody needs to look at it is to help the next person they're going to see, and not just to beat you in a competition.

But, the dean said, the dissenting faculty predicted that despite all of those "fringe benefits," the worst possible thing would also happen: objective test scores would go down. And, he said, no field is more filled with objective testing than medicine.

Then he said, "Guess what?" Of course, I could guess, because in the academic community you don't take people out to dinner to tell them about your failures. "Not only have the test scores not gone down, but they've gone up. Every year since we've started practicing this curriculum [and it had been five years by then] the objective test scores have risen."

He and I then began a fascinating conversation about why it is that this form of community in higher education makes people smarter faster. And this is the image of education-in-community that I'd like to offer you, the concrete and practical image of educational community that goes beyond what the skeptics like to call "fringe values"—you know, "fringey" things like compassion and ethics and human decency! This form of educational community is also about people's capacity to grasp and understand and be able to employ complex, rigorous, demanding information in a way that makes them *smarter faster* than the old top-down objectivist models of higher learning can do.

There is a strong case for educational community that's based not only on human compassion, not only on ethical behavior, not only on our ability to be good citizens in a very difficult world—though God knows those arguments should suffice. But you can make an argument for community that's deeply connected to the core mission of higher education, the mission called knowing, teaching, and learning. I mean knowing, teaching, and learning around demanding and difficult things that range all the way from the humanities to the sciences to vocational subjects to making a difference in the world. You can make a case for education-in-community that is not only about affect but also about cognition, not only about the heart but also about the head, not only about ethics but also about information. Ultimately, it seems to me, this is the case we have to make if we want education-in-community to prevail.

Why is it that this communal model makes people smarter faster? Why is it, I asked the dean, that you have had such success with a form of education that everyone thought was simply about the soft stuff and not about the hard stuff at all? As I bring these remarks to a close, I want to make a few comments about what's underneath or behind this model.

It seems to me terribly important that when we look at a model like this, we not ask ourselves what I think is a dead-end question, which is, "How can we replicate this exact approach in our situation?" I don't think that's the issue here. I think the issue here is to understand the underpinnings of the model itself. How it is that knowing, teaching, and learning are enhanced, not just by a particular form of community, but by engendering a "capacity for connectedness?" Our challenge is not to reduce good teaching to a particular form, model, methodology, or technique, but to understand its dynamics at the deeper levels, the underpinnings, to understand the dynamics that make connectedness a powerful force for learning in whatever form it takes.

I want to make a brief parenthetical comment here, because the turning point I'm trying to make is to me very important, and I feel like I haven't said it very clearly yet: good teaching cannot be reduced to technique. Good teaching comes out of the identity and integrity of the teacher—as that identity and integrity find ways to create the capacity for connectedness that is the magic of this model.

Different teachers are going to create those connections in different ways. Different subjects are going to demand different ways of creating those connections. I'm very worried that we are so addicted to methodology, so captive to the tyranny of technique, to reducing all questions to matters of methodology, that, as the culture war starts to wane, we have merely replaced it with the methodology war, the pedagogy war. People who advocate collaborative learning are lining up against people who are devoted to lecturing as arch enemies, and vice versa.

I think that's fruitless nonsense. I think the standard we all ought to be held to is not our adherence to a particular teaching method, but rather how we are helping create this capacity for connectedness no matter what method we are using. That capacity is at the heart of the model that I've just offered you, and that capacity can be engendered by many different teaching methods—if the method emerges from the identity and integrity of the teacher.

Let me give you a concrete example from my education at Carleton College. (I know some Carleton folk are here, and I hope that I'm not embarrassing the college with what I am doing this morning!) I had a professor at Carleton who lectured non-stop. He just couldn't stop. He was so aflame with a passion for his subject that we would raise our hands with a question and he would say, "Wait a minute, I'll get to that later..." But later in the hour, later in the week, later in the month, later in the year, he still hadn't gotten to it—and now it's thirty years later and my hand is still up and he hasn't called on me yet! What that means, of course, is that my mind is still engaged with some of the things he was teaching about—a powerful testimony to his non-collaborative form of teaching!

This man taught the history of social thought, and it was absolutely extraordinary. He would stand over here and make a Marxist statement and argue for it vigorously while we were taking notes like crazy, and suddenly he'd get a quizzical look on his face and stand over there and argue with himself from an Hegelian standpoint! Years later, I understood: he didn't need us to be in community! Who needs eighteen-year-olds from the North Shore of Chicago when you're hanging out with Marx and Hegel?

I was the first person in my family to go to college. I had never seen such a model of the intellectual life, offered up with such passion and such rigor—and I wanted more than anything in the world to get into that world, the world this professor inhabited and carried inside of him. That was the incredible gift that he gave me—and, believe me, he was casting pearls before swine! There was no way for us at that time to understand what he and his life were all about, and yet some of us were awakened from our dogmatic slumbers and wanted to come into this engaged life of the intellect that also constitutes a capacity for connectedness.

This professor drew us into connectedness in the most remarkable and mysterious way—and had someone sat him down and said, "You *won't* get tenure unless you learn collaborative teaching techniques," the result would have been both grotesque and tragic, tragic both for him and for us. In talking about good teaching, we have to open the methodological questions into a wider and more generous way of honoring many modes of teaching, while asking the same question of all of them: how does this method help create the capacity for connectedness that's at the heart of a truly educated self?

So what is behind this medical school model? What is the infrastructure that supports students in getting smarter faster? I'll just tick off a few things, and then I want to open up a time for dialogue.

What's behind it, first of all, is that communal, connected methods of higher education simply reflect the web-like nature of reality in all of the fields we study. We came into this century with non-communal models of reality. We came into this century with a model from physics that imaged reality as constituted of little discrete "bits" called atoms floating around in the void—a model that has had tremendous power over the fragmentation of imagination in the twentieth century.

But that's not what physicists are telling us today about the nature of reality. One of my favorite professors at Carleton, Ian Barbour, quotes a physicist named Henry Stapp who says, roughly speaking, "You can no longer talk about atoms as if they were isolated discrete particles. You can now only image an atom as a set of relationships reaching out for other relationships." In systems thought, in ecology, in the Gaia hypothesis: wherever it is you want to look, both in orthodox and unorthodox science, community is the name of the very physical reality in which we are embedded.

I was at the University of Michigan a couple of years ago. I was giving a talk on community in higher education and noticed in the audience a very distinguished looking gentleman with a three-piece dark suit and long white hair. In the conversation period after my talk he arose and introduced himself as "the Distinguished Professor of Biology Emeritus." He used those very words, and I thought,

"I'm about to catch my lunch..." But in his comment, he said, "I don't understand what all this fuss about community in higher education is about. After all, he said, it's only good biology." And he sat down.

For a minute I thought I'd been attacked, and then I realized I had been supported and affirmed! He and I proceeded to have a dialogue about how the metaphors of biology have evolved from competition, and nature red in tooth and claw, and all of those images that fed Social Darwinism, into a new understanding of ecosystems, of collaborative living and dying. It's not that death is no longer happening out there, but that it's now understood as being in the service of larger life.

When we study things in ways that are not isomorphic with the things themselves, there's disconnect, there's dissonance, and the hidden curriculum isn't working on our behalf. In the disciplines that have most to do with our elemental condition, in physics and in biology, the very realities we study are best represented by communal models. If reality is communal we must teach and learn them in ways that are communal—that is one secret to helping people get smarter, faster.

My second point is that this kind of model of community in higher education also reflects our newest and deepest insights into epistemology, into how human beings know. The model that I was educated with was an epistemology of objectivism which insisted that in order to know truth, you must maintain a radical separation between the knower and the known—and that translated into radical separation between the student and the subject. But in every discipline I know about today, this objectivist epistemology, this epistemology of distance, is being challenged and changed. It's not just that such an epistemology is ethically deforming by removing us from the world we know—it's that such an epistemology simply does not describe how human beings have ever known anything! Human beings do not know things at a distance. Human beings know by holding together a very complicated paradox of the subjective and the objective, of the intimate and the removed.

Some of you know my favorite story along these lines—the story of the great biologist Barbara McClintock who died a couple of years ago at age 93, arguably the greatest American scientist of the twentieth century, responsible for breakthrough findings into genetic transposition that have given us a whole new understanding of the life process. When McClintock was in her early eighties, another scientist, Evelyn Fox Keller, came to her and said, "I want to write your intellectual biography—how did you do this breakthrough science? What is the secret of your journey into genetics?"

McClintock thought for a moment and said, "Well, all I can really tell you about the doing of great science is that you somehow have to have a feeling for the organism."

Keller, the biographer, pressed her again: "What more can you tell me about this journey into great knowing that you have taken in your life?"

McClintock, thinking back to the ears of corn she had studied ever since she was in her early twenties because they were cheap and plentiful and she had a hard time getting grants, said, "All I can say about doing science is you have to somehow learn to lean into the kernel."

Obviously, you don't win a Nobel Prize if you *don't* honor logic and data, and Barbara McClintock was one of the most logical, rigorous, and empirically precise scientists we have ever known. But when she's asked to choose those images and metaphors that describe the heart of the scientific enterprise for her, she talks about "feeling" and "leaning into." That is, she chooses images of connectedness, of community, with—of all things—an ear of corn.

In the book that Keller wrote about McClintock, Evelyn Fox Keller wrote a sentence that I find brilliant. She said, "Barbara McClintock, in her relation with ears of corn, practiced the highest form of love—which is intimacy that does not annihilate difference." Keller names love as an intellectual virtue—when it enables us to hold together the paradox of subjective engagement with objective understanding. That's great knowing and that's part of what underlies the success of that medical school model, where students become intimate with a person who has a problem *and* are asked not to reduce that person to their own convenient ways of thinking, to step back and look again.

There's so much more to say but my time is almost gone. I'll just say one more thing and then we'll have a little time for conversation.

If we ask ourselves why it is that we have such struggles with community—however we define it or understand it—in higher education, I think that one of the most compelling answers has to be that we live in a culture of fear. Fear, more than anything else, is what keeps us from getting connected.

Fear keeps us from getting connected too deeply with our subjects, lest they make a claim on our lives. Fear keeps us from getting too deeply connected with our students, lest they make a claim on our lives. Fear keeps us from getting too deeply connected with each other, lest we make a claim on each other's lives.

I think that conferences like this, and work like this, and the new movement for teaching and learning, are, at bottom, efforts to move beyond fear, to break the academic culture out of the fearful bonds that have held it in rigid place for far too long. We have all kinds of reasons to want to move beyond fear. Some of them are moral and ethical, some of them are personal and humanistic, and some of them are intellectual and scholarly. Neither persons nor ethics nor great thinking thrive in a climate of fear.

I wish you well in your journey into ways of teaching and learning that transcend fear, and that can take us toward forms of community that are real and compelling and healing for us and for our wounded world. Thank you very much.

References

Fein, Kommilyn G. *Hitler's Death Camps: The Sanity of Madness.* Holmes & Meier, 1981.

Keller, Evelyn Fox. *A Feeling for the Organism: The Life and Work of Babara McClintock.* W. H. Freeman, 1983.

Palmer, Parker. *To Know as We Are Known.* HarperCollins, 1983, 1993.

_____ *The Active Life.* HarperCollins, 1990.

_____ "Community, Conflict, and Ways of Knowing: Ways to Deepen Our Educational Agenda," in *Change Magazine,* Sept/Oct, 1987.

_____ "Good Teaching: A Matter of Living the Mystery," in *Change Magazine,* Jan/Feb, 1990.

_____ "Divided No More: A Movement Approach to Educational Reform," in *Change Magazine,* Mar/Apr, 1992.

_____ "Good Talk about Good Teaching: Improving Teaching through Conversation and Community," in *Change Magazine*, Nov/Dec, 1993.

The Use of Stories in Teaching

Nel Noddings

Nel Noddings became interested in the use of stories in teaching through her own experiences as a teacher, both in high schools and in universities. She now serves as Lee L. Jacks Professor of Child Education at Stanford University, where she tells teachers-to-be about the value of using stories in their teaching. Her latest books are *Educating for Intelligent Belief or Unbelief* (1993) and *Philosophy of Education* (1995).

Good teachers have always used stories in their teaching, and often stories turn out to be more effective than arguments and explanations. Some subjects seem to lend themselves more easily than others to story-telling, but this apparent difference may be the result of practice—not something inherent in the subjects. I have taught mathematics, teacher education, feminist studies, and philosophy, and I think stories are valuable in all of those fields. For those of us who teach future teachers, stories become doubly important because they are likely to be used again and again across a spreading network of teachers and students. (On the use of stories in teaching and teacher education, see Clandinin et al., 1993; Witherell and Noddings, 1991).

Stories should not be construed as time-out from the serious business of teaching. Rather, they should be an integral part of lesson planning and presentation. I will discuss five categories of stories and their uses here, and, although my examples will come mainly from the fields in which I have worked, the categories apply quite generally. In all subjects, we can draw on historical and biographical stories, on personal stories, and on literature. We can use humorous stories as ice-breakers and to relieve tension. We can use other stories to get at the psychology of learning and help students to understand their own capacities and habits.

Historical and Biographical Stories

It would seem natural for teachers who love their subjects to study the history of those subjects. One might also expect teachers to be fascinated by the biographies of great thinkers in the field. However, when I look back on my own mathematical training, I am sad to say that none of my teachers shared such interests with their classes. It was not until I turned to the study of philosophy that my interest in the history and philosophy of mathematics was aroused and, with that interest, a parallel one in biography also grew.

It seems obvious that if college teachers do not use historical and biographical stories, it is unlikely that precollege teachers will use them. Why should it matter? First, one could argue that such stories add substantially to our students' cultural literacy. I think this is true, but I would not make stories the focal point of my instruction, test students on their content, etc. Such focus might well spoil the attractiveness of stories. Thus, although I believe that stories make a hefty contribution to cultural literacy, I prefer to let them contribute indirectly and with seeming spontaneity. (We will see in a moment that one must, paradoxically, plan for effective spontaneity.) Second, stories enliven a presentation, and this is in itself a reason to use them. Third, and for me the most important reason to use them, stories help to expand interests, connect with other fields, and relate otherwise esoteric subject matter to the universal problems of living. They help to reveal the teacher as a person and establish a climate of care.

With some planning, stories can be used to extend a theme over several units of work. Stories tend to accumulate around the personal interests of teachers, but by observing their effects on student listeners, we can expand our repertoires to include interests expressed by students. I'll give some examples.

I have long been fascinated by the fact that so many mathematicians have had religious and theological interests. Because almost all human beings—especially high school and college age students— have such interests (often in an anti-religious form), these matters should be part of academic discussion. (See Noddings, 1993.) But, of course, religious topics can be highly controversial, and many of us understandably avoid them. At the high school level, teachers often believe (wrongly) that they are constitutionally forbidden to address such matters. However, there is no legal restriction on sharing biographical information, and the biographies of mathematicians are often replete with theological interests.

Whenever a mathematics teacher introduces or uses a coordinate system, it is reasonable to tell stories about the life of René Descartes, inventor of the rectangular coordinate system. There are many stories to be told: of multiple interests (how many people get to make major contributions to more than one field?), of personal idiosyncracies—matters of style and dress, of political intrigue and religious bigotry, and of theological interests.

In addition to his work in mathematics, Descartes did monumental work in philosophy, and some of that work focused on theological matters. One of his efforts is especially appropriate for discussion in a mathematics class. Descartes revived and perfected St. Anselm's proof of the existence of God. The proof can be presented in all its sophistication and elegance to some classes at the college level, and at the high school level, it can be presented in skeletal form. The basic idea is that perfection implies existence; that is, a perfect entity must exist because nonexistence would imply a flaw and, thus, nonperfection. The chain of reasoning, greatly simplified, looks like this:

1) If an entity is perfect, then it must exist.

2) God is a perfect entity.

3) Therefore, God exists.

Students in mathematics classes often enjoy looking for the flaws in this proof, and it is not unusual for some students to suggest flaws that have been identified and described by great philosophers. Needless to say, this can be a gratifying experience for students. Teachers who discuss this facet of Descartes's work need not declare their own status as believers or unbelievers. Further, they should be careful to point out that a flaw in the proof does not justify the conclusion that God does not exist.

Teachers who want to sustain the theme of religious interest or theology might follow up with stories about Blaise Pascal. Whether to do this immediately or to wait for a relevant mathematical topic—probability or statistics—is a matter of teacher's choice. In contrast to Descartes's approach through logical proof, Pascal approached the question with a wager. Befitting his interest in probability, Pascal suggested that we put our bets on God's existence. If we bet that God exists, live our lives accordingly, and he does exist, what do we stand to gain? If he doesn't exist, what have we lost?

In approaching the question of God's existence this way, Pascal made two important points: first, he argued, we can't ever *prove* that God exists; it is something we have to take on faith. Second, proof does not appeal to ordinary people and, if we hope to influence the bulk of our populace, we should use language and methods likely to reach them. This is an important point even today because there is considerable evidence that people are more likely to be moved by stories than by arguments. As teachers, we can infer from such evidence that we have to work harder at teaching students logical reasoning. Or we can decide that we should use stories and other methods more freely. Or, of course, we can do both and try to achieve a balance that is effective in our own teaching.

Once launched on a theme of this sort, one should be prepared to follow up, if student interest warrants it. Newton and Leibniz, who independently invented the calculus, both had keen theological interests. Newton was apparently more interested in theology than in mathematics, and he spent considerable time trying to show that biblical chronology and historical accounts could be made compatible. He also studied the problems and theological accounts of creation.

Leibniz analyzed the problem of evil. How can an all-good, all-knowing, all-powerful God be reconciled with the obvious existence of evil in the world? His *Theodicy* introduced a word that still describes an important field of theological investigation, and the topic is of vital existential interest because many, many people have rejected religion over just this issue. They cannot reconcile for themselves the simultaneous existence of a perfect God and evils in the world. The cruelty of the *Theodicy* (accepting the consignment of many souls to hell) is in part a legacy from Augustine, but the reasoning is typical of a mathematical thinker. Here, too, even high school students may identify the logical possibilities. If we do not deny that the evils of the world are really evils (as Leibniz did), what else might we do? "Process" theologians have variously suggested that we relax the overly-stringent criteria describing God. Suppose God is not all-knowing, but exists in time as we do. Does that help? Suppose God is not all-powerful and actually needs human help in overcoming evil. Or, finally, suppose God is not all-good. Students may find this last impossible or at least distasteful even to entertain, but they should know that some important thinkers (e.g., Carl Jung) have explored the possibility.

To reiterate the principles with which we started, such discussion may contribute to students' cultural literacy, enliven daily presentations, expand interests in and connections to other fields, and clarify the image of the teacher as a person. Every time we make connections to another field, we increase the possibility that students will find our own subject more relevant and interesting. No one topic will appeal to all students, but the entire set of topics may well span the space of student interests.

Having mentioned Newton and Leibniz, it makes sense to note that we could consider a theme other than theology. Available evidence supports the claim that each man invented the calculus. It was a case of simultaneous, independent creation. There are similar stories to be told about the invention of logarithms and much of the work on non-Euclidean geometry. An interesting question arises about the preparation of a "collective mind." Is there such a thing as a collective mind? How can it reasonably be described? Are there periods when the collective mind is ready for a new concept, skill, or device? Does that explain simultaneous invention?

Still another topic that can profitably be explored in connection with Newton and Leibniz is professional and national jealousy. The battle between followers of the two men—both groups insisting that their man did the creative work and the other was guilty of intellectual theft—was one of the most disgraceful episodes in the history of mathematics. Even Newton and Leibniz, who held themselves above the fray initially, descended to nasty personal attacks. (See the account in E.T. Bell, 1937/1965.) This battle over what we call today "intellectual property" is all the more deplorable when we remember that Newton is said to have commented, "If I have seen farther than others, it is because I have stood on the shoulders of giants." Generous credit is sometimes easier to give to those already dead than to contemporaries. Teachers can build effectively on this theme to help students understand how interdependent intellectual life is, how pervasive jealousies and antagonisms are, and how generous some great thinkers can be in their acknowledgement of others.

The Use of Literature

Thoughtful teachers often seek ways to introduce political and social themes into their regular classroom work. Because this material almost never appears in standard textbooks, teachers have to be persistent in looking for it. Sometimes it pops out unexpectedly. For example, many math teachers use the delightful science-fiction work *Flatland* (Abbott, 1952) to introduce notions of dimensionality and relativity. But *Flatland,* the story of a two-dimensional society, is filled with illustrations of sexism, classism, and religious mysticism. Indeed, I have heard teachers say that they refuse to use it *because* of its sexism (even though the sexism is probably satirical). My response is that its sexism gives us an excellent reason to talk about sexism in math class. Imagine a society in which all the males are polygons, and class status depends on the number of one's sides. Isosceles triangles are the working poor, so to speak, and those polygons with so many sides that they approximate circles are the priests at the top of the social hierarchy. Every father in Flatland hopes that his sons will have more sides than he has. In this highly classed society, women are mere line segments, and special rules govern their behavior. They are, essentially, nonpersons.

In addition to sexism and classism, *Flatland* introduces a good bit of mysticism. The narrator of the story, an upstanding square, is visited by a three-dimensional entity. Of course, no one believes him, and he finishes his tale in prison—treated as either mad or subversively dangerous. In the mystical tradition, he longs for another visitation, something to reaffirm what he knows really happened. But how can one explain a third dimension to people living in a two-dimensional world? How would we describe a four-dimensional entity to our peers?

Alice in Wonderland is another book filled with stories that can be used by teachers interested in logic. Whether logic is taught in math, philosophy, or in a class that emphasizes critical thinking, *Alice* abounds in examples of both sound and faulty logic, and there are many references to philosophical problems that are current even today, such as theories of meaning.

In some fields—feminist ethics, for example—stories may provide the main content. Women's traditions have not been articulated as men's have been. In philosophy, feminist writers are just beginning to produce frameworks that arise directly out of women's experience. In such fields, stories are used to elaborate a perspective that grows out of lived experience. Philosophers working in this area do not reject reason and argumentation, but they use both to elucidate and harmonize lived experience and thought. Reason and argumentation are not primary modes.

To paint a vivid picture of a tradition (in my own work, the care tradition) that has not been cast into discursive language, we might draw on Mrs. Shelby in *Uncle Tom's Cabin*, on Doris Lessing's Jane Somers (*The Diaries of Jane Somers*), on Lucy Winter in May Sarton's *The Small Room*, on the loving friends in Mary Gordon's *The Company of Women*, on Virginia Woolf's Mrs. Ramsay in *To the Lighthouse*. In extracting parts of these stories, we separate features we find admirable from those we deplore or feel ambivalent about. We may argue for our choices, and then we return to literature to find further examples to support our position.

The search for exemplars of the care tradition reminds me that, in the discussion of biography and mathematics, I did not mention the possibility of finding stories of women mathematicians. Surely, as we read and discuss *Flatland*, we will be moved to consider the role of women in mathematics. Some effort will uncover fascinating stories of Hypatia, Sonya Kovalevskaya, Emmy Noether, and many others (Perl, 1978).

I mentioned earlier that teachers have to plan for spontaneity (Hawkins, 1973). A teacher searching through familiar literature for examples of the care orientation will almost certainly begin to think about real women who have embodied this tradition, and then there will be a natural turn to history and biography. From *Uncle Tom's Cabin*, we turn to its author, Harriet Beecher Stowe, and from Stowe to her sister, Catherine Beecher. We think of Jane Addams and, perhaps, contrast her moral orientation with that of her good friend, John Dewey. We are reminded, as I was above, of omissions in earlier discussions. As we read biographical material, we are led to consider the times and historical background of each life and, from there, we move into literature that further enlivens the central topics we plan to discuss.

College teachers can profit from the example of good elementary school teachers. Such teachers are always on the lookout for materials that will interest their students. Vacationing, shopping, reading, watching television, they are always collecting objects, stories, pictures, coupons, and all sorts of ideas that may come in handy some day. In contrast, we college teachers seem to plan in a much more linear and constrained fashion. To break out of that mold, we have to think more broadly, perhaps even syncretistically. To be useful pedagogically, things do not have to fit together in a deductive chain. As David Hawkins (1973) put it in his discussion of planning for spontaneity:

> Everyone knows that the best times in teaching have always been the consequence of some little accident that happened to direct attention in some new way, create a brand new interest that you hadn't any notion about how to introduce. (p. 499)

To be ready for such accidents, teachers must build a repertoire of stories.

Good teachers are hardly ever off-duty. If that sounds too demanding, there is a bright side—overly conscientious teachers can now find permission to read for fun and to read over a broad range of topics. In a very real sense, such reading, if it is watchful reading, may enhance one's teaching for years to come.

Personal Stories

Students like to hear stories about the personal experiences of their teachers. Of course, no responsible teacher devotes whole class periods to such stories, and the overuse or injudicious use of personal stories may cause a lack of respect for the teacher and a loss of interest in the subject. But students can profit from learning what attracted you to your field, why you chose the school at which you did graduate studies, whom among your professors you admired and why. They may also profit from hearing what you had to give up, who encouraged you, what you hope to accomplish, and it can be especially reassuring for them to hear that you did not always succeed and how you handled failures or near-failures. Obviously, these stories should not come out all at once—like "true confessions"— but they should be introduced when they are relevant. This means that you have to be sensitive to the needs of your students and maintain a steady concern for what they are going through.

I have used the pronoun "you" above because I am talking directly to my readers, particularly you professors and teachers new to the field. Students like to hear stories from all their teachers but they especially appreciate stories from their younger teachers. Stories from well established older professors are more like fiction than possibilities for their own lives. Students can identify more closely with younger teachers, and their anticipated experience in graduate school will be more nearly like theirs than like that of their older professors. In all of this, we have to remember that not all students will go on to graduate school, and so our stories should not overemphasize that experience. Struggles with career choices, moral dilemmas, and existential questions are usually of interest to most students.

I can still remember vividly a moment from my own undergraduate years when a young professor of earth science briefly described his own view of mortality. To die, to decay, and replenish the beloved earth seemed to him entirely fitting and quite beautiful. I had never heard anyone express such a view. It astonished me, but even then it did not strike me as heretical. Rather, as a quiet statement of commitment, it impressed me greatly and set me to thinking in ways I had never before dared.

All teachers can contribute stories about their own growth as teachers. I often tell prospective teachers about my early years as a math teacher. I worked very hard, and I expected my students also to work hard. Although I was scrupulously fair, I was much too strict. I remember with considerable pain grading a geometry student's exam a "13." Well, I argued, that is all she earned—13 points out of a possible 100. I wouldn't give such a grade now. Anyone capable of the simplest arithmetic knows that it is almost impossible to recover from such a grade. All incentive to work harder is lost. In later years, I made "50" the bottom grade. It says "failing" very clearly, but it allows for recovery, and it saves a bit of the student's dignity.

I also learned that positive grading is more appreciated than negative grading; that is, instead of scoring problems "-3" or "-6," I learned to score them "+7" and "+4." This practice encouraged students to share their thinking. They knew that I was looking for what they had learned, not just for their mistakes. There were even times when students got a full 10 points for a problem solution that ended in a wrong answer. If all the work was right and clearly laid out and some tiny error (usually computational) was made, I charged that to "the heat of the examination." This sensible generosity did much to alleviate test anxiety.

Reflecting on my own testing and grading practices led to more than the changes mentioned above. I decided that, if I really wanted students to learn the material, it shouldn't matter whether they demonstrated competence on the first try or at some later date, and so I allowed students to retake tests as often as they needed to (within the parameters of school district marking periods). Today, in my university teaching, I do not give letter grades at all, and I ask students to resubmit papers that are not satisfactory.

In the opening paragraphs of this section, I urged young professors to share their personal-professional experiences with students. I said that such experience is usually regarded as interesting and relevant because the differences in age and status are not quite so great as they are between students and full professors. However, older professors can give a special gift in discussing their development as teachers. The importance of this discussion is obvious for those who teach future teachers. But many students appreciate hearing that professors reflect on their work as teachers and that they have changed, grown, and matured in their thinking about that work.

Again, sharing personal stories may be encouraged by reading the stories of others. In my own development as a teacher, I have found particularly useful Sylvia Ashton-Warner's (1963) *Teacher* (elementary school reading), Carl Rogers' (1969) *Freedom to Learn* (teaching at every level), Wayne Booth's (1988) *The Vocation of a*

Teacher (college English), and Bruce Wilshire's (1990) *The Moral Collapse of the University* (philosophy at the college level).

Humorous Stories

Stories in the first three categories can, of course, be humorous, but the stories I have in mind here are usually very short, and they are rarely part of an extended theme. They are relevant to the moment, and they serve mainly to relax tension, establish a warm pedagogical climate, and keep students awake. They are often corny, and students frequently respond with groans, but then they go on to tell the stories themselves—sometimes as examples of bad jokes.

One of my math professors told the story of how and why Noah had invented logarithms. It seems that as Noah was saying farewell to all the animal pairs after the flood and enjoining them all to "go forth and multiply," a pair of snakes demurred. "We can't multiply," they apologized. "We're adders." Thereupon Noah invented logarithms so that all the "adders" of the world could multiply.

There was another story about a brilliant mathematician who tried hard to be a good teacher. One day a student asked for further discussion of a result the mathematician had presented in his usual laconic form. The professor accepted the request genially enough, stepped to the side of the room, stroked his beard, and wrinkled his brow in concentration. Then his eyes lit up, he strode to the chalkboard and wrote the answer again. "See!" he exclaimed, "there's another way of doing it!"

The above story would fall in nicely with a discussion of one's own development as a teacher. Sometimes stories from a repertoire of humor do fall into a theme we have decided to explore. For example, math teachers who choose to elaborate on the theological interests of mathematicians will surely want to include a story about the great algorist, Euler. He, too, concocted proofs of God's existence, but the one for which he is remembered is a nonsense proof. Story has it that Catherine the Great implored Euler to do something about the atheistic influence of the prominent French philosopher Diderot. Therefore, in front of the gathered court, Euler presented a proposition to Diderot: "Sir, $\frac{a+b^n}{n}=x$, hence God exists;

reply!" It is said that Diderot, like so many of our students today, recoiled at the sound of mathematics and fled, humiliated, from the scene. True or not, it makes a good story. However, students should be aware that Euler also devised serious proofs of God's existence— none of which, of course, is accepted today.

Stories of this sort are best used sparingly and never with the same class twice. Most good teachers do not include these stories in their lesson or lecture plans; rather, they store them in ready memory, and pull them out on suitable occasions.

The Psychology of Learning

It is odd that professors who are obviously entranced with their subjects rarely consider or discuss the psychology of learning those subjects. By "psychology of learning" I do not mean formal psychological experiments on memory and the like but, rather, questions and issues that should interest any serious student: Under what circumstances do I learn best? At what time of day am I sharpest? When is it best to put a problem aside? Are there strategies that can reduce the burden on memory?

Jacques Hadamard (1954) explored the phenomena of invention in mathematics. In an appendix to his study, he included questions from a well known questionnaire. Mathematicians were asked whether they were affected by meteorological conditions such as temperature, light, season, and the like; whether they engaged in regular exercise and of what sort; whether they worked best standing up, seated, or lying down. Commenting on Hadamard's study, James R. Newman (1956) noted:

> Hadamard...considers whether scientific invention may perhaps be improved by standing or sitting or by taking two baths in a row. Helmholtz and Poincaré worked sitting at a table; Hadamard's practice is to pace the room ("Legs are the wheels of thought," said Emile Angier); the chemist J. Teeple was the two-bath man. Alas, the habits of famous men are rarely profitable to their disciples. The young philosopher will derive little benefit from being punctual like Kant, the biologist from cultivating Darwin's dyspepsia, the playwright from eating Shaw's vegetables. (p. 2039)

Almost certainly Hadamard is right when he says that cultivating the habits of famous thinkers will do little to enhance the inventiveness of students. But studying their own habits and the conditions under which they work best may help students to improve their work. Notice, too, that Newman could not have made the above comments if he had not been familiar with stories about Kant, Darwin, and Shaw. Those stories can be used to get students thinking about their own working and learning styles. Hadamard explored at length the possible contributions of the unconscious mind to problem solving and invention. Drawing heavily on the account of Henri Poincareé (1956) and the analysis of that account by Graham Wallas (1926), he described the stages of thought called preparation, incubation, and illumination. In the state of preparation, a thinker works hard to solve a problem; he or she formulates plans, entertains alternative hypotheses, exercises all sorts of strate gies, and, with no success, sometimes gives up. However, the "giving up" is temporary. One has to get on with other matters, and so the problem is set aside for a while.

A remarkable thing often happens. As the thinker is seemingly fully occupied with something else, the answer springs to mind. Hadamard and others have explored this phenomenon. What accounts for it? Some have suggested that resting the mind does it. But the mind is not actively re-engaged, so this explanation is not convincing. Others have suggested that the subconscious mind continues to work on the problem even while the conscious mind is busy with other matters. We are not sure what accounts for the happy result, but the stage has been labeled "incubation." The "aha" experience that follows in successful cases is the stage of illumination.

There are many wonderful stories of discoveries made through preparation, incubation, and illumination. (See Hadamard, 1954.) If teachers can add stories about their own experiences, students may be convinced of the reality of the events. In my days as a high school teacher, I told many of these stories. Some students, of course, wanted to skip the stage of preparation. These were people who were also attracted to learning foreign languages in their sleep. Of course, without the hard work of preparation, no results were forthcoming. Perhaps the most important idea that students gained from these discussions is that hard work, even if it does not pay off in immediate results, is likely to produce something eventually. Students have to learn not to measure their scholarly efforts in terms of gross productivity. Teachers should help by refraining, occasionally, from assigning grades. Some assignments, or parts of assignments, should be undertaken without fear of penalties.

It seems likely that most students do not use their minds well. They settle into drab modes of coping with academic work. It can be exciting for some to hear about the visual methods used by mathematicians and scientists and to learn that, despite the claims of many philosophers, some great thinkers (e.g., Einstein) have insisted that the core of their new ideas was established not verbally but visually or even kinesthetically.

In *Awakening the Inner Eye* (Noddings and Shore, 1984), my co-author and I have suggested ways by which students can enhance intuitive modes and thus add to their powers of thinking. First, one must have a congenial setting. Most of us need at least fifteen minutes of gradually deepening concentration in order to enter an intuitive mode. Pearl Buck, for example, needed fresh flowers and a peaceful view in order to get started on her writing. Descartes often worked (thought deeply) while lying abed mornings. Pablo Casals got in touch with his own musical muse by starting every morning by playing Bach fugues. Students should be encouraged to explore what works for them. (Again, there will be some who will copy Descartes by lying in bed, but not by thinking.)

Second, we must encourage receptivity. Receptivity, as I am using it here, should not be confused with passivity. Today we are so aware of the evils of passive learning that we sometimes castigate ourselves for lecturing. But students and listeners can be very active; they can generate and construct during a lecture, and these capacities should be cultivated. To be receptive is to be wide awake, open to ideas, willing to believe. Too often, especially in philosophy, we require students to analyze and raise objections prematurely. A receptive attitude induces a consummatory experience, one of enjoyment.

Third, an intuitive mode is aimed at understanding and not just the production of a particular result. Stories of artists and scientists working in this mode can be very valuable. Such work is not rushed; it is not guided by specific learning objectives. One of the worst suggestions made by professional educationalists is that all teaching and learning should be directed by pre-specified objectives. This approach takes all the romance and fun out of learning and leads to the debilitating notion that all intellectual effort must culminate in a measurable result, under specified conditions, in a particular span of time. Stories of genuine intellectual effort should help to dispel this pernicious notion. (This is not to say, of course, that no academic work should be guided by specific learning objectives. Some work is well suited to that method.)

Discussion of the psychology of learning in a particular field can be as important as teaching the content. Such a discussion is greatly enhanced by stories, both biographical and autobiographical. Hearing the stories opens new vistas for students. Searching for them adds pleasure and relaxation to the lives of teachers.

Summary

Stories can be used to increase the cultural literacy of students, to enhance our presentations, to extend the influence of our subject to other fields and into existential questions of universal interest, and, overall, to establish a climate of care in our classrooms. I will close this chapter with the analysis of a paragraph that illustrates the points I have made here.

In an exploration of his own theological interests, Martin Gardner (1983) scoffed at "fake immortalities." He, like many of us, wants a continuation of his own consciousness, not a conceptual imitation of immortality. He wrote:

> It does not fortify my soul in the least to know that after I die all unmarried men will still be bachelors, that 37 will still be a prime number, that the stars will continue to shine, and that forever I will have been just what I am now. Away with these fake immortalities! They mean nothing to the heart. Better to say with Bertrand Russell: "I believe that when I die I shall rot, and nothing of my ego will survive." (p. 282)

Sharing this paragraph with students tells a personal story of sorts; it reveals my interest in mathematics, philosophy, biography, and theology. It has the potential to increase students' cultural literacy. Do they know that "All unmarried men are bachelors" is a famous tautology used repeatedly in philosophy? What will they say if asked whether 37 is a prime when it is written as a numeral in base 5? (It is, of course, but because it appears as 1225, many students will say that it is now divisible by 2!) Do they know that some prominent theologians have described immortality in terms of the record of our experience in the mind of God (an ultimate form of permanent record or transcript)? Have they heard of Bertrand Russell?

Students who are fortunate enough to hear such stories from their teachers may find their intellectual lives enormously enriched. They may read more widely and find soul-mates among writers who share their own idiosyncratic interests. They may even find satisfying answers to some of the persistent existential questions that all of us, as thoughtful human beings, face.

References

Abbot, Edwin A. 1952. *Flatland.* New York: Dover.

Ashton-Warner, Sylvia. 1963. *Teacher.* New York: Simon and Schuster.

Bell, Eric Temple. 1937/1965. *Men of Mathematics.* New York: Simon and Schuster.

Booth, Wayne C. 1988. *The Vocation of a Teacher.* Chicago: University of Chicago Press.

Clandinin, D. Jean; Davies, Annie; Hogan, Pat; and Kennard, Barbara. 1993. *Learning to Teach: Teaching to Learn.* New York: Teachers College Press.

Gardner, Martin. 1983. *The Whys of a Philosophical Scrivener.* New York: Quill.

Hadamard, Jacques. 1954. *The Psychology of Invention in the Mathematical Field.* New York: Dover.

Hawkins, David. 1973. "How to Plan for Spontaneity." In *The Open Classroom Reader,* edited by Charles E. Silberman, 486-503. New York: Vintage Books.

Newman, James R., ed. 1956. *The World of Mathematics.* New York: Simon and Schuster.

Noddings, Nel, and Shore, Paul. 1984 *Awakening the Inner Eye: Intuition in Education.* New York: Teachers College Press.

Noddings, Nel. 1993. *Educating for Intelligent Belief or Unbelief.* New York: Teachers College Press.

Perl, Teri. 1978. *Math Equals: Biographies of Women Mathematicians.* Menlo Park, CA: Addison-Wesley.

Poincaré, Henri. 1956. "Mathematical Creation." In *The World of Mathematics,* edited by James R. Newman, 2041-2050. New York: Simon and Schuster.

Rogers, Carl R. 1969. *Freedom to Learn.* Columbus, OH: Merrill Publishing Company

Wallas, Graham. 1926. *The Art of Thought.* London: J. Cape.

Wilshire, Bruce. 1990. *The Moral Collapse of the University.* Albany: SUNY Press.

Witherell, Carol and Noddings, Nel, eds. 1991 *Stories Lives Tell.* New York: Teachers College Press.

The Braiding of Classroom Voices: Learning to Write by Learning to Learn

Wendy Bishop and Toby Fulwiler

Toby Fulwiler became interested in writing to learn—the basic principle of the writing-across-the-curriculum movement—as a young professor of English at Michigan Technological University in 1977, when he attended an NEH Summer Institute on "Writing in the Humanities." He and department chair Art Young created a model writing-across-the-curriculum program at Michigan Tech, demonstrated that writing can help students learn in any discipline, and began giving workshops on writing-across-the-curriculum techniques around the country. Those workshops, and the articles and books written by Toby, Art Young, and others, have touched large numbers of teachers in every discipline. Today, Toby teaches writing and directs the writing program at the University of Vermont. His most recent book is *When Writing Teachers Teach Literature*, co-edited with Young. He has also written *The Working Writer*, *Writing Across the Disciplines* (with Young), *College Writing*, and *Teaching with Writing*, and edited *The Journal Book*. His email address is <tfulwile@moose.uvm.edu>.

One of the teachers affected by the work of Fulwiler and Young was Wendy Bishop. She uses writing-across-the-curriculum techniques in her own classes, but sees herself as a proponent of writing-within-the-curriculum—i.e., teaching new teachers that writing to learn is an essential component of literature courses. She currently is Professor of English at Florida State University. Forthcoming books include *Elements of Alternate Style: Essays on Writing and Revision* and *Ethnographic Writing Research: Writing it Down*,

Writing it Up, and Reading it. She is also completing a text-book (*Thirteen Ways of Looking for a Poem: An Introduction to Poetry*) and a collection of nonfiction essays about writing and relationships called *The Shape of Fact.* Her email address is <wbishop@garnet.acns.fsu.edu>.

I. Learning to Learn

We both tell the same story: How, when as first-year teachers we met our first classes, we worried about the same things: "Am I prepared? Do I have enough to say? Will anybody listen?" Questions that all circled around our more fundamental question, "Can I teach?" And we both found relief, at the end of those first classes, that we had managed to keep their attention for most of the period and still had material we hadn't covered—a start on the content of the next class. In those early classes and, actually, for much of our teaching lives, we worried more about our needs as teachers than their needs as students.

John—You know it's the same day every Monday, Wednesday, and Friday—you get to class on time, you sit near the front & plan today to really pay attention to what he says, but pretty soon you're drawing cartoons in the margins and realize you haven't taken a note in twenty minutes.

Their needs, as students, being to enter the community of literate learners to which we now comfortably belong. Their needs to become comfortable and confident speakers for the new knowledge they daily encounter, to tell us and each other back, that history means this, geology this, literature that. At the same time, they're being asked to sit quietly, take good notes, care little about classmates sitting to right and left, speak up when questioned, write when tested—being shown their own words are not theirs at all, and our lectures, long answers to questions no one had asked.

Jose—Another C on a test I really studied for. I really don't get it—I studied the text, studied my lecture notes, and even memorized some good quotes to throw in. When we get the exams back, it says at the bottom, "competent, but no evidence of original thinking." What does she want, anyway?

They need most their own words and questions, not ours. In spite of all we know and wish them to know, in spite of all we tell them carefully and cleverly to think and take notes about, and in spite of all the texts we require to be read, reviewed, and remembered, their best learning happens in their own words, in spite of our needs and illusions as first or fifteen year teachers, not by copying our notes and memorizing profound quotations, when and where do you make these ideas your own? When do you put the ideas you receive into your own language? Where, in a copybook, do you argue and rebut and critique and retort and test what you hear against what you know?

Molly—The only class where I actually know the other students is my writing class. It's fun sharing papers in my group and I really like hearing theirs as well. I don't mean it's fun only in the social way either, because we really give each other good ideas and help each other out. I like a class where I can talk about ideas and have fun at the same time.

Students talking to students makes a difference. Saying back, discussing, trying out, re-saying—often, at first, wrongly—aloud in fragments to seat-mates, then louder to classmates—three, four, five times—challenges, and proves what has been heard, read, copied. Their talk helps our authority become (sometimes imperfectly, but always personally) theirs. Small group talk, by the way, runs the world—groups of people in small rooms clustered around tables—exploring, questioning, answering—in corporations, universities, government. We do our students no favors when we do all the exploring, all the questioning, all the answering. We encourage a mixture of learning opportunities for our mixed sets of students, each of whom learns differently.

Brenda—I never really never feel comfortable talking in a large group. Blame it on shyness, some weird hang-up of mine or whatever, but I really do not do well in large groups, in

ANY of my classes. I do think I do well in small-group work-shops, though, or working with one other person.

Authority is what authors have and students need more of, but can only get, finally, by writing. What many inexperienced writers do not understand is that the act of writing is often the business of taking the half thoughts that run around your mind and fashioning them into full thoughts. Remember E.M. Forester's question? "How do I know what I think until I see what I say?" Putting down one idea suggests another, and that another, until the words you write help tease out of you the fully-developed thought you want—which is usually better or more complete than the half thought you started with. And there don't seem to be any shortcuts—without writing down the half-thought, the full thoughts seldom come—and if they do, not as completely as had you written them out. It's in the writing that students learn what they have learned.

Lucille—I think that we are very closely linked to our texts. It comes from inside us and is part of us. I feel that my writing is definitely a part of me and that is why I am often very self-conscious about it. I'm not always pleased with my writing and I wish I could be better at it. I don't think I'm that BAD of a writer, I just know I can, or wish I could be better at it. It is the same way with me as a person—there is always something more I can do to help others in order to make me a better person—sometimes I just need a swift kick to get me going.

Writing also tells writers when they're not making sense of. A writer's text reveals what's missing in the learning, the flaws in flawed arguments, the halfness of half-conceived thoughts. The fragmented thoughts and missing information are just as important, demand attention, and become what good authors focus on next, the writing revealing the malady, the need for continued writing also suggesting the cure.

Jason—I say to myself, "Can this be done? Well the only way to know is to write it and see. Like all writers, I am still searching for a voice, a place to call home.

The phrase "writing to learn" is the foundation of writing across the curriculum. It means simply that the best way for students to learn history or chemistry or business is to write history, chemistry, and business as often and in as many forms as possible—but always first to themselves to make sure of their own understanding. Later, of course, they must write to you. If you want students to learn your subject in the most thorough manner possible, you will add writing to your course at all those points where their understanding is most required and crucial. Provide your students with chances to explore their understanding in their own language, see if they think it makes sense, then ask them to communicate it to you. Writing and thinking honestly for themselves is the necessary precursor to writing and thinking effectively for you.

Neil Postman: "Writing gives birth to the grammarian, the logician, the rhetorician, the historian, the scientist, all those who must hold language still so they can see what it means, where it errs, and where it is leading." (Amusing Ourselves to Death.)

How do students learn to be grammarians, logicians, rhetoricians, historians, and scientists? They have to move from a state of not knowing to a state of knowing, move from a position outside these professional communities to a place inside. With these students who are first learning your discipline, share how you learned to write, talk, think, how you entered your community. Make time to explain the tacit ways that community works. Tell your own first awkward stories, share copies of your work in progress—your own drafts in rough and developing states—share with them that you too were once a novice, that you're still a learner.

Raphael—Last semester I learned that I need to put the primary load on students. Instead of standing in front of the class, I try to get class discussions going. If they don't get going, I have students write on the topic and read their responses. I try to get the students more involved with each other. I know that group work failed somewhat because I didn't give the students a chance to get to know each other before throwing them into groups. I'm trying to ease into group work a bit more this time.

The emphasis on the value of each learner's own language developed from the research conducted by James Britton, Nancy Martin, and their colleagues at the London School of Education, whose research revealed that most language used in school was for examination rather than exploration. They categorized the language as 1) expressive (personal language to explore—informal conversation, journals, notes, first drafts); 2) transactional (language to convey information—oral reports, research papers, critical essays, and most "school writing), and 3) poetic (language used aesthetically such as poetry or Martin Luther King's "I have a dream" speech). However, Britton and his colleagues suggest that the expressive—language for the self—is basic, the matrix from which transactional and poetic language must grow and develop. What they found in schools, was that teachers did not encourage nor value expressive language, orally or in writing.

> *Marc—I used to write more for my own enjoyment than for anyone else's. But once I got to high school, I stopped writing for me and began writing to please each particular teacher. I would find the formula they approved of and write it for them.*

Other influential research for the development of language for learning grew from early work done by M.L. Abercrombie who found British medical students performed better when allowed to make collaborative diagnoses. And psychologist Carl Rogers who developed an influential client-centered group counseling method, believing that his clients were the best solvers of their own problems. Their work was applied to classroom learning by Kenneth Bruffee, who argues that students must develop collaborative learning communities, using their own talking and writing to find, extend, and communicate their learning—the same model we use in department subcommittees, workshops, task-forces, panel presentations, colloquia. Our own speaking, listening, reading, and writing advances our knowledge, so too must students' language advance theirs.

> *Don Murray: "Process cannot be inferred from product any more than a pig can be inferred from a sausage."*

When students attend to the processes of writing and learning, they learn the difficult and messy journey, from discovering to drafting to revision to editing to—finally—final draft. However, when they attend only to the products of writing and learning—studying, for example, only published texts, listening in lectures to the elegant end products of someone else's trials and errors—they are kept from learning the magic of learning. That's natural since professional writers spend most of their time smoothing over the trail, obliterating the missed turns and exploratory forays they undertook on the way to constructing their text. The problem with hidden processes—students will try to construct the appropriate looking texts without really exploring, analyzing, thinking critically about the material they encounter:

> *Robin—You have the due date looming over you so you latch on to the obvious and easy things first, you drop in some notes, and then go into the text and find only what you need—"This quote matches what I want to say, this quote doesn't." So you copy every quote out of the text, put them on a couple of sheets of paper and stick them in where they'll look good.*

Process classes strive to make the journey understandable—to provide some maps and equipment. There is a simple yet important good result that comes from process instruction: Inexperienced writers learn that they have a process—one that may be less than efficient, but the faults are in their habits or their lack of practice and not in them as humans as they too often have come to feel:

> *Mia—My right foot is a half-size larger than my left foot. For a long time, I thought that this meant there was something very wrong with me. When I learned that it is normal for one side of a person's body to be larger than the other side, I felt so much better! This is the way I felt after our class discussion on the writing process. I have always felt that I wasn't very good at it, because it is such a struggle for me . . . . Maybe there is hope for me after all.*

Some students in our classes will already know how to work in groups: they know that they need a focused task or else daily talk may overwhelm learning through talk. They can tell you that some students get bossy or too quiet in groups, so groups have to have instructions on member roles: how to keep track of time, how to collect material and report back to the class (have a group historian and time keeper, for instance). And students know that they have to do their part—if they haven't read assigned material, they'll not be able to join the discussion. Students know too that in groups they can solve problems they can't solve singly—whether the subject is math, history, or public administration. They know in groups they can't sit back and let the teacher present information to them—to accept or reject— instead, they have to jump in and be active.

Jason—Group discussion (in our group at least) is going well, although sometimes it is hard to decide what to discuss, or to stick to the story.

Mia—Groups would work better, of course, if everyone would get more involved. Some members are always coming to class unprepared. If they haven't read the work it is hard to discuss.

Robert—The group discussions work very well and class discussions stimulate new ideas. Personally I feel like my first paper was an accomplishment—and my group gets part of the credit.

All of us, no matter how good we are, need to keep growing as writers. And as instructors we can encourage our students to do so as well. None of us can learn to do everything all at once, and few can attend simultaneously to organization and evidence and clarity and disciplinary conventions. In fact, there's no reason to pay attention to wordy constructions or inappropriate punctuation until what is needing to be said is said—is explored, examined, understood, rethought, figured out finally with a reader in mind. We erase many of those lower order errors in our writing, just by returning to our drafts and rewriting to get the larger conceptual matters straight, sometimes by simply cutting out the passage in which the offensive language occurred, sometimes by simply re-reading our first draft and now noticing (Oh, I left out a word). Why not encourage our student writers to do the same?

Cal—The paper was due today, so I started it right after supper last night, figuring I had plenty of time to type up five pages. But nothing seemed to work until I finally read chapter twelve again—then it clicked—then I saw why my argument went in a circle. But it was already midnight and I was really tired and so I just put together what I had and went to sleep.

We all learned to write differently and also the same. As children, we were immersed in language,* liked to talk, be talked to, wanted to enter the discussion, sometimes interrupted (often not raising a hand) got frustrated if not understood, saw others looking at words, paper, texts, that unclear code, that powerful one. We started memorizing words, began to break the code, pushed our way in (I know, I know what this means!) and did this both alone (paging through a first book *Gregory the Terrible Eater* or *Green Eggs and Ham*) and together, that is, found we were no longer alone. We had spoken and printed words, had other worlds, pushed our way into a textual conversation going on before us, that will go on after us. We write to learn about social work, nursing, music, whatever. Sharing letters, sharing drafts, capturing fears hopes conflicts and agreements, we cover our subjects, meet our needs, meet their needs—belong together.

> *Sue—Our texts are "safe" when we do what we know we've gotta do to get a good grade, rather than approaching a paper creatively. Regardless, you must make your point, but a safe paper is one you write, stylistically, for others, not yourself. I hate safe.*

Sometimes we don't invite our students into our discussions because we're scared, have just barely arrived here ourselves, feel like we have to save face, be the authority, never show that our authority is surprising to us, and rarely acknowledge that what we're doing most is worrying about our effectiveness as teachers and our mastery of our own field—again, worrying more about our own needs, not those of our students.

> *Tina—I am in front of a large group of people who expect me to say something but I have lost my voice. I can't reach for the glass on the podium because I don't want them to see that my hands are shaking. I can't move to the blackboard because sunlight pours through the windows and I remember that I don't have any slip on and my skirt is sheer. My knees are knocking and the one that was broken locks into place and I know if I walk it will be with a limp. The limp is most noticeable in my cowboy boots because the heels are hollow, so you hear the limp more than you see it.*

II. Writing to Learn

We don't think teachers have to limp through the curriculum in hollow-heeled cowboy boots. Consider some of the following suggestions for providing students more opportunity to use writing for learning in your class—that is, writing for *them* not you, to clarify their thoughts to themselves, not to you, writing you don't grade, maybe don't see. Try the ideas that best match your personality and suit your purposes:

- Start, end, or interrupt your classes by asking your students to write about the subject of the day. Tell them to keep their pens and pencils moving, not to worry about false starts, digressions, or the mechanics of writing. Writing fast and freely, trying to answer questions or solve problems, turns off the editor and critic in your mind and lets you focus on larger ideas and relationships. Good questions include: What did you learn from reading the chapter assigned for today? What is your opinion, belief, insight, or objection to the ideas discussed in our last class? What questions do you have so far? This technique, called freewriting, can be done daily to engage students in your class by using their own language.

- Ask students to talk to each other—to seat-mates, in small groups—after they've written something, to share their opinions, discover who their classmates are, to solve problems you might otherwise solve yourself for them—doing for them, in the bargain, favors. Fifteen minutes of class time invested in private student writing, then collaborative talk, changes your class by inviting all of your students into the conversation and by suggesting that their ideas are worth expressing and sharing—only in small groups will everyone have a chance to talk in a non-threatening manner. It's a good idea to have students talking to each other after freewriting.

- To keep student abreast of assigned course reading, ask them to keep journals instead of giving quizzes. Journals reveal the movement and growth of a writer's mind from day to day, week to week (small loose-leaf notebooks work well). Respond to selected entries and ideas—not style or mechanics—in a friendly voice; and grade them only quantitatively. Journals are good places in which to write informally in class, good places to keep freewriting.

- Write letters with your students. Personal, informal, non-graded letters that begin, Dear Toby or Dear Wendy, assume or create a friendly, equal stature between writer and audience, allowing the writer to share ideas and problems honestly. In small classes, ask for a letter from each student every Friday; read them over the weekend and write one collective letter back, that you deliver (Dear Classmates) on Monday. Invite comments on lectures, readings, discussions, personal issues related to your class material. Write back using passages from their letters to you, answering those you want, asking new questions yourself, allowing the back-and-forth nature of the letters to help broker your weekly class meetings. Letters are journals with an audience.

- Don't grade writing-to-learn activities (in-class writing, freewriting, journal and letter writing) in the conventional sense; if you want your student learners to be honest and free to take risks, count their informal writing as done or not done—they must be free to sometimes be wrong without being clobbered for it. They will consider it purposeful, not busywork, if you use what they have just written as the basis for further class discussion or to help them find paper topics.

- Write some of your assignments with your students to find out how interesting they are and to demonstrate that you remain a learner yourself. If you ask students to write in class, be sure to write with them and sometimes to share what you wrote—watching you write too gives credibility to the value of the writing.

II. Learning to Write

We think students need to learn to write first for themselves—to sort out their own thoughts; next they need to learn to write for a wider, more public audience. The following ideas will help students improve their ability to communicate when they write formal papers—critical essays, research papers, lab reports, book reviews, and the like:

- Make writing assignments to students that you would like to do yourself, that are interesting, and to which you do not already know the answers. Put samples of excellent student writing on projectors for class critique (friendly) and discussion. Talk briefly about ways previous class writers have approached and succeeded at a class assignment.

- Revision is, in fact, the key to all good writing, theirs as well as ours. Revision is "a way to open up material and draw more edges into the material, as opposed to sanding the material down so that you end up with something smooth, polished, and featureless" (Clayton Eschelman). Build serious writing assignments around revision; comment on papers with that in mind; withhold grading until you both call the paper done.

- Don't be the sole reader for student papers. Every classroom contains other potentially interested readers of each others writing and learning—the other students in the class. Set your class up so that students have regular opportunities to share drafts— one day with seat-mates—the next with out-of-class study groups. Reading papers aloud helps both writer and reader.

- Make student learning part of the course content: publish student writings in a mid-term class "book" through a local copy shop. Instead of grading this work A-F; base the grade on willingness to publish (S/U—it's in the packet or not) and let students experience the real evaluation of being read by other knowledgeable, critical, interested readers.

- Include student voices in all classroom conversations: discuss the class written books in small groups, discuss the class book as a whole class, as preparation for end-of term projects, write letters to each other about texts in the class book, review the class book in a lecture—pointing to the accomplished disciplinary aspects of what has been said, what needs to be said further or differently.

- When you read early drafts of student papers, comment on conceptual matters, but don't comment at all on the spelling, punctuation, or grammar. When you read later drafts, comment on whatever needs attending to. When you read final drafts, comment finally—the student is through with writing the paper and you should be through making rewriting suggestions.

These practices allow our students to learn in their own words to see what they think and what they know and what they don't; they also allow our students to communicate this full or partial knowledge to us and so enter in to our disciplinary conversations. Their learning, like our teaching, is an amalgam of thoughts, voices, and influences, braided together to create new and important understandings. And they must do the braiding, yes, with our help but for themselves.

References

Bishop, Wendy. *The Subject Is Writing*. Heinemann, 1991.

Bazerman, Charles. *Shaping Written Knowledge: The Genre and Activity of the Experimental Article in Science*. U. Wisconsin Press, 1988.

Elbow, Peter. *Writing Without Teachers*. Oxford U. Press, 1973.

Emig, Janet. "Writing as a Mode of Learning." *College Composition and Communication* 15 (1977) 122-28.

Fulwiler, Toby. "How Well Does Writing across the Curriculum Work?" *College English* 46, 2 (February, 1984), 113-125.

_____."Interactive Writing and Teaching Chemistry." *Journal of College Science Teaching*, February, 1987, 256-262.

_____. *The Journal Book*. Ed. Boynton/Cook Heinemann, 1987.

_____. *Programs that Work: Models and Methods for Writing Across the Curriculum*. Co-ed., A. Young. Heinemann, 1990.

_____. *Teaching with Writing*. Boynton/Cook, 1987.

_____. "Writing Is Everybody's Business." *National Forum*, The Phi Kappa Phi Journal (Fall, 1985), 21-24.

_____. "Writing Workshops and the Mechanics of Change." *WPA: Writing Program Administrator* 12 (Spring, 1989) 7-20.

Gere, Anne, ed. *Roots in the Sawdust: Writing to Learn Across the Disciplines.* NCTE, 1985.

Herrington, Ann, and Charles Moran, eds. *Writing, Teaching, and Learning in the Disciplines.* New York: MLA, 1992.

Maimon, Elaine. "Writing in all the Arts and Sciences: Getting Started and Gaining Momentum." *Journal of the Council of Writing Program Administrators* 4.3 (1981) 9-13.

_____. "Collaborative Learning and Writing Across the Curriculum." *Journal of the Council of Writing Program Administrators* 9.3 (1986) 9-15

McLeod, Susan H., ed. *Strengthening Programs for Writing Across the Curriculum.* New Directions for Teaching and Learning No. 36. Jossey-Bass, 1988.

Russell, David. *Writing in the Academic Disciplines, 1870-1990.* Southern Illinois University Press, 1991.

Walvoord, Barbara E. *Helping Students Write Well: Strategies for all Disciplines.* Modern Language Association, 1986.

Young, Art, and Toby Fulwiler. *Writing Across the Disciplines: Research into Practice.* Boynton/Cook, 1986.

Tools For Tampering With Teaching's Taboos

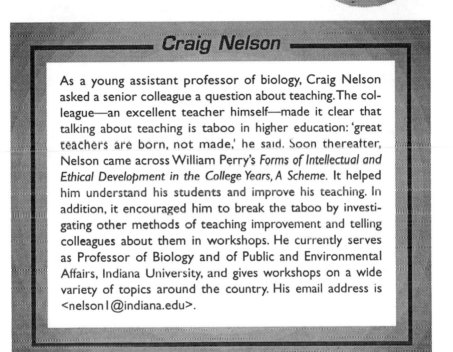

Craig Nelson

As a young assistant professor of biology, Craig Nelson asked a senior colleague a question about teaching. The colleague—an excellent teacher himself—made it clear that talking about teaching is taboo in higher education: 'great teachers are born, not made,' he said. Soon thereafter, Nelson came across William Perry's *Forms of Intellectual and Ethical Development in the College Years, A Scheme*. It helped him understand his students and improve his teaching. In addition, it encouraged him to break the taboo by investigating other methods of teaching improvement and telling colleagues about them in workshops. He currently serves as Professor of Biology and of Public and Environmental Affairs, Indiana University, and gives workshops on a wide variety of topics around the country. His email address is <nelson1@indiana.edu>.

Teaching is like other forms of loving in at least two important ways. First, different concerns emerge at different levels of mastery and maturity. And second, just as detailed knowledge of pair-wise love and love-making were more or less taboo when I was growing up, knowledge of teaching has been essentially taboo in many academic cultures. And I mean taboo in the strong sense—not just failing to teach prospective faculty about teaching and teaching resources, but pretending that there is nothing to be known that can make a major difference in teaching. Beyond the mastery of content, great teachers are born and not made, in this view. Just like Don Juan, it would seem. I have been quite lucky in my teaching career, as I have serendipitously encountered some important alternatives at pivotal moments in my development. Or, perhaps more likely, encountering the alternatives made the moments pivotal.

The extent of the change in my views is epitomized for me by the contrast between the answers I would now give to two questions and the answers that were implicit in the ways I initially taught. One of these questions is: "Should we evaluate teaching by what the teacher presents or by what the students learn?" Coming out of graduate school I gave well organized, dense lectures that covered a lot of ideas quickly—lectures that were just what I thought I would have learned best from at that time. Indeed, they were much better than most of the lectures that I had learned from! And they were well received by a good portion of my classes. I assumed that the students who did not learn well from them were either dumb, lazy, ill-prepared, or, to be more generous, otherwise engaged—although I would never have put it so bluntly, even to myself.

Although I have since observed that many faculty feel this same way, I now see two main problems with it. The most fundamental is that it abdicates all power for change and makes any improvement depend on getting different students. And it is not unusual to hear faculty blame the problems they have in teaching on insufficiently rigorous admission policies. The second main problem with this approach is that it assumes that one's own experience is all the guide one needs to teach effectively, and thus takes one's self as the measure of all things. (I will turn to the second of my two questions at the end of this chapter).

Initially in all kinds of loving, including teaching, a lot of attention usually falls on basic structure. There are a number of guides to the basic anatomy of teaching ranging from short treatments of basic lecturing and variations thereon (Cashin, 1985; Frederick, 1986) to full blown handbooks (Eble, 1988; McKeachie, 1994; Lowman, 1984). Indeed, most of us learn in graduate school how to organize content and present it in talks, seminars and lectures. But often when we leave graduate school, lecturing is really the only teaching mode in which we are semi-competent.

However, a key to outstanding teaching, and outstanding love-making generally, is to move beyond basic anatomy—to be able to do more than one thing well. The acquisition of alternative teaching moves thus becomes central. In most classes this means somehow mastering a variety of discussion and other active learning techniques. A few of us come naturally to discussion, finding it easy to keep track of who said what while guiding the discussion and managing the class. I was not—and am not—one of those people, and I do tend to think of that talent partially as something one is born with, a facet of personality if you like. What the rest of us need are active learning techniques that are robust enough not to depend on our personalities—robust enough to be largely goof-proof.

Active Learning Example: Quick Pairs

Perhaps the single most useful teaching move I have learned is a technique that seems able to elicit engagement and discussion from any class. For mnemonic reasons let's call it Quick Pairs or PWPH: pulse, write, pair, and harvest. The pulse is an initial stage that gets each of the students prepared for discussion. It can be, for example, a brief silent (i.e. individual) consideration of a paragraph in the reading or a segment of lecture. I then give the students a question to answer and time enough to formulate their answers in writing. I usually wait until about half have quit writing. With experience one can announce the time first ("take two-minutes to sketch your answers")—though I still tend to adjust the time according to the students' non-verbal behavior. I then ask the students to "compare your answers with your neighbors, in groups of two or three." I time this paired phase by listening to several pairs of students and watching the non-verbal behavior of the class as a whole. After these brief collaborations many students spontaneously participate in class discussion. Moreover, students typically regard it as fair for faculty to further harvest the results by calling on them individually for a report on their pair's ideas—even though they would often resist being called on individually without the prior, preparatory interchanges. Typically, this will allow me to engage any and every student in whole group discussion, if my purposes are well served thereby.

This example illustrates the kind of active learning that I have found both most effective and easiest to use, especially with students with little prior experience in serious collaboration. I think of it as teacher-structured and student-executed. I see three main tasks that teachers usually need to take responsibility for: assuring preparation, structuring social roles, and providing intellectual scaffolding.

Making Active Learning Work:
1. Assuring Preparation

The Quick Pairs or PWPH approach as applied in a large group illustrates how teachers can be responsible for having the students prepared for discussion. In lecturing to freshman courses, I find it very helpful to stop every five to ten minutes and use this technique. The initial lecture segment prepares the students for the writing exercise (and the knowledge that an exercise is coming focuses their attention on the presentation). The writing exercise in turn prepares them for the discussions with their neighbors.

The importance of this move is evident in the flip definition of an extrovert as someone who really likes to start a sentence outloud hoping to find out where it ends. Introverts, in contrast, hate the very idea of starting before they know where the sentence ends. An initial period of writing thus prepares the introverts for talking with their neighbors and helps the extroverts refine what they are going to say—thus improving the small-group participation of everyone. The discussions with their neighbors in turn prepare the students for participation in the larger group, partly by letting them rehearse what they will say, partly by getting feedback that they are on an interesting track, and partly by letting them decide to talk about their partner's ideas if they find them more interesting than their own initial efforts. At each stage the teacher has thus taken responsibility for having the class prepared for the next step.

As an alternative starting point, I often have students read an assignment before class and prepare several questions for a possible quiz. The discussion in class can then focus on the more interesting of the prepared questions. And the frequency of actual quizzes can be adjusted to maintain a satisfactory level of preparation (I prefer nearly 100%).

Having students prepare a one- or two-page written analysis before class and then modify it in class will profitably sustain a period-long discussion. I allow modifications in class that count for the grade. However, I either require that the preparation be printed or insist that the students use in class a color of ink that contrasts markedly from the one in which they prepared the assignment—this makes it quite easy to see whether each student has prepared for class. And by making the fraction of the course grade proportional to amount of effort required in preparation for discussion, and by giving zeros for failure to prepare, I find that on most days all of the students will come to class with the assignment prepared.

Again, this illustrates the idea of the teacher taking responsibility for setting up a system in which the students are prepared for active learning. And the central point is not that one should use any particular technique. Rather: active learning works best when the teacher takes this responsibility seriously.

Making Active Learning Work: ───────────────────
2. Structuring Social Roles

Once the students are prepared, the teacher must structure the discussions so that they work socially. Quick Pairs (PWPH) and similar methods rely for social structure on the students forming groups and taking turns. In the group formations phase it is often helpful to say "look around you and make sure everyone is included in a group of two or three." Turn taking can be greatly facilitated by announcing, "one more minute" or "two more minutes," at which point anyone who has not yet participated fairly will usually be asked by their partners to share what they have written or thought. Frequently the discussions become even more animated at that time, and I often allow them to extend beyond the announced time, relying on the intensity of student engagement and on listening to student comments to pace the ending time, which I usually announce as "20 more seconds—finish your sentence" and "10 more seconds—let's pull back into the large group." Sometimes I have to then begin talking to fully regain the classes attention—frequently by asking a student to share what her group concluded. Out of a desire to hear this student, others in the large group will then hush anyone who is still talking in a small group.

The essential point here is not any particular move by the teacher. But rather, discussions and other active learning arrangements will work better if the teacher is monitoring the social interactions and has at hand ways to make the interactions more effective.

When student interactions are relatively brief—a few minutes— groups can be small. The main tasks are typically sharing ideas and finding and modifying partial understandings of the material and its applications. Many topics benefit from more prolonged discussion than pairs can reliably sustain, often because the task requires more understanding than the average pair of students brings to it. In these situations more of the responsibility for the social processes must be explicitly built into the groups.

One of the pivotal moments in my development as a teacher was a demonstration by the late Dr. Judith Hanson of an approach to discussion that she used in classes as large as 125. She had the class prepare a written assignment. She then broke the class into groups of five and had them discuss the topic and modify their work (using ink of a different color than the one they had used in preparing the assignment). This allowed her do a rough assessment of the extent of preparation simply by scanning the papers during the discussions. She and one graduate student would monitor the groups and give each student a grade for participation dynamics and, later, a grade on the written work that took account of both preparation and the modifications. The students were deeply and effectively engaged in the demonstration discussions and I was inspired to try this in my own classes.

I have found several teaching moves that help make the social dynamics work when using Hanson's approach with groups larger than two or three. One is managing the group size. I try to keep the groups to fewer than eight students, with five or six being ideal: Large groups often fragment into side conversations and groups that are too small may not have enough insights and differences in perspective to sustain a period-long discussion.

I have also found it helpful to assign students to groups. Usually I do this by deciding how many groups I want and then having the students count off. One time we count off along the rows. The next we count off in some erratic pattern—thus making it impossible for students to control who they will be with. When in contrast I have let groups form spontaneously and last for several weeks, I have often had problems. Some groups will include too many students who are trying to disengage from the course. Some groups will be disproportionately good students—they will be pleased but other good students who are not in such groups will feel disadvantaged. And most of my classes seem to include at least one person (in addition to myself) who is hard to get along with. With permanent groups, other students feel trapped with this student whereas when the groups reform for each new task they typically feel they can take their turn almost happily. Rotating group membership also increases the number of their classmates whom students know well enough to consider including in out-of-class study groups.

In some classes longer discussions may tend to wander progressively off course. This can be fairly easily prevented by providing a more structured agenda or another more carefully specified task— for example, going over a worksheet or set of questions. It is also quite interesting and effective to wander slowly around the room listening to some groups while watching others part of the time and actively and visibly watching the group you are listening to at other times. The first allows better monitoring and the second allows more direct encouragement.

For larger groups to work well, it is essential to make the group responsible in part for keeping everyone involved. One can easily monitor the dynamics of up to a dozen groups of students as long as one is not trying to keep track of the content of their discussions (evaluation of content is handled by evaluating the worksheets). If a student seems not to be participating actively in the discussion (not just actively listening), I lower the participation grade for every student in that group unless the other students are repeatedly inviting that student to share what she or he has written. Even quite extreme introverts can usually participate if they can read what they have written and if the group spontaneously asks them to share it. With the group taking responsibility, I almost invariably get 100% participation in group discussions.

However, it often takes more active intervention to keep some students from monopolizing the discussion. I eventually learned to suggest to people who were dominating discussions that since they were good at getting the floor, they needed to learn to use this skill to involve those whose views they did not yet understand. I give them an A- the first time I note this on their paper, a B and a more elaborate set of comments the next time if necessary, and a C and invitation to come and see me if the B and associated comments were insufficient. I have found that almost everyone can learn to pass the floor in the face of rapidly declining grades. Although this sounds harsh, I have never had a student complain about it on the course evaluations. Instead, I have had a number of students comment that this approach to group dynamics led to the first real discussions they had ever experienced.

Once again, the central lesson here is not that one should use a particular approach but rather that active learning will work better if the teacher has taken responsibility for providing a framework that structures social roles. One further example will show how large the benefits can be.

Active Learning Example:
Complete Turn Taking

Active Learning Example: Complete Turn Taking. The benefits that can be gained from structuring social roles is illustrated by a method I think of as complete turn taking. I learned it in a workshop given by Dr. Barbara Olive of Concordia College. For preparation, the students read an assignment and write answers to some open-ended questions. In discussing their answers and reactions in groups of three to five, each person in turn gets to continue without interruption until she formally announces "I'm finished." On the second round, each in turn notes the positive things she gained from her collaborators' insights, terminating again with "I'm finished." Thereafter the collaboration is unstructured.

This produces unusually effective communication. In less structured modes, if I have a new idea and pause to get it straight, someone else starts talking. If, alternatively, I suddenly realize how the material at hand sheds light on my personal history and pause to decide whether and how to share it, someone else usually starts talking. Moreover, in unstructured exchanges, we often put more energy into thinking about what to say next than into listening. But here what one is going to say depends on one having listened closely to what one's peers have to say. The complete turns approach thus fosters more careful listening, greater freedom to develop ideas, and clearer statements of consequences and values. Some dreamers even argue that such an approach might be applicable to faculty committee meetings.

A number of books are now available that provide additional approaches to active learning and additional methods for assuring that one's students are really prepared for structuring the social dynamics (Bligh, 1986; Gabelnick et al. 1990; Johnson et al. 1991; Myers and Jones, 1993; Whitman, 1988)

Making Active Learning Work: ─────────────────
3. Intellectual Scaffolding

Once we have structured our classes so that the students are almost invariably prepared for the active learning opportunities and so that the social roles work during active learning, we can turn to the question of how to maximize the gain. This might seem like an unnecessary question since active learning itself tends to be better than lectures in producing retention, comprehension, application, synthesis and student enthusiasm and satisfaction (McKeachie, 1994). However, my own first attempts at using discussions were not very successful because I mistakenly thought that all one needed to do was have the students talk amongst themselves. I find instead that providing some intellectual scaffolding or framing can radically improve discussions.

Consider first the Quick Pair method. Rather than simply saying discuss this with your neighbors, it is more effective to ask particular questions. I usually either use questions that draw out connections and implications or ones that are like questions, or parts of questions, that I might put on the exam (or other assessment) over the material being discussed. This has three effects. It increases the importance of both the preparation and the discussion in the students' eyes. It allows the students to think together more effectively. And it allows them to rehearse kinds of thinking that you want them to do but which might otherwise be beyond many students' reach.

Longer discussions will require more careful scaffolding to achieve these same goals. This can be in the form of an outcome that must be produced—a report to the larger group, for example. Or it can be in the form of more demanding analyses to be done and reviewed. Let me give an example of the latter.

Active Learning Example: Worksheets for Intellectual Scaffolding

When I want to produce deeper understanding of complex issues, and of ways to deal with complexity or controversy, I often have a class fill out an evaluative worksheet before class. A typical worksheet asks for the author's main points, the support offered for each, an evaluation of the strength of that support, and a statement of the burden-of-proof that the student advocates for each point. Burden-of-proof is a choice between the skepticism of the scientist who usually "rejects the point until it is shown to be probably true" and an alternative that "accepts the point until it is shown to be probably false." Either choice must be justified by an explicit statement of the consequences on which the student bases the choice and by a statement of the strength of evidence that would cause the student to reverse her conclusion. This approach takes uncertainty and adjudication as foundational and further asks the student to justify choices in terms of the consequences and their value (see Nelson 1986 and 1989 for examples). It thus uses intellectual scaffolding to elicit higher-order critical thinking.

Critical Thinking

There are several different major approaches to fostering critical thinking in college (Kurfiss, 1988). I have earlier discussed how to fit three of them with active learning (Nelson, 1994). I want to concentrate here on the approach that sees fostering critical thinking as a process of producing cognitive development. This approach was as fundamental to the transformation of my own teaching as was the discovery of failure-proof discussion methods.

In this approach the deepest difficulty in fostering critical thinking comes from our unchecked expectation that students already have developed the intellectual capacity to understand the ways our disciplines work. It is helpful to distinguish several capacities that we want students to master. One includes such basic right-answer reasoning skills as syllogisms, understanding area and volume in terms of unit squares and cubes, and understanding (not just executing) mathematical operations. I term this level complex-correct thinking: there is a correct answer and usually a correct way to get there but a lot of thinking is required, as anyone who has learned at least some calculus can testify. Arons (1990) provides a longer list including both general and quantitative reasoning skills.

Piaget (e.g. 1967; see also Arons 1990) provides a framework that explains many of the problems delineated by Arons and others. Children initially acquire skills in concrete tasks and only with more experience and maturation become capable of dealing with ideas and reasoning operations in the abstract—i.e. "formal operations." Understanding mathematical equations without needing to think of specific concrete examples and understanding the concept of a tragic hero rather than just picturing particular heroes provide examples of formal operations. In many institutions a majority of entering college freshmen are not yet ready for courses based on formal operations (e.g. Arons), but many first-year courses require them. Herron (1975) lists 16 "competencies" integral to freshman chemistry that appear to require formal reasoning. Arons provides extensive examples of how we can help students master complex-correct formal reasoning tasks.

However, even students who are fully competent at formal operations may still not be capable of many of the tasks faculty usually characterize as critical thinking. I have asked over 3,000 faculty in workshops to envision the critical thinking skills they would like to teach. Well over 90% of the tasks specified require understanding beyond the right-answer focus of basic logic and formal operations. Perry's (1970, 1981) scheme of intellectual development helps us understand some central tasks faced by students after they become capable of formal operations.

Perry found that students typically enter college with a simple view of knowledge, one that greatly limits their ability to understand complex issues. Subsequent studies have confirmed the basic pattern he found while considerably enriching our understanding of the varieties of experience subsumed under the overall pattern (e.g. Basseches, 1984; Baxter-Margolda, 1992; Belenky et al., 1986;,

Kitchner and King, 1994). As a first approximation to understanding some of the significance of these studies for learning in college students, I find it useful to simplify the findings to a series of four approaches that the students take to learning and to focus especially on the three transitions between the four approaches.

Approach One:
Dualism or Sergeant Friday

In this approach, the intellectual world is seen almost exclusively as red or white with few things being pink. Real knowledge is assumed to be unambiguous, discovered, and eternal truth and falsity is equally clear and permanent. Misspelling and wrong additions provide concrete examples of what is taken to be the general state of knowledge. Perry termed this approach "dualism."

In such a universe the roles of teacher and student are quite clear. Students, like the famous TV detective sergeant, want "just the facts ma'am" and mostly expect to memorize them, at least for long enough to pass the exam. Teachers are seen as gigantic fluorescent yellow highlighters. We are supposed to tell students what parts of the text are important enough to be memorized. We are not supposed to add anything to the text—there is plenty there already. And we are certainly not allowed to disagree with the text. The students have a clear view of the hierarchy of authority and if we were that smart we would have written the text. Right? And besides, if the text isn't right why are we using it? And, worse, how could anyone decide what part of the text to trust and what to discard?

Although this approach severely limits students' abilities to understand complexity, partly by seeing complexity as due to the incompetence of some authorities, it does allow students to do two things that are helpful as a base for complex thinking. First, a dualistic approach can be used to master a base of information, though the significance of the information may be quite elusive. Second, even though students are taking this approach to a course, they can learn to do the form of critical thinking that I termed above "complex correct thinking"—the thinking required to solve problems where there is a single right answer and the teacher has taught the students "the way" to find that answer.

Much teaching of freshman courses, especially in the sciences, focuses on the two tasks that dualists can do well: memorizing information and solving right answer problems. Partly, I think, this is because teachers have found that such teaching works, in the sense of letting the students pass exams. However attractive this seems, I now question its appropriateness. Students seem too often to mistake knowing something for the exam with having usefully learned it—and are often insulted if one wants them to remember it later.

──────────── Transition One: Legitimate Uncertainty

Sometimes students take the Sgt. Friday approach to an area because it is new to them and they have no mastery of its complexity. Sometimes they take that approach because it is the core way they think about most or all intellectual matters. Either way the first key intellectual task in a course is understanding that uncertainty can be legitimate and is often pervasive, even in areas such as science that are popularly thought to be laden with truth. No one can think critically about things that seem unquestionably true. However, dualistic students so resist uncertainty that they may suspect a teacher's competence if shown two ways to work a problem!

Therefore, a basic question for teachers is, "How can we help the student understand the extent of the uncertainty in what we teach and its legitimacy or sources?" And understanding of both the extent and the sources is essential. If the students just understand the possible sources without understanding the extent, they will often assume that the uncertainty is just a theoretical possibility and that for practical purposes the material is eternal truth. More sophisticated students often take this approach to science, for example. On the other hand, if students see that uncertainty is rampant in a course but do not understand its sources they often seem to assume that this is the teacher's fault—if the teacher were more competent, the truth would be clearer. Alternatively they assume that a particular area of knowledge is aberrant. When I began trying to teach ecological biology so as to produce intellectual development, students repeatedly said things on their evaluations such as "Nelson is a pretty good teacher but it is a shame that ecology is so uncertain—they should let him teach some real science sometime."

One very powerful tool for helping students understand that knowledge is in practice quite uncertain, even in "real" science, is to focus on the long term and short term history of knowledge. I sometimes ask students what physicists 100 years ago would have "known" to be absolutely and certainly true and beyond all possibility of doubt but that we now know to be wrong nevertheless. Important answers include: space was thought to Euclidian, motion was thought to be Newtonian, and matter was thought to be indestructible. It is of course important to focus on more recent shifts also, bringing these to bear on the course at hand. In biology the history of the "central dogma" in which information can flow only from DNA to RNA (precluding HIV) and of our explanations of why sex exists provide telling examples. More generally, the gradual demise of the dominance of "modernist" ideas and the emergence of "post-modern" alternatives provides a plenitude of examples (Anderson, 1990).

A discussion of the sources of uncertainty also depends closely on the material in the course. In science we can focus on the failure of logic to yield certainty. If logic provided truth about reality (rather than about imaginary universes which ours only approximates), then space would be Euclidian, rather than being a function of the distribution of matter, and two quarts of alcohol added to two of water would be a gallon rather than distinctly less (they dissolve in each other).

A central question then becomes: "How can knowledge be both uncertain and useful?" I like to take this one level further and ask how scientific knowledge can be wrong and still be useful—since if wrong ideas can be useful then uncertain ones surely can be useful too. For this I turn to the brilliance of the flat earth model.

A Key Example: The (Nearly) Flat Earth. In understanding the flat earth model, it is good to begin by asking how the curvature of the earth compares with the flatness of a small pond on a still day. How much would the pond dome up in the middle if it were rounded like the earth instead of being so wonderfully flat? The answer, of course, is that the pond does dome up in the middle to exactly match the earth's curvature. As indeed it must if the oceans are to encircle the globe.

One can also ask how smooth the earth is. Physicists have assured me that if one wants to understand how smooth the surface of the earth is, one should first look at a large ball bearing that has been carefully hand polished until it is everywhere a mirror. If it were blown up to the size of the earth, keeping the surface irregularities the same proportionally as they are on the ball bearing, it would then be much rougher than the surface of the earth. So the earth is as flat as the surface of a pond and smoother, proportionally, than polished steel.

Moreover, the flat earth model is the most widely used model of the shape of the earth in practical human applications like architecture and engineering, just as Newton's laws of motion, and not the more current relativistic models, are typically used in designing cars and airplanes.Indeed, I first began to really understand the importance of uncertainty in our knowing when I realized that the flat earth model currently has the same scientific status as we enter the 21st century as Newton's laws of motion. Both capture important pieces of reality. Both are of immense practical importance. And both are quite wrong and wrong in exactly the same sense: each is a quantitatively-good first approximation that fails on larger scales.

It gradually dawned on me, and I try to use this example to help students understand, that all of our current scientific models may ultimately turn out to be useful in this same sense and wrong in about the same sense too. It matters that the subjects we teach are largely current versions of ideas that will probably eventually be seen to be humorous half-truths, as the flat earth model is now regarded.

I have found that the significance of the flat-earth example eludes even some faculty. In discussing this, it has often become evident that they are trying to make sense of it within a realist or modernist view (Anderson, 1990), where science is seen as a mirror of nature. However, the key point here is precisely that the example shows that such an approach is too limiting, that science is too uncertain and its models too temporary to fit comfortably within such a model. Students have the same problem and clearly will need to discuss this model with each other in order to fully appreciate its significance.

Some theorists emphasize the importance of tangible stories or examples in our students' understanding of new ideas.[1] I have devel-

---

[1] For example, see Nel Noddings, *The Use of Stories in Teaching*, chapter 1 of this book—*eds.*

oped the flat earth idea here as an example of the kind of touchstone we need to provide our students if they are to apperceive the ubiquity of uncertainty and the way that things can seem true and be quite useful while still remaining uncertain or even being wrong. Alternatively or additionally, stories like this illustrate how theories can match a lot of data without being proven: almost any attempt to measure the curvature of the surface of a small pond (without the use of lasers) will erroneously show that it is indeed quite flat.

Approach Two:
Multiplicity or "Baskin Robbins"

When the students first see that there is no guaranteed right answer in an area, they typically conclude that all opinions must be equally valid. Lacking any better standard, they pick an opinion because it feels intuitively OK, much as one might pick a flavor of ice cream. Perry termed this stage "multiplicity". Most graduates from most four year programs have multiplicity as the most sophisticated mode they use spontaneously in thinking about real problems (King & Kitchner, 1994). In this sense, liberal and professional education generally fail even for most students we graduate!

Transition Two: Comparisons and Criteria

The transition from dualism to multiplicity requires that students recognize the inevitability of important uncertainty on many questions. The transition from multiplicity to greater sophistication requires the recognition that despite this uncertainty, one can often select one or more ideas or other human productions (be they poems, scientific theories, nursing plans or whatever) that are superior to most other comparable productions or, alternatively, that although there is a fair range of acceptable productions, many others are demonstrably terrible. Our primary teaching task becomes showing how we recognize better from terrible or vice versa in our disciplines.

How do we separate better from terrible? Most people have heard of the big bang theory for the origin of the universe. Relatively few know that this model predicts that matter will have been initially spread so evenly that galaxies would never form, a prediction that has been understood for decades. Despite the elegance and power of the big-bang theory, there are of course a few individuals who believe in the existence of galaxies simply because they can see them or see photos of them! Put differently, the big-bang theory has been known to be wrong for decades. How can it then be that everyone is still taught it? It is taught not because it is right but because it is better.

When we claim that one theory is better than others, two questions immediately arise. Better than what alternatives? And better on what criteria? The big bang set of models is better than models that assume an unchanging universe and better than models that assume a steady state of endless change—better because they account for the cosmic background radiation, the changes in the average composition of stars through time and certain other features of the universe that are left unexplained by the other models.

The contrast with modernist views may help us understand the significance of this example too. Under a modernist approach the big-bang model would be seen as clearly truer. Under the approach I find more helpful to students, it is seen as clearly better, with progress towards truth regarded as very difficult to ascertain.

Under either a modernist or a more tentative approach, however, we can foster critical thinking more effectively if we explicitly delineate both the alternatives and the criteria we use to adjudicate among alternatives (Nelson 1986, 1989, 1994). Thus in teaching evolution my goal is not student belief. Rather, my task is to help students master the criteria used in science to judge which theories are better so that they can compare evolution with any proposed alternatives (Nelson, 1986).

In teaching, I attach special importance to ways of testing theories that are "fair" both in the sense that they are based on new discoveries and in the sense that they could have supported each of the alternatives being compared. Radioactive dating provides a good example of a fair test. In this case the competing theories are that the earth is quite young, that it has to be less than 100 million years old as advocated by Lord Kelvin, and that it has to be of much greater age. Radioactive dating estimates the time since a rock crystallized. It is fair because none of the original theories are based on radioactivity and fair because it could have shown that all the rocks on earth are less than 10,000 years old (and some do date this young, due to very recent crystallization) or that they are all less than 100 million years old. Instead it showed that the oldest rocks are about four billion years old.

Approach Three: ――――――――――――――――
Contextual Relativism or "Teachers' Games"

As students learn to use criteria to separate stronger and weaker productions, they begin to treat intellectual activity as games, either teachers' games or disciplinary games. These are seen as games in two senses. First, there are good and bad moves and the student can tell the right moves within the rules of the class or discipline. Further, students have a choice of playing or not playing. There is a strong element of sophistry: instead of the "any opinion is equally good" of multiplicity, students now often still think privately that any framework is equally good but that within a disciplinary framework one can tell better from worse and otherwise proceed to make sense of the chaos of uncertainty in a way that is satisfying to the teacher if not to oneself. "Contextual relativism" describes this stage.

Why Games Are Not Enough: Developing Intellectual Empathy
The necessity for further development can be seen if we examine the development of empathy (Belenky et al. 1986). When we treat issues as dualists, we rely on an authority to provide the answers. We see no validity in asking why authority chose those answers: authority chose them because they are the truth. Since we don't understand why our group believes as it does, we have no basis for understanding why other groups believe differently—they are simply wrong. Indeed, we frequently regard other views as not just factually wrong but also as morally wrong—as evil (Perry, 1970). Thus we have no base for either intellectual tolerance or empathy.

In areas we treat with multiplicity, we believe that authority cannot provide dependable answers. If we must pick an answer, we do so unreflectively (again, like choosing ice cream). Thus, we have no articulated understanding of our choice and, hence, no grounds for intellectual empathy. But we want others to tolerate our choices and thus expect to tolerate theirs. This leads us to try for unlimited tolerance in areas where we see that there are no clear answers.

In the intellectual "games" of contextual relativism, we understand that people living in different contexts often legitimately believe differently. We may even take as one of our central tasks the attempt to understand how intelligent, even brilliant people (past and present) ever came to believe things that are so different from those we currently believe (Russell, 1945). We are thus rapidly developing the capacity for intellectual empathy. But we still have unlimited tolerance for different frameworks of belief. Great tolerance might seem to be a virtue, but students here often carry it to extremes. Given an introduction to modern German history, they can see that in many ways Hitler was brilliant and effective. But they are reluctant to say that key parts of what he did was wrong or crazy (Belenky et al. 1986).

─────────────── **Transition Three: But Games Matter**

To make such judgements, one has to assert one's own values as preferable. One has to begin to take stands again, as one once did in dualism, but based now on an articulation of one's own values and analyses and not just as an echo of authority's positions.

How can we best foster this third transition, the one that allows deep professional competence and sophisticated ethical judgement? One way is to provide students with a model of how to make such judgements. Indeed the provision of just such an intellectual scaffolding was the rationale underlying the development of the burden of proof worksheet described above.

But intellectual models are not enough! In verbal presentations of his findings, Perry often emphasized that students at this level have just one question of you as a faculty member: "Are you alright?" The student can see that this new approach to knowing requires both that she leave behind many of her earlier views of why things should be and that she accept considerable responsibility for herself and her world. She wants to know if you are happy enough and moral enough. Who the teacher is becomes an essential part of the learning experience in a new and deeper way.

Put differently, students need to see us as faculty modeling the taking of stands securely grounded in our values in the face of uncertainty and complexity. One way to do this is to articulate for ourselves the answers to questions such as: "How are my personal values reflected in the choices I make as to what content to teach and what not to teach?" and "How are they reflected in the choices I make as to what pedagogical approaches to use and not to use?" Once we have articulated these for ourselves, we can share them with the students, thereby modeling mature thinking in the area that matters most to them—the ways we teach them.

By now we have blithely crossed several layers of the taboos that surround teaching. Not only are we looking at ways that teaching can be done better, but we must ask whether the ways our disciplines have traditionally been taught, or the ways our graduate professors taught, are the most effective ways for our particular students. And in many fields there is a further taboo against seeing that teaching is always at least implicitly teaching about values—both in the content choices and in the choices of pedagogies.

Approach Four:
Personally Affirmed Games

To operate as sophisticated adults, we must combine "games" and adjudicate among various combinations of these games in different contexts. Thinking becomes more complex. We come to see knowledge as constructed rather than discovered, as contextual, as based inevitably on approximations, as involving tradeoffs among conflicting values, and as requiring of us that we take stands and actively seek to make the world a better place (Belenky et al., 1986; Anderson, 1990).

We come to understand that to do significant good one must risk doing harm and that to do great good one must do significant harm (Levinson, 1978). We understand that a doctor who is unwilling to risk harming us is useless to us. Aspirin kills people. Other powerful drugs also have significant, occasionally lethal, side effects. Doctors must accept that some of their patients will be harmed or die from the side effects of drugs and treatments appropriately administered and from the consequences of appropriately withholding drugs and other treatments. And that is without any mistakes! Tradeoffs and risks are the rule not the exception in important real world decisions.

When we as faculty fail to get students to this level of critical thinking, we leave them poorly prepared to deal with personal and professional decisions and with the major issues of our times. Diversity, social problems, environmental issues, and the changing geopolitical system all require minds that can grapple successfully with uncertainty, complexity and conflicting perspectives and still take stands that are based on evidence, analysis and compassion and that are deeply centered in values. This ability must be a major goal of liberal and professional education. I have one more major tool to offer in this regard.

Maps for Students (and Teachers)

Ideas of conceptual maps have gradually acquired a central place in my thinking about teaching and its improvement. In proposing an introductory freshman seminar last year, I asked myself what maps I could provide that would help students frame their educational tasks—help keep things in a larger perspective and thereby make them both more doable and more educationally effective. Three quite different sets of idea came to mind.

The first is a one-dimensional map, a spectrum. It is useful to consider the span from naive realism to full social constructivism. In naive realism, of course, our ideas accurately represent an external reality. Descriptions of mineral crystal axes or legs on a grasshopper serve as nearly indisputable examples. And, from the students' point of view, so would the names of the characters in book and its basic plot structure (when unambiguous). At the constructivist extreme, our ideas are subject to few or no constraints from external reality and what we collectively think is (almost) totally a matter of social agreement. At the concrete level, examples are provided by the questions of what hair styles or clothing choices are appropriate for what modern interior environments (where neither hair nor clothes address any physiological needs). The shocking thing, from a freshman's point of view, is that most of this range is now "contested terrain."

Hence the power of this one dimensional map. It allows us to ask questions like: Where does the author (or the professor) think this issue or question falls along this gradient? And where do I think it should be placed along it? Anderson's (1990) book, *Reality Isn't What It Used To Be,* provides a fine, student-level introduction to the issues at stake in this contested terrain. For science, see also the chapter on "Believing where we Cannot Prove" in Kitcher (1982). For more advanced students, depending on discipline, try Kline (1980; the preface is widely useful and thought provoking), Strahler (1987), or Novick (1988, Chapter 13 "But the Center Doesn't Hold") and references therein.

A second map of the modern intellectual landscape is that of disciplinary discourses. A major problem for many students is that faculty often act as if (and may even believe that) they are teaching and thinking in English, rather than in some arcane disciplinary dialect. The dialects, of course reflect larger cultural distinctions. It is sometimes helpful to describe science as dealing with questions of external reality and pretending that questions of internal response and meaning have no relevance or even no validity. Much of the humanities, in contrast, deals with internal reality. Here the questions of correspondence to external reality are reduced in many cases to the issue of plausibility. No fact in a work of fiction need be literally true, only plausible in context. We judge the work by its correspondence with or relevance to an internal reality of motivations, feeling and emotions, and values.

A closer look at this landscape shows that disciplines (and subdisciplines) differ in the questions emphasized and in the standards for judging answers to those questions. Freshmen typically think that a text means what it says. But the same novel used in literature, women's studies, economics, and sociology classes means quite different things across the different courses. Students can be quite surprised and empowered by the ideas that the significance of a book is determined to a large extent by the questions one brings to it and that these questions differ markedly among courses; similarly for the standards by which one judges the quality of an answer. Bruffee's works (e.g. 1984, 1994) provide an introduction to this perspective.

Ideas of intellectual development (Perry and other references above) provide yet a third map that is quite helpful to students. At one level, these ideas help students articulate for themselves the differences between how they would have tended to think of the material in a course and the ways in which faculty typically want them to approach the material.

These three maps allow me to illustrate four points that are central to the processes of improving teaching. First, many faculty are like most freshmen. They are perforce on a journey but they have often not acquired any maps. With no maps, with no sense of where one is trying to go, one often mistakes any movement for progress or, worse, mistakes where one is for the center of the universe, the only reasonable place to be, the only reasonable way to think or to teach. Second, teachers often find that maps such as Perry's scheme provide powerful guidance in deciding what teaching moves are more appropriate at a particular time for a particular student. Third, the provision of new maps as students are ready for them can be a critical teaching move. So too, the issues presented by new maps of teaching can be a critical move in changing our own teaching or in fomenting change in others. Fourth, the three maps I have presented are fundamentally each about the same larger terrain, but each brings out a different perspective. The overall question is not which map is right, but rather which set provides the most useful guidance and promises the most enjoyable journey. Moreover, as Allan Watts once remarked, we in the West are always in serious danger of mistaking the map for the terrain. Having a set of overlapping maps helps us avoid unduly reifying any one map, whether as students or as teachers.[2]

Values and Teaching

The existence of multiple maps and the unavoidability of a guided do-it-yourself or constuctivist approach highlights a central issue for teaching: Is one inevitably engaged in a process of values modification or reinforcement? It is attractive to claim that the goals of teaching are really value-neutral. In reality, maps like these let us see that college teaching is always a process of values inculcation and values advocacy.

What values? Whose values? The values taught vary with the pedagogical and content choices the teacher makes. One pervasive value in higher education is that we should prefer a position sup-

---

[2]cf. Donald Dansereau and Dianna Newbern, *Using Knowledge Maps to Enhance Teaching*, chapter 7 of this book—*eds.*

ported by evidence, justified by comparisons with other positions, and checked for consequences. We should prefer this position over, for example, one chosen because authority tells us it is right.

This fundamental value of academia conflicts with the values students bring to us from many sub-cultures and the training many of them have received in previous schooling. Teachers may choose not to challenge authority-based universes for a variety of reasons, but this choice has severe consequences. It leaves students with less powerful ways of dealing with the complexities of professional, social and personal lives. And it leaves them less capable of understanding current intellectual and political landscapes. This is especially problematical for those issues where informed and effective responses and initiatives are crucial to the quality of our lives in the next several decades. In my mind these include: social structure and the limits of permissible economic disparity, environmental quality and resource use and conservation, and the appropriate applications of limitations for new medical and information technologies.

In the introduction to this chapter I emphasized that the extent of the change in my views is epitomized for me by the contrast between the answers I would now give to two questions and the answers that were implicit in the ways I initially taught. The first question was: "Should we evaluate teaching by what the teacher presents or by what the students learn?" My answer has switched from the former to the latter. The three main approaches I have treated here, teacher-structured active learning, fostering intellectual and ethical (cognitive) development, and providing students with maps that allow them to take an overview of their education as a whole, are the most powerful ways I have found to foster student learning.

Once we focus on fostering student learning, a second question arises naturally: "To what extend do we want to sort students and to what extent do we want to foster high levels of achievement by as many students as possible?" Although we would like to be able to answer "both," I have found that these two goals can be in substantial conflict.

For example, in courses I teach I often give out the question pool, or much of the question pool, as I assign the readings and other work. Similarly, when I write an exam I often write a second exam over the same material. Students who don't like their grade on the first exam (or who wish to skip the first one to concentrate, for example, on other courses) may take the second one with the higher grade prevailing.

These approaches considerably increase the proportion of the class that achieves the level of work that I have customarily called A. It decreases my ability to sort students, however. I also believe that it increases the accessibility of my courses to students from non-dominant backgrounds (see also Nelson, 1993). I have even begun to wonder if our goal should not be to see if we can eventually come to evaluate our teaching by the proportion of our classes that legitimately earn an A.

That radical thought deserves some pause. A mature Carl Rogers (1961), in sketching his own views on teaching, noted "when I consider the implications . . . I shudder a bit at the distance I have come from the common sense world that everyone knows is right." I think that all of us who have made major shifts in our pedagogies have shuddered a bit at times. Such is the force of taboos. And thence the constant need for a loving reconsideration of what we are about—to make sure our teaching reflects our intentional, caring choices rather than the shadowy dance of taboos brought unthinkingly forward from earlier contexts and times.

References

Anderson, W. T. *Reality Isn't What It Used To Be: Theatrical Politics, Ready-to-Wear Religion, Global Myths, Primitive Chic, and Other Wonders of the Postmodern World.* Harper and Row, 1990.

Arons, A.B. *A Guide to Introductory Physics Teaching.* John Wiley and Sons, 1990.

Basseches, M. *Dialectical Thinking and Adult Development.* Ablex Publishing, 1984.

Baxter Margolda, M. B. *Knowing and Reasoning in College, Gender-Related Patterns in Students' Intellectual Development.* Jossey-Bass, 1992.

Belenky, M., B. Clinchy, N. Goldberger, and J. Tarule. *Women's Ways of Knowing.* Basic Books, 1986.

Bligh, D. (ed.). *Teaching Thinking by Discussion*. Taylor & Francis, 1986.

Bruffee, K. "Collaborative Learning and the "Conversation of Mankind." *College English*. 46 (7), 1984.

_____ . *Collaborative Learning. Higher Education, Interdependence, and the Authority of Knowledge*. Johns Hopkins, 1994.

Cashin, W. E. "Improving Lectures." *Idea Paper* No 14. Center For Faculty Evaluation and Development, Kansas State University, 1985.

Eble, K. E. 1988. *The Craft of Teaching: A Guide to Mastering the Professor's Art*. 2nd Edit. Jossey-Bass, 1988.

Frederick, P. J.. "The Lively Lecture—Eight Variations." *College Teaching* 34:43-50, 1986.

Gabelnick, F., J. McGregor, R.S. Matthews and B.L. Smith. *Learning Communities: Creating Connections Among Students, Faculty and Disciplines*. Jossey-Bass, 1990.

Herron, J. D. "Piaget for Chemists: Explaining What 'Good' Students Cannot Understand." *Journal Chemical Education* 52:146-150, 1975.

Johnson, D. W., R.T. Johnson and K.A. Smith. *Cooperative Learning: Increasing College Faculty Instructional Productivity*. ASHE-ERIC Higher Education Report 1991-4, 1991.

King, P. M. & K. Strohm Kitchner. *Developing Reflexive Judgement: Understanding and Promoting Intellectual Growth and Critical Thinking in Adolescents and Adults*. Jossey-Bass, 1994.

Kitcher, P. *Abusing Science: The Case Against Creationism*. MIT Press, 1982.

Kline, M. *Mathematics: The Loss of Certainty*. Oxford, 1980.

Kurfiss, J. *Critical Thinking*. ASHE-ERIC Higher Education Reports, 1989.

D. Levinson, D., et al. *Seasons of a Man's Life*. Random House, 1978.

Lowman, J. *Mastering the Techniques of Teaching*. Jossey-Bass, 1984, 1990.

McKeachie, W. *Teaching Tips. A Guidebook for the Beginning College Teacher.* 9th Edit. Heath, 1994.

Meyers, C. and T.B. Jones. *Promoting Active Learning.* Jossey-Bass, 1993.

Nelson, C. E. "Creation, Evolution or Both? A Multiple Model Approach." In R. W. Hanson (ed.) *Science and Creation.* Macmillan, 1986.

_____. "Skewered on The Unicorn's Horn, The Illusion of a Tragic Tradeoff Between Content and Critical Thinking in the Teaching of Science." in L. W. Crow (Ed.) *Enhancing Critical Thinking in the Sciences.* Society of College Science Teachers, 1989.

_____. "Valuing Diversity in the Educational Process" and "Every Course Differently: Diversity and College Teaching: An Outline". Both in *The Role of Faculty from the Scientific Disciplines in the Education of Future Science and Mathematics Teachers.* National Science Foundation, Publication 93-108, 1993.

_____. "Collaborative Learning and Critical Thinking." In: K. Bosworth and S. Hamilton, Eds.: *Collaborative Learning and College Teaching.* Jossey-Bass, 1994.

Novick, P. 1988. *That Noble Dream : The "Objectivity Question" And The American Historical Profession.* Cambridge University Press, 1988.

Perry, W. G. Jr. *Forms of Intellectual and Ethical Development in the College Years, A Scheme.* Holt, Rinehart and Winston, 1970.

_____. "Cognitive and Ethical Growth: The Making of Meaning." In Arthur W. Chickering (ed.), *The Modern American College.* Jossey-Bass, 1981.

Piaget, J. *Six Psychological Studies.* Vintage, 1967.

Russell, B. *A History of Western Philosophy.* Simon and Schuster, 1945.

Strahler, A. N. *Science and Earth History: ,The Creation/Evolution Controversy.* Prometheus, 1987.

Whitman, N. A. *Peer Teaching.* ASHE-ERIC Higher Education Reports. 1988-4, 1988.

For Openers...
An Inclusive
Course Syllabus

Terrence Collins

Terry Collins was a first generation college student who took a long time to figure out how the university works. Consequently he felt like an outsider throughout his undergraduate career. He currently is Professor of Writing and Literature and Director of Academic Affairs in the General College, University of Minnesota—an open admissions unit designed to provide first generation, poor, minority, and otherwise disenfranchised students with equitable access to higher education. He believes that 'full disclosure' is the only way to ensure that students understand the ground rules of colleges and universities. His email address is <tcollins@maroon.tc.umn.edu>.

Background

To work in higher education is to work in a closed system. Those of us who are insiders to that system go about our business, occasionally surprised by a tacit ground rule we hadn't yet internalized, but for the most part we have been quietly socialized by extended stays in college, then graduate school, to norms we cannot name.

In general, this closed system feels comfortable to us. Even those members of the professorate who have built their careers as critics of the academic establishment make their livelihood within the comfortable security of tenure and the largely self-defined workscope of the academy. A bit of the monastery, a tinge of the jet set, a piece of the marketplace, a dollop of politics, a touch of the shopping mall—the closed system of higher education is a comfortable congeries of the arcane and the pedestrian.

To the newcomers who are our students, however, the norms and ground rules of higher education are neither clear nor valued. Granted, some few have had a chance to peer into our world. Perhaps their parents were successful in college; perhaps they've been privileged by co-enrollment in college courses while in secondary school; perhaps they're just quick studies. To the majority of our students, and especially to the so-called "new students" (those historically under-represented in higher education, such as older students, members of ethnic and racial minority groups, first-generation college students, single parents), our courses make real the pain of being strangers in a strange land. Not surprisingly, there is evidence that self-perception of outsider status among students leads to alienation and contributes to dropping-out (A. W. Astin. *What Matters in College*. San Francisco: Jossey Bass, 1993)

While we might not be able to do a lot about the complex social forces that contribute to insider/outsider dynamics, we can make our own courses sites where outsiders become insiders. We can demystify the obscure processes of the academy. Most importantly, we can make explicit the befuddling mores, assumptions, work habits, background knowledge, key terms, or other markers of the academic subculture too often left implicit, inaccessible to outsiders. And the starting place for that is the course syllabus, built on the principle of *full disclosure of the terms of success.*

Most often, I've found, course syllabi aren't given nearly enough thought. With word processing, it is easy—too easy—to play it safe, to call up a previous semester's entry (a file we might have inherited from a colleague who teaches the same course, who in turn may have inherited it from a professor in graduate school who taught the course, who may have...). We plug in some new dates or a new title, and *presto!* we're deluded into thinking we're up to date.

I'd like to propose that we think about the syllabus more complexly, for the sake of our students and for the sake of our own professional development. The syllabus lets us help students think of themselves as insiders in the strange world built by academics, and the process of its construction and revision affords us periodically recurring opportunities to be self-critical about our course, its content, and our approach to it. As much as any research monograph, the syllabus is a site where our professional integrity is tested and where our professional identity is formed.

Preparation

Before looking at the parts of a syllabus or at the language which forms it, let's step way, way back and begin with what might seem like artificially simple *basic assumptions* about our individual syllabus, the *goals and objectives* we have for the course, and the *resources at our disposal in the course site.*

Basic Assumptions

I'll offer the following as points of departure, recognizing that there are few universal basic assumptions, hoping that you might supplement this list with others which reflect your own circumstances.

Assumption 1: My syllabus enacts my theory of teaching—even if I didn't know I had a theory of teaching. Actually, all of our teaching enacts our theory of teaching, but the syllabus is the place where it gets codified tangibly, publicly. Whether I think teaching is a process of individual discovery or a matter of dispensing knowledge to passive students or a construct of interdependent collaborative communities, that theory will, and should, show up in my syllabus.

Assumption 2: My syllabus functions as a figure of the course and its theory. Its recursive nature (i.e. students consult it daily) gives it significant defining power, both connotatively and denotatively. If I want to know what the course looks like from the outside, what the course looks like to colleagues, to students, to the parents of students, the syllabus will show me.

Assumption 3: Students are not usually telepathic. I have to be very careful about what I assume students know or what I take for granted about their knowledge of how my course works. In general, the closer the students are to having just entered my institution, the less they will know about how things work; the more experienced they are, the more they are likely to know. This is especially true as I address increasingly diverse students in courses I teach.

Assumption 4: Faculty are responsible for building courses that promote the success of all students who legitimately enroll in their courses, not just the most experienced, the most familiar, the most attractive, or the most highly achieving. A syllabus that discloses all the terms of participation and the nature of all work to be performed establishes an assumption of inclusion of all members of the class.

Assumption 5: As faculty, it is our job to disclose as much insider knowledge as possible to promote the success of all students, and the syllabus is an important tool in such disclosure of tacit knowledge. This is especially true in courses that enroll freshmen or beginning majors, and in settings, such as large urban, commuter institutions, where we might reasonably expect to find many of the new students most likely to come to college without intellectual, social, and cultural insider status.

Your own situation will no doubt create different versions of these assumptions and additional ones. It's not likely that all assumptions about students on an urban commuter campus like mine, for instance—with 38,000 students across the full range of ACT scores, social classes, life situations, and ethnic-cultural backgrounds—will apply in smaller, residential, more homogeneous, more highly selective settings. *Regardless of the specifics of your situation, it is good to list explicitly your tacit assumptions as you begin to think about constructing a syllabus.*

Goals and Objectives

In addition to listing unstated assumptions, it is a good idea to force yourself to articulate *goals and objectives for the course* well before you begin to put together the syllabus. Most typically, courses exist because they have gone through a faculty/administrative process peculiar to a local institution. In nearly all cases, courses in colleges and universities get reviewed by departmental curriculum committees, and in that process it is usually the case that general goals and objectives have been stated rather formally for review by the curriculum committee or similar body. If you've not done so, you might want to review what these foundational documents say about the course for which you are preparing a syllabus. Knowing what your colleagues have imagined a course to be and what their rationale might have been for approving its general shape and objectives will help you define your own approach.

Additionally, you will want to articulate as fully as you can the following sets of goals, perhaps for disclosure to students through inclusion in your syllabus, perhaps solely for your own benefit as you prepare to create the syllabus:

What are the content or mastery goals for the course as defined by the department? This will usually be apparent from the foundational documents for a given course, but you may have to consult colleagues or your notes from faculty meetings to get the full picture. Usually, these departmental goals will be somewhat general. For example, in a course on the history of slavery in the U.S., the departmental goals and objectives might stipulate treatment of topics such as the geography of African origins, the geography of American slave economies, economic impacts and changes over time in such impacts, philosophical arguments used to justify slavery, abolitionism, and emancipation. Specifics of sequence and methods would not likely be detailed. In the syllabus you prepare for your particular offering of the course, you should assume that colleagues expect you to address these general goals explicitly.

What additional content or mastery goals do you bring to the particular version of the course you will teach? Since departmental goals and objectives are typically rather general and focussed on the minimum collegial expectations, you should define for yourself (and perhaps for the students) more specific goals and objectives you might have. To build from the example of a course on the history of slavery in the U.S., you might wish to add content goals about the family in slavery, differences in the legal status of slaves from colony to colony and state to state, the slave trade and middle passage, women in slavery, and religion. These additional goals and objectives might reflect your own interests or specialty, your values, new thinking in the field since original departmental approval of the course, your students' special interests, or other influences.

What are the process or skills goals for the course as defined by the department? In addition to content or mastery goals set out by the department, you might find that there is departmental or collegiate direction on other matters. It might be that our hypothetical course in the history of slavery also serves to introduce the students to work with primary sources, with departmental skills goals stipulating that students work with slave narratives as a way of coming to know primary source material in historical study. Or it may be that the course serves a "writing intensive" purpose in the freshman curriculum, etc. Granted, it is unlikely that a clean division between content and skills goals can stand close scrutiny, but it is a helpful distinction from which to begin a process of reflection.

What additional process or skills goals do you bring to the course as you teach it? In addition to those processes or skills stipulated by the department, you may have additional goals in this domain. For instance, you might wish to introduce students to on-line databases or CD-ROM bibliography tools in your discipline—in our hypothetical course on slavery in the U.S., various social sciences indexes. Or you might value highly collaborative work, and might need to build into the syllabus directions and time to cover overtly the communication processes and skills needed to carry off productive collaboration. In any case, to build a coherent syllabus and to support students' success in the course, you should be overt about such skills acquisition, whether the skills goals emanate from departmental dicta or your own values.

■ *Resources: Taking Inventory of the Course Site* ■

Courses change shape as a function of many things. Class size may determine the amount of student writing you can manage; the availability or absence of teaching assistants or lab assistants may shape your thinking about active learning strategies to use; the amount and type of computer access and support you have will determine whether you use simulation software or live labs; designation as an honors section may affect your baseline expectations of students; the time of day the course is offered or the length of the class period may make some approaches practical and eliminate others from consideration. In most cases, your syllabus should detail for students any number of resources and procedures for their use, and therefore the syllabus will change as resources dictate. In short, you'll likely consider lots of things external to the subject matter or goals of the course prior to designing an effective syllabus for a specific offering of a course.

To advance this process of course site inventory, you might want to begin by articulating answers to the following questions. Indeed, until you come to know fully the ins and outs of all sectors of your campus, you might want to make actual lists in preparation for writing your syllabus. While it may seem artificial to do so, it is nonetheless essential to plan course specifics in view of particular settings, rather than from a generic or dated ideal situation.

Individual situations vary widely, to be sure. The following inventory items provide only a start:

Who will enroll in the course? How many of them? A colleague who teaches courses in Fluid Mechanics had first taught these large lecture courses as if all those enrolled were majoring in Mechanics and Aerospace Engineering—her home department. Frustrated with relatively high dropout and failure rates, she looked closely at information supplied by the registrar and learned over the years that only about 30% of those enrolled in her course actually conformed to her imagined profile. Fully two-thirds of those who enroll are from diverse backgrounds she had not anticipated, ranging predictably across engineering disciplines, but also including students in Physics, Natural Resources, and Mathematics. To make the course workable, she has added tutorials, has spent more time with foundational materials, has provided a wider range of problems in her problem sets, and has radically changed the examples and simulations from which she moves toward theoretical clarity.

Quite predictably, the syllabus has changed as a reflection of her new realization about the population in the course and her new approaches to them. She cannot assume familiarity with how her department's tutorial operation works, since most of the students have not taken prior courses in that department. She now includes in the syllabus a section on how to access tutorial help and make best use of tutorial sessions. Formerly a one-page sheet with office hours and abbreviated daily readings and problem numbers from the textbook, her syllabus is now a multi-page document. Since the syllabus addresses what she knows to be a very sophisticated group of students (all are in at least their third year of university, and all of them are fairly advanced in Mathematics, for instance), it is not as fully explanatory as would be a syllabus for a freshman introductory course. But, since her digging through information on enrollments resulted in the discovery that English is a second or third language for nearly half of her students, she has made stylistic and vocabulary choices which are accessible across a fairly wide range of reading levels. Her syllabus for the diverse lecture course with its 80-120 students is, of course, now quite different than it was prior to her inquiry about whom to anticipate in the course!

What courses are prerequisite for my course? What procedures can I assume my students to be familiar with, or what specific knowledge can I bank on? What procedures etc. will I treat only briefly, and which will I need to address specifically in full? Some courses stand alone and do not define a predictable baseline of prior learning; others build on prior knowledge made specific by attaching requirements that students must have completed other courses prior to the course in question. If your course has prerequisite courses, you may want to examine recent syllabi for those prerequisites, being sure to note how your syllabus can and cannot build from what you find there. For example, building a syllabus for the first course in a three-course sequence in Chemistry for non-majors requiring only college level algebra, for which you might be able to make no assumptions whatsoever about new students' prior learning in Chemistry, will likely be quite different from building a syllabus for the third course in that sequence. While you need to build the syllabus for the first course from the ground up, elaborating on procedures and policies, in writing the syllabus for the third part of the course sequence you can probably make some assumptions about familiarity with the function of homework, safety equipment, lab procedures, or tutorial centers.

What human resources are available to me in teaching this particular section of the course? The vagaries of budget allocations and competition across departments for limited human resources lead to shifts in availability of help in course management—people such as clerical support, computer technicians, and skilled teaching/lab assistants. This, in turn, determines in part how we teach and how we design and present our course to our students in the syllabus. In the same vein, we should realize that not all students know how to use tutors or teaching assistants productively. Too often for beginning students (especially non-traditional students), being referred to the teaching assistant for help evokes images of detention in high school or unfortunate assumptions of stupidity based on skin color, hairstyle, or gender. In making an inventory of available human resources for your syllabus, categories overlap—here, in planning the syllabus document, you should consider not only whether you have access to assistants etc. to help with the load of a large course or with labs, but also whether students likely to enroll will know how to take advantage of this resource. A course for beginners might need a very different presentation of tutors and assistants than would a course for more advanced students familiar with departmental support personnel and their functions. Your syllabus will eventually need to address not only whom is available for help, but how students might use them.

What non-human resources are available to you in teaching this particular section of the course? In making this list for yourself, consider the full range of tools accessible by you or by the students. Where relevant, these resources might include computer facilities, locker rooms, livestock barns, slide collections, listening rooms, specimen vaults, map collections, simulation software, theaters etc. As a working academic who is in daily contact with such resources and materials, it is easy for you to overlook the fact that students who are outsiders don't know about such resources or their location. You may need to list in the syllabus detailed directions to some facilities, or you may need to specify such things as the size or optimal density of computer disks. Given the responses you provided to earlier inventory items about who will enroll in the course, you may need to give some attention to things which seem to you to be perfectly obvious, such as the location of library materials especially useful to the course or procedures for procuring items you might have placed on your library's "reserve reading" list.

Naturally, the inventory that *you* do will reflect your subject matter and the level at which the course is offered. How much of the inventory gets translated into syllabus material will likewise reflect the particulars of the course. But without knowing what's available and how it supports the work of students in the course, how can you build your syllabus?

Building the Syllabus

Getting down to making the text that will be your syllabus should go a lot more smoothly if you have done your preparatory work. You'll have made explicit what you and your colleagues want the course to do, what you can expect the students to know or not know, what resources you and the students will be able to access to carry forward the work of the course, how you hope to approach the content and skills goals of the course, how the various parts of the course fit together—even whether the room in which you teach has moveable tables and flip charts for collaboration or bolted benches designed for lectures before large audiences. Putting all of this into a coherent, effective document is the next challenge.

Generally, syllabi have at least three parts. The goal of each part is to make explicit how the course operates and how students can best succeed. The three basic sections are

(1) Background Information,

(2) Schedule and Assignments, and

(3) Procedures.

We'll discuss each of these sections in turn. Before getting into specifics, though, you need to make a key decision about how you plan to distribute the syllabus. Because the choice you make determines length and content, the *medium of distribution* for syllabi in your situation is important to know before writing the syllabus. While paper handouts are the common medium, it is no longer safe or smart to assume that this is the *best* or *only* medium for you and your course.

Increasingly, electronic text transfer has become the norm of professional discourse, and syllabi are no exception. Basically, you need to know whether your institution is one where all students have computer access and reliable electronic mail or file transfer access. In the fairly recent past, how much information you could include in each section of a syllabus was a function of many factors, including constrained photocopy budgets in some departments. *Prior to writing your syllabus, you should determine whether there are limits on how long the document can be, whether it is to be distributed for free or included in a course packet to be purchased, or whether you can simply post it on a departmental electronic bulletin board, gopher site, or World Wide Web homepage for student retrieval via computer prior to the start of class, avoiding the paper duplicating process entirely.* Needless to say, file transfer distribution, as opposed to paper preparation, provides some freedom from length restrictions. Moreover, such a system might well save you the trouble of replacing lost syllabi (and the students the embarrassment of asking for a replacement). And perhaps more importantly, electronic distribution facilitates access among people whose preferred medium is not print, such as visually impaired students who use Braille or voice output.

Having resolved the question of distribution medium, you're ready to build the syllabus.

1: Background Information

As is the case for writing each of the three sections of a syllabus, how much and what kinds of information you include in the background section will depend on who enrolls in the course and what assumptions you can make about their prior knowledge of the subject matter and about you personally. Other circumstances might also dictate how you approach this section. In any event, you can use this section to set a tone for the course, establish your classroom persona, and get across some essential information.

A: Instructor Information

At a minimum, include the following information about yourself in the text of your syllabus:

- your name and title
- your preferred form of address

- your office location
- information on wheelchair accessibility of your office
- your office hours
- your phone number
- your FAX number
- your TDD number or relay access
- your department's message system (do you have voice mail?)
- your e-mail address
- your mailbox location for delivery of materials
- your full mailing address for U.S. mail or courier service

Keeping in mind that students come back to the syllabus for essential information fairly often, you can use the syllabus text for such seemingly straightforward information to *set a tone that invites inclusivity and which promotes success*. Items included as instructor information can be stated simply as a list of facts. But you might also use this list as a chance to set a tone for your course. Over the years, I have seen colleagues and graduate teaching assistants do a marvelous job of using this introductory part of the syllabus to set just such an inclusive tone that invites the success of all. Consider how you might approach the following items from the instructor information section. For instance,

Instructor: Jane Doe

tells students who you are. But consider the difference between that short version and this longer possibility:

Course instructor: Professor Jane Doe (I prefer 'Ms. Doe' and will address you as 'Ms.' or 'Mr.' unless you prefer another form of address).

Note that the longer form leaves no doubt about how you wish to be addressed, giving the students explicit cues about how to operate, putting them on secure ground in approaching you. As to use of titles and formal or informal address, you should give some thought to what is most appropriate to your situation. For example, I deliberately ask students to use "Terry" rather than "Dr. Collins" or "Professor Collins" as a preferred form of address. As a very tall white male in middle age, with tenure and full professor rank, I have to work hard to make myself accessible to students. On the other hand, some women with whom I have worked identify themselves quite clearly and deliberately as "Doctor Doe" or "Professor Doe" because they have perceived a need to establish their persona's authority in view of culturally embedded patterns of trivialization of women.

Or, again, consider the very real differences in tone and success-orientation suggested in the following example:

Office hours 8-930 T Th in Old Main 104

This is pretty standard syllabus shorthand. In a limited way, it's clear. But it's also minimal to the point of seeming brusque or incoherent (What is "T" to the uninitiated?). Compare it to:

Office hours 8:00-9:30 a.m. on Tuesdays and Thursdays in my office, Old Main 104. The wheelchair accessible entrance to Old Main is on the east side.

If you cannot make these hours, you are welcome to see me in class to make an appointment at another time. You can also schedule meetings with me outside of office hours by exchange of e-mail.

Please do not see office hours exclusively as a time to address problems with the course. You can use them to clarify points you don't understand, to get additional readings, to talk about the subject matter in relation to your special interests, or to go over work in progress. You don't need a crisis to make productive use of these hours.

While the shorthand version at the top provides the minimal information *about you*, it doesn't provide the essential information *about the student* in relation to the course that is likely to promote success.

Finally, consider the tonal and content impacts of how you present something as trivial as your phone number:

Phone: 555-1234

versus

Phone: 555-1234
The best time to reach me by phone is during office hours, and
on Mondays and Wednesdays from 3:00-4:15. The phone rings
through to a secretary when I am not in the office, and you can
leave a message with him. Be sure to include your name, your
number, and good times to try to reach you if you would like
me to return your call.

B: Books and Materials

Most often, faculty simply list the author, title, and edition of books required for their course. In some cases, that is sufficient—the institution is small or the environment is coherent enough that even the newest of students will know that the sole bookstore on campus has ordered the books. But in other environments, additional information will be needed. Keep in mind that if you teach courses to first-year students, they will have been provided with their books on loan in public high schools, and may therefore have had no prior experience with the process of identifying books for purchase in a campus bookstore. If there is more than one bookstore on campus, you should be explicit as to which one will have stocked books for your course. And you might want to note if the books are available in one of your campus library reserve reading rooms (a good idea if you have doubts about whether all students can afford to purchase all books).

Very often, you will need to list other, non-book essentials. If photocopied course packets are used, be sure to note where students are to purchase them and how they are filed (by course number? by instructor name?). If specific non-text supplies are needed, give students enough information so that they can get the right stuff the first time they try. For instance, if they need safety goggles, give the minimum tolerances and the recommended or required type of materials. If they need computer disks, give the size and density you require. If they need to keep a journal, be explicit about required or preferred size and format or colors of ink you hate to look at. If you have very specific materials which are required and which have been ordered for purchase, be sure to note where and when they can be purchased. If deposits are required for additional materials or lab breakage, be sure to note that so students know without question what they need to do.

C: Resources

If you are building a syllabus that promotes student success and have done the background inventories suggested earlier, you will be able to include in your syllabus helpful information on resources available to students and how or when students might access such resources. You should include names, locations, office hours, and a statement about appropriate roles for teaching assistants, if you have them, or you might invite assistants to prepare a separate sheet about themselves in parallel with information you provide about yourself. If your department has a tutorial center, or if there is a campus-wide learning center, you should be explicit about its availability and its relationship to and appropriate uses for the course. For instance, it is one thing to write

Assistance with course papers and lab write-ups is available in the reading and writing skills center in J. Garcia Hall.

It is quite another matter to write,

Tutors in the reading and writing skills center in J. Garcia Hall have met with me, have gone over the writing assignments for this course and my expectations for those assignments, and are prepared to review drafts or work in progress either in person or via e-mail exchanges.

As another example, if librarians or specimen curators offer orientation sessions about special collections relevant to and required for your course, be explicit about when and where such sessions are held and your expectations about student participation in them.

Colleges and universities, and the faculty who teach in them, are required to provide appropriate reasonable accommodations when they are requested to do so by students with disabilities. On nearly all campuses, there is an office with responsibility for insuring access and assisting in identifying appropriate reasonable accommodations.

More and more, faculty are finding it to be in their best interests and in the best interests of students with disabilities to include in their syllabus a statement about reasonable accommodations. Such statements have the effect of notifying students with disabilities of the channels designated for pursuing accommodations and create an inclusive tone for the course, apparent to all those enrolled. Your institution may have a carefully worded boilerplate statement aimed at legal compliance with regulations. If that's the case, use it. In other instances, you may need to create your own. Consider language such as the following:

Students with Disabilities: If you have a disability which requires accommodation in this course, please see me as soon as possible. I am happy to make appropriate accommodations, provided timely notice is received.

To receive a copy of this material in alternative formats such as Braille or text file, please contact me immediately. Our system requires 72 hours for these services.

In addition to these fairly common subdivisions of the background section of a syllabus, some faculty find it useful to state clearly for students the goals and objectives of the course. In so doing, they disclose the direction they have in mind for the course and give some sense of how the various parts of the course work toward a thoughtful set of outcomes. Moreover, such goals and objectives disclose some of the "insider knowledge" of the organization of learning in disciplines and the perception of coherence among the various discrete items being studied. Other faculty, however, are reluctant to state so explicitly the goals and objectives of a course. To them, such statements seem to foreclose possibilities of discovery and autonomous outcomes among students who bring diverse motivations and aspirations to the course. In general, your decision to include or omit such statements will likely reflect your theory of teaching and the specific situation you find yourself in.

2: Schedule and Assignments ━━━━━━━━━━━━━━

As is the case for most decisions you make in building your syllabus, how much scheduling to build into the syllabus prior to the start of a course and how much to do after meeting with the class is a function of the complex interaction among institutional characteristics, students' profiles, teaching theory, and course goals. In his widely consulted *Teaching Tips* (Lexington, MA: D.C Heath, 1986), Wilbert J. McKeachie asserts that you'd want to provide a minimal outline of the course. By outlining things only lightly, he claims, you reserve the capacity to be flexible and responsive. This may well be useful advice in many situations where a residential, homogeneous population without outside demands of job and family can be anticipated.

My own experience, however, is the opposite. Students in urban commuter universities, in most community colleges, and, increasingly, in weekend and after-hours programs at small liberal arts schools won't often welcome or benefit from loosely scheduled situations. In my site, with my students, I've come to see that I need to create a coherent schedule for the course, commit to it, and be explicit in making it available at the very start of the class. For students who work nearly full time, who have young children, whose lives take them away from campus for the majority of their days and nights, success in our challenging courses often depends on their capacity to plan ahead, to schedule precisely, and to manage competing demands. In such a situation, students benefit from getting as much information as they can get as soon as they can get it. They need advance notice of due dates, reading assignments, labs, time spent in groups pursuing collaborative projects, studio requirements, field work, exams, study group meetings. More and more students are attending postsecondary institutions on the fly, making it less and less likely that they can be flexible in response to your mid-term shifts in direction or late announcement of new assignments or requirements.

The nitty-gritty of scheduling assignments and required work in the syllabus lends itself to a kind of thoughtfulness about tone and inclusivity very similar to observations made earlier. You can be clear and thorough in making assignments *and* create at the same time a supportive tone which says, quite directly, that you are serious about student success. Do not confuse this seriousness about student success with mindless coddling or unnecessary caretaking. Rather, think of it as being parallel to what you expect from professionals who interact with you. Which would you prefer to hear from the physician you pay to treat you, for example:

Take two of these brown pills twice a day. Call me next week.

versus

You have some minor inflammation and swelling in the knee, but I don't see signs of anything more serious. I'm prescribing a seven day supply of a mild anti-inflammatory called "swelldown." You should take two in the morning and two at night. It has no likely side effects, but if they make you tired or irritable, call me and we'll try something else. The swelling should go down over the period of a week, and if you'll take it easy on the knee you should get full relief from the pain by then, too. If the symptoms haven't diminished in seven days, be sure to call. Any questions or other concerns?

Quite naturally, we prefer the fuller, more respectful explanation, and we would be incensed if a physician failed to explain things fully for fear of "coddling" us or "stooping" to over-explanations of what is "completely obvious."

Back in the world of syllabus schedule writing, consider the following scenarios, in which a sample of typical syllabus shorthand is once again contrasted with a more generously elaborated treatment of the same scheduling material:

Feb 22: Read pp. 112-67

versus

Feb 22: Read pp. 112-167.
This is a particularly difficult section on American historiog-

raphy and theory, followed by application to competing histori-
cal representations of the Sand Creek massacre. You may find
it most useful to review notes from the lecture on January 30
and pp. 77-91 in the textbook prior to doing this new reading.

Granted, the first take does indeed make clear that students are to have read a certain body of material by a certain date. With it, you will have addressed the minimum of what they have to do. But with the second, you will have accomplished the same goal, with the additional clear indication that additional time might need to be budgeted to do the work well and that it is especially important that the concept be grasped. The second, in short, invites students to become insiders to the workings of the course.

In scheduling, whether fully elaborated at the very start or provided via bi-weekly handouts, always alert students not only to the daily requirements of reading or problem sets, but also to major due dates, exam dates, lab schedules, studio hours, small animal clinics, and the like, as they are relevant to your course. With the availability of formatting features even on low end word processing software, nearly any faculty member can use highlighting via bolds or shifts in font size or boxes or white space to draw attention to particularly important items on the schedule.

3: Procedures

In addition to full exposition of what work is to be done in what sequence if a student is to succeed in the course, your syllabus should also spell out as clearly as possible the policies and procedures which guide the course. In creating this part of your syllabus, you will need both to consult institutional regulations and to articulate your own expectations. Once again, if your goal is to promote the success of all students by taking the time to write a disclosive, inclusive syllabus, your section on procedures should set out to dispel any fog that might hold back the progress of those who haven't yet mastered the insider knowledge of college or university operations. Quite conveniently, a syllabus which spells out in detail the procedures under which a course operates will go a long way toward protecting *you* from surprises, too, since clear communication about how things work will minimize complaints that arise from misunderstandings.

Course policies

As I said at the beginning, academics are very often unable to imagine that someone wouldn't know the unspoken ground rules of academia. Like all closed systems, ours seems perfectly logical and reasonable to those of us who live within it. The result is that many things go unsaid which students need to know, particularly in the area of behavior and performance policies. The following is a sampling of course policies which usually need to be spelled out. In your situation, you will no doubt have others to address in your syllabus (I was surprised to see a weapons policy on a syllabus, for instance, but after a colleague explained it to me, it made sense in the situation). In nearly all cases, your syllabus section on policies should answer the following kinds of questions.

- **Grades:** How do students earn grades in the course? What counts for what portion of a grade? Are all papers, problem sets, labs, studio sessions, quizzes etc. equal? How does a student find out how she's doing? Are materials returned with grades? Are lab scores posted? Who is the final arbiter of contested grades in courses with teaching assistants?

- **Late work:** How do you handle late work? In what circumstances will it be accepted? With what notification? With what documentation?

- **Attendance:** Does your college or department have any guidelines on attendance? Have you initiated a policy of your own? Why is attendance important in your course?

- **Academic honesty:** Does your institution have a statement on academic honesty and plagiarism, which both defines unacceptable conduct and states the consequences? If so, you would do well to reproduce it in, or attach it to, your syllabus so that everyone knows and is operating within the same rules. Do you have additional strictures or policies about academic honesty which apply to your situation?

- **Classroom climate ground rules:** Increasingly, institutions and individual faculty are finding it necessary to spell out in course syllabi ground rules for individual conduct in classrooms. Such ground rules, usually put in place to protect class members from abusive but not illegal speech or conduct, have caused a great deal of controversy about limits or lack of limits on free speech in classrooms. Do you have such ground rules? Why? Are they yours individually or do they reflect public positions taken by the institution as a whole? How do they apply specifically to the course for which you are preparing a syllabus?

- **Student conduct in general:** All institutions have a *student conduct code* or similar document. In a syllabus section on course policies, it is usually a good idea to anticipate problems related to the student conduct code which might arise in the course, or what areas of the code relevant to your course are *not* likely to be familiar to newcomers—students without "insider knowledge" of academe. Such aspects of the code should be addressed overtly in the syllabus. For instance, if your institution has sexual harassment policies which put in place a standard beyond your local laws, it might be good to note that in relation to collaborative requirements where interdependencies among students are essential to course completion and success. Any number of parallel situations will become apparent with reflection.

Course procedures

Depending on what you teach and how you teach, your syllabus should include a section on procedures which must be followed if students are to succeed in the course. The procedures essentially advise students about operational expectations that are in place to insure their success and well-being in the particular course. In some situations, syllabi sections on procedures are necessary to reduce institutional liability in cases where students are exposed to potentially harmful situations and materials.

In some courses, these procedural issues are minimal—they are no more than friendly reminders that reading is to be completed before class starts or that problem sets are to be done collaboratively or that studios are to be locked after instrumental practice to prevent theft or the like.

In other cases, however, procedures comprise the bulk of the syllabus. In some cases, this is so because faculty have put in place pedagogies which require elaborate procedural guidance because they are unfamiliar to students for whom lecture halls are the norm. For instance, if you are undertaking a shift toward collaborative learning in cooperative groups, you may find it necessary to devote considerable time and effort toward making your syllabus effective in guiding group activity and shared task-specific responsibility. Procedures for operating in collaborative groups in a large course, for instance, would need to be very specific in allocating responsibility and shared effort—it is not very likely that oral instructions would be effective amidst the creative noise of face-to-face collaboration.

In other instances, safety considerations help shape the syllabus section on procedures. In taking inventory prior to writing the syllabus, you would no doubt gather information on this. The complex interaction among student characteristics, course site, and teaching methods indicate the sorts of things you might need to address as procedures. In some medical and lab situations, this is most obvious, and it is likely that in such situations institutional procedures are codified in a required boilerplate—for example, procedures which must be followed by clinical students when handling blood products or when exposed to body fluids. Similarly, but perhaps not so obviously, lab science and applied engineering courses, some art studio courses, many physical education courses, and others require that you spell out safety procedures. Especially in beginning courses, where novice students are likely to find themselves in situations to which they have no prior exposure, the tone of the explanation of procedures can be as important as the content. Again, the goal of explaining such procedures is twofold: first, to insure the safety of the students in our course; second, to help students see themselves in relation to the business of higher education in ways which foster success. For example, consider the following abbreviated and elaborated paired samples. In each case, the safety issue is addressed through statement of a procedure to be followed. But note the tonal differences:

NO FOOD and NO DRINKS in the LAB

versus

Eating and drinking are not allowed in the lab. Please do not bring any food or beverages into the lab. We will be working with hazardous materials throughout the term. Eating or drinking during lab puts you and your classmates at increased risk of accident and injury from breakage or toxins. You will be asked to remove any food or beverage you bring into the lab.

The former appears to be arbitrary, gratuitously forbidding. The latter is no less emphatic, but offers a student-based explanation for a demand that is certainly not made in all classes. Again, consider the following:

Appropriate garb is required at all times in the sculpture foundry.

versus

When working or observing in the metal sculpture foundry, you must wear the following safety gear for your protection in the presence of the furnace and molten metals, and to insure consistent safe procedures all around:

> *Steel toed safety boots*
>
> *Leather chaps tied over boot tops*
>
> *Leather apron*
>
> *Insulated sheathed leather gloves extending not less than eight inches above wrists*
>
> *Safety goggles*
>
> *Hard hat*

Except for safety shoes, all items can be checked out in the foundry foyer during the ten minutes prior to the start of each class. You must provide your own boots. You will be required to leave your student i.d. with the foundry assistant when checking out equipment. Students who do not wear appropriate safety gear as listed are not permitted in the foundry. No exceptions.

In this instance, the contrasting feature is the fullness of the explanation about what constitutes "appropriate garb" in the foundry and where the student can get it. It will produce both a safe environment and understanding on the students' part of how they can comply—how they can move toward insider knowledge of life in the metal sculpture foundry.

Whether your class requires use of computer networks, map rooms, free exercise weights, preserved animal specimens, microscopes, observation rooms, language tapes, or collaborative groups, your syllabus should spell out the terms of student participation and the procedures through which appropriate participation can be achieved. As noted, these procedures are frequently dictated by others, and your syllabus will simply attach institutionally generated procedural statements. In other instances, you should write your own procedures or add to institutional boilerplate procedures to make them less mean spirited, less gratuitously authoritarian in tone. In either case, keep in mind that while the initial—perhaps even primary—impulse in writing procedures might be to protect institutional property or to reduce institutional liability, the final test is whether your statement of procedures achieves its institutional goal at the same time that it discloses to the students the terms of their own success in your course.

It would be foolish to ascribe to the syllabus for your course more significance than it deserves. A badly taught course with a great syllabus is still a badly taught course. A too-busy student who knows clearly and supportively what is required of her still lives in a world where there's always too much to do. Nonetheless, the syllabus sends a clear—albeit partial, albeit preliminary—message to our students and colleagues about our professional values and about our attitudes toward the students we teach. As a public document, it does indeed serve as a significant figure of our approach to our work.

Student Management Teams—The Heretic's Path to Teaching Success

Edward B. Nuhfer

Ed Nuhfer became interested in management teams before he began teaching. While serving as a research supervisor at the West Virginia Geological Survey he learned the value of informal discussions among everyone involved on a project: technicians and student workers through senior managers. When he began teaching geology he tried to incorporate the principles he learned, eventually incorporating the ideas of Tom Peters (*In Search of Excellence: Lessons from America's Best Run Companies*), William Glasser (*The Quality School*), and Edwards Deming (*Out of the Crisis* and other works). At the University of Wisconsin-Platteville he established a faculty development center. The center's first project was developing the idea of student management teams and assessing it's efficacy.

Ed currently is Director of Teaching Effectiveness at the University of Colorado at Denver. He also teaches courses in geology—using student management teams—and does research in environmental geology and geology education. He is the only geologist in the nation to have received three presidential certificates of merit from the American Institute of Professional Geologists; he has also received the AIPG John T. Galey, Sr., Public Service Award for his work in university education. His E-mail address is <enuhfer@carbon.cudenver.edu>.

■ Successful Teaching and Successful Management ■

Teaching success is not insured by mastery of our content area; doing that extra research paper probably will not translate into better teaching—heresy! Our teaching success is not insured by a knowledge of pedagogical theory—more heresy! Subject mastery is essential and knowledge of pedagogy is of great value, but sorry, folks—we can have lots of both and still get eaten alive in the classroom. If the key to becoming an outstanding teacher really were mastering a content area and passing graduate-level courses in educational psychology, learning theory and teaching methodology, then the student ratings of faculty in the education colleges at every university would consistently excel those of faculty in other colleges, but such is not the case—heresy and blasphemy!

If you have already found a statement to hate in this chapter, let me provide comfort in a promise to behave myself—after this paragraph. My heretical tendencies on the issue of teaching improvement began when I noted academia's fascination with a form of distance management (otherwise known as losing touch). I suspected that bizarre behavior, such as a small town college chancellor's eight year commitment to locking the administration building at 4:00 P.M. and never being seen in a local grocery store or restaurant, arose from a cult perception of the mystique of leadership. The perception seems to be this: the less I interact with the people I am supposed to manage, the more I will enhance my image as their leader. Chancellors like this can survive best where their own boards of trustees or regents also practice distance management.

In contrast, teaching by any means, even teaching through television, carries admonishments that we maximize interaction with our students. But when the issue of *teaching improvement* arises, we're back to distance management as usual, with endless creativity for devising ways to avoid students. We are taught to go to our chair's office, to our dean's office, to the faculty development center, to lock ourselves in our own offices with self-help books, to view teleconferences and videotapes of how others succeed, and even to fly across the country to attend workshops to help us improve. In short, we are told to try to consult with virtually everyone about our teaching except our own students!

The heresy I propose is to break with such nonsense. First, work directly in a structured way with your students to improve your teaching. Discover the solutions to problems together and experience the changes that working with students can produce. Second, look to external sources for new ideas, inspiration, and answers to problems that you cannot resolve by working with your students in a structured way.

Individuals who are recognized as consistently outstanding teachers by peers and by students can be found in any discipline. These teachers achieved their status through continuous focus on practice rather than through a study of theory. Practice eventually enabled them to become expert managers—not simply experts at managing classrooms but, more precisely, experts at managing people engaged in the enterprise of learning. Physician and author William Glasser (1990) refers to teaching as the hardest of all management jobs. Management cornerstones include achieving excellent communication, mastering the art of listening, conveying caring for others, inspiring confidence, and promoting enthusiasm. These traits are as important to teaching as to any management enterprise.

Many professors who make incredible effort still find themselves receiving poor teaching evaluations from both students and peers. Successful teaching is not, unfortunately, the guaranteed outcome of dedication and hard work, but rather comes from focusing our efforts on areas that will produce the needed changes and yield reasonable returns. There is a considerable amount of research to show that most of us, particularly at the beginning stages of our teaching, are not good at determining, by ourselves, where our own efforts should be focused. We evaluate ourselves by our intentions, whereas others evaluate us by our actions. Therefore consultation with instructional experts about our teaching does help us to focus on our actions. Without this focus, we can enter into a cycle of trying harder that translates into working longer hours without rewards or much success, and this only leads to cynicism and burnout.

Recent experiences show that regular, structured discussion about teaching with our students can also provide the needed focus. We may be tempted to dismiss students' suggestions out of hand on the basis of their traditional status in the hierarchy of colleges and universities. Although we place great stock in the authority of expertise, consider: What chairperson, mentor or faculty developer has the first-hand, in-depth experience with our teaching that can compare with that of the students enrolled in our own courses? Learning to tap the human resources present in our classes to help us to improve our teaching is not an issue of content knowledge or pedagogical knowledge, but is indeed an issue of applied management.

A Worst-Case Scenario

Consider a case in which a student gives his/her best efforts toward a difficult class. The professor ignores the student all semester, never suggests how to improve, and gives the student a bad grade on the last day along with a few insulting and very personal remarks. Few of us would consider that as helpful practice for creating better scholars, but this hypothetical student's situation is parallel to that in which many universities place professors. To wit: you may have devoted nights and weekends to your class preparation, delivered what you judged to be impeccable lectures, maintained high standards, kept all your office hours, even achieved the standard grade distribution championed by your dean, and felt that you really had done your best. Then you discover that about a third of your students have roasted you on their final evaluations—making degrading comments that ran the gamut from 'not caring,' 'not being available for help,' 'being disorganized and unclear'—maybe even for exhibiting poor taste in clothing! This is devastating, but it occurs when there is a serious disparity between what the students and the professor perceive is actually going on inside a class.

Who is at fault in the scenario? Could it be the university's fault? It might at least have provided a program of mid-term formative evaluations. But some universities have washed their hands of any development of their own faculty. Could it be the students' fault? By not expressing their difficulties and dissatisfaction to you, they concealed their needs so that you could not meet them. And could it be your fault? If you relied only on your own labor, your own perceptions, and your own values, and you ran the course on your own schedule and desires from syllabus to final period, then you may never have actually managed the people in your course. In this age of scapegoating and victim-defining, we could assign blame endlessly to everyone involved, but the message of this chapter is to deal with disappointments by doing something effective rather than by blaming or initiating a flurry of wasted effort. If we were caught haplessly in such a scenario, and we were to ask ourselves what we really want to happen next, few of us would list assigning blame or increasing our labor in penance as our heart's desire. Most of us would want success and a way to assure that the scenario never happens to us again.

How Edward Deming Achieved Success from Worst-Cases

Management, like teaching, has had its own history of theories, recommended practices, methods and techniques. I like the model proposed by Edwards Deming because it has a track record of success and it is so applicable to managing the college classroom. The core tenet of Edwards Deming's participatory management (see Deming, 1986) is that the people closest to any problem/situation have the greatest incentive and potential to understand and solve or improve it. Deming's methods contrast greatly with those of the once traditional boss-managed corporations. Those corporations were strictly hierarchical and characterized by one-way, chain-of-command communication from supervisors (or hired experts) to workers. The workers were supposed to do as they were told passively and to leave their creativity at home.

Deming's opportunity came when he was engaged by Japanese corporations who badly needed to improve the quality of their products. He found that most factories were the typical boss-managed variety and relied on inspection of the product at the end of the assembly line to achieve quality. If flaws in widgets were found, the bosses tried to improve quality by scolding workers. Deming studied the outcomes and confirmed that more final inspection, more blaming and more scolding did nothing to improve the quality of widgets; in fact it made things worse. Deming sought alternative ways to get improvement; in the process he redistributed management so that it became everyone's responsibility.

He soon found that quality could be increased by promoting two-way oral communication and respect between bosses and workers. The workers, in fact, possessed valuable knowledge that went unrecognized and not utilized. Further, they wanted to exercise creativity to make their workplace better, but the boss-managed structure discouraged this. Deming learned to tap this knowledge and creativity by having regular meetings where bosses and workers met as equals to listen respectfully to problems and to pool their knowledge to obtain solutions. He eventually called these meeting groups "quality control circles." Inspecting for flaws at the end was replaced by constant attention being given to every step of the manufacturing process.

As the suggestions given by the workers were implemented, flaws began to disappear from widgets. Managers also began to discover that they didn't have to come up with master plans in a lonely office and then force change down the throats of resistant workers. They began to build support through the team connections; when a plan was implemented, little forcing was required. The plan was understood because the workers themselves helped to create it.

Deming's overall approach was to create an encouraging environment built on regular, purposeful communication and a respect for the contributions made from all levels. Deming stressed the concepts of shared empowerment and ownership. *Empowerment* is the dynamic that increases participants' ability to make positive changes in their own work environment and in the ongoing enterprise. Empowerment enables responsibility; charging someone with responsibility without providing enabling empowerment is a way to bring frustration, not results. *Ownership* is a status conferred by empowerment. Ownership arises from the personal satisfaction and pride that comes from being able to share credit for success that results from involvement.

This summary in no way implies that good management began with Edwards Deming or that he invented effective teamwork. Effective teamwork dates back through prehistoric times and accounts for the very survival of the human species. Principles of quality circles also have long been used by academics in their collaborations, and small group discussions were respected for the results they produced in research centers for years before they became a basis for a formal system of management. In teaching, close parallels exist between Deming's participatory management and cooperative learning in the classroom as espoused for nearly 30 years by David and Roger Johnson at the University of Minnesota[1].

---

[1] and by others—see chapters 9 & 10 of this book

While both Deming and the Johnsons built on earlier work and experience, there is good reason that they are recognized as authorities almost synonymous with their areas of study. They approached their topics in a scientific manner, amassed considerable data, formulated testable hypotheses, and eventually produced resources based upon coherent sets of principles that could be taught to others (Deming, 1986; Johnson, Johnson and Smith, 1991). While the use of learning teams still remains a less common practice than lecturing in college classrooms, the Johnsons and their colleagues must be given major credit for the awareness that now permeates all disciplines within higher education—that the power of group dynamics can be used as a viable, and often superior, alternative to the lecture. In a similar manner, Deming's published principles (summarized below) now enable nearly all prospective managers, including professors, to enact proven ways to use effectively the power of structured groups. We can use this power not only to produce higher-level learning through cooperative learning, but also to help us achieve better success in teaching.

■■ Application of Deming's Principles to Academia ■■

Academia has its own equivalent to reliance on final inspection and scolding through its use of end-of-course student evaluations for purposes both of improving teaching and for rewarding or punishing faculty on the basis of merit pay, tenure or rank. Mixing the two purposes is known to be bad practice, but still remains common. If evaluation is done just at the end of the course, then it only provides information after all opportunity for improvement is gone. In many institutions, giving the summative evaluation is still the chosen means through which to improve faculty, even though both educational research and management experience consistently indicate that such a choice promises disappointment.

Deming developed fourteen principles of management over nearly fifty years of diagnosing and curing management problems. (Condensed from Walton, 1986.)

1. Create constancy of purpose.
2. Adopt a new philosophy of quality.

3. Cease dependence on final inspection.
4. Consider total cost, not just initial price.
5. Find problems; improve constantly.
6. Institute on-the-job training.
7. Institute leadership across the organization.
8. Drive out fear.
9. Break down communication barriers between units.
10. Eliminate slogans, targets, and exhortations for workers.
11. Eliminate numerical goals.
12. Encourage pride of workmanship.
13. Encourage education and self-improvement.
14. Take actions needed to make transformations.

In higher education, we can use these principles as guidelines to help students work together in ways that are productive and satisfying.

When faculty are not taught how to improve through every day of the year, but are only taught to improve by being evaluated, then principles 3, 5, 14, 4, 6, 1, 2, and 10 are being violated, in that order of severity. When informal communication about teaching is not actively fostered between us and our students, principles 9, 7, 8, 1, and 2 are violated. When students feel they have no control over what happens to them in the classroom, principles 7, 8, 12, and 13 are violated. If our teaching environment puts excessive emphasis on grades (in the case of students) or student credit hours (in the case of administrators) and not on quality teaching and learning, then all the principles are prone to being violated wholesale, 11 and 12 most obviously.

It is sobering to note that Deming's principles were established at a price. These principles were verbalized only after violation of each brought its own set of serious consequences.

Student management teams draw heavily from the experience of participatory management as developed by Deming, expressed in the fourteen principles listed above. For purposes of this chapter these fourteen principles can be reduced to six key concepts:

1. Students should be enlisted as colleagues in improving the teaching and learning enterprise.
2. Good management practice can lead to good teaching practices.
3. Teaching skill is not conferred at birth, but is learned through focused effort and experience.
4. The ability to teach well is maintained by continuous effort to improve and will atrophy unless so maintained.
5. Communication problems are the most common obstacles to successful teaching.
6. Improving teaching is easier to do with the help of others than alone.

All six of these concepts have foundations in practice and research.

Can Our Students Help Us to Improve Our Teaching? ──────

Historically, student helper roles have ranged from single observers (Fink, 1973) to teams of observers (Sorenson, 1994; also summarized in Rhem, 1993), who were actually trained student employees of faculty development centers. The latest reports show good results from these student helpers. But the distinction of whether one uses students from inside or outside one's own class is not trivial. As soon as one composes the team from outside the class, the students are placed in the role of monitors, observers, and consultants, but in no sense are they operating under Deming's principles of participatory management. Improving classes through outside interveners or through a student management team are as different in concept as managing a company by an external consulting firm or by its own employees.

The results from over 100 student management teams affirms that our students in a participatory management structure can indeed be suitable colleagues in bringing about significant improvements in our teaching. The teams have a very high success rate in producing specific improvements. About 85% of teams produce notable improvement during their ongoing semester. If teams that formulate major improvements that can only be enacted the follow ing term are added to the 85%, then about 98% of teams are successful in generating notable improvements (data from Nuhfer and others, 1990-96).

There is an unchallenged assumption in the literature of faculty development that hints that progress can only be made with the aid of an expert consultant, but industry's successful quality circles are not composed of outside experts. They are made up of involved people who are empowered to continually improve their own work environment through pooling experience, insights gained through introspection, and creativity in a structured group environment. Teams of average people working together establish synergy that enables them to accomplish surprising results. Such teams have a habit of discovering, on their own, the solutions that an expert would provide. A single student cannot serve a faculty member as well as an expert consultant, but the presumption that a structured team composed of a committed faculty member and his/her own students cannot generate much improvement is reminiscent of the time when bosses pooh-poohed the concept that teams of workers could improve quality. Presumptions like these have been refuted repeatedly.

Some reasons that student management teams enable faculty to improve without experts are (1) the members meet regularly over a sustained period of time rather than for the customary single consultation with the expert; (2) the team members are committed to improvement and quality; (3) teams may acquire data through formative evaluations (Murray, 1984) and class room assessment techniques (Angelo and Cross, 1993), which is the same data available to expert consultants, and (4) the synergy of regular, purposeful group discussion produces insights that an individual would not likely achieve alone.

The Student Management Team — Using Deming's Principles for Ourselves

Student management teams are rough equivalents to Deming's quality control circles. The benefits of using these teams are to polish our own teaching practice so that our classrooms are more suitable places in which to teach and learn. Teams provide mutual empowerment, wherein both we and students give ourselves permission and structure to communicate about teaching in order to study, transform, and improve what is taking place in class. Teaching cannot be improved by guessing at what our students' needs may be. In order to learn our students' needs, our students must be assured respect so that they can safely communicate their needs. We must be assured respect so that we can work safely with those needs to formulate the best possible solutions. The formal structure of the team provides this safety. As improvements occur, all should be able to own the pride that comes with success. If failures occur, it is then no longer satisfactory to merely blame the professor. Instead, the failure is owned by the entire class and the appropriate response is not defined by unproductive evaluating or blaming, but instead by finding a remedy so that the failure cannot happen again.

Student management teams consist of the professor and several students. The students are selected from within a single class, and the team is convened for the specific purpose of improving the classroom teaching and learning environments. The teams are a means to vest students with more responsibility for the success and quality of their own education and to help build academic community through total involvement. They are also a way of stimulating in students an interest in teaching, beyond the self-serving experience of obtaining content or formal credit. Serving on a team is a step up from being a scholar to becoming a scholar-citizen with an increasing awareness of the importance of caring about students, about professors, about teaching and about learning.

Student management teams

- Consist of 3-4 students (usually) plus the professor; one student is chosen by the professor on the basis of energy, desire, leadership; other members are selected in a variety of ways, including election by class.
- Students are all from same class of the professor; an external facilitator is optional.
- Students have a managerial role and assume responsibility for the success of a class.
- Students meet weekly; the professor attends only every other week. Meetings generally last about one hour.

- Meetings are all held in a neutral area away from classroom and professor's office.
- A written log of suggestions, actions, and progress is maintained; the professor retains the log at the end of the term.
- The team is provided with its initial task by the professor; these tasks can relate to delivery methods or to the content of the course.
- Teams utilize the group dynamics approach of quality circles.

Small numbers of about four students plus the professor are ideal, but some teams are larger. Regular attendance at meetings is essential, as is maintenance of a written log which is retained by the professor at the end of the course. This log proves invaluable when rewriting the syllabus for the next course offering. The professor should consider the initial task proposed to the team as an opportunity to ask for help in a specific area. This area could arise from a present concern such as poor student attendance or lack of discussion; it might come from an area of concern defined from an evaluation tool such as a formative evaluation instrument or last term's student evaluations.

The operation of the team is based on a global charge of shared responsibility. The manual for the development of student management teams we use states: *Students, in conjunction with their instructor, are responsible for the success of any course. As student managers, your special responsibility is to monitor this course through your own experience, to receive comments from other students, to work as a team with your instructor on a regular basis, and to make recommendations to the instructor about how this course can be improved.* (Nuhfer and others 1990-96.)

It is obvious that such an arrangement empowers students. For most this will be their first experience with a formal structure that assigns high positive value to students' involvement in enhancing their own learning environment and enables them to see the suggestions they make successfully enacted in class. Students constitute the major population on any campus, and classes are the part of the campus in which students are most intimately connected. Academic community is promoted by a campus culture in which all members of the campus see themselves as important contributors. The act of empowering students to work with faculty to improve their own classes is a major asset to the nurturing of academic community.

The structure also empowers faculty. It frees us from dependence on student input obtained at the end of a course. It provides us with an opportunity to discover specific ways in which to improve, to consider multiple alternative ways to present material, to make changes while the class is ongoing, and most important, to practice developing better classroom communication with our own students. No matter what kind of institution that we teach in, we can have support and improvement by setting a structure for it in our own classroom.

Some professors are at first apprehensive about sharing power with students, but they have not considered that the image of a professor's power in the classroom is like that of the boss within the older boss-managed corporations. Boss-managed arrangements rarely operated at their true potential because employees' available ideas, energy and creativity were scarcely used. Deming produced such strikingly effective results because he found a way to tap these unused human resources. A classroom structure that casts the professor as the boss who controls all power, all information, and assumes all responsibility for success of the class, also is likely to be operating far below its potential. The students' own human resources go unused and unappreciated, and there are few worse indictments of inept management than an inability to use available resources. Viewed in this light, it is small wonder that research shows that what is actually going on inside the classroom and what is important to successful teaching are usually perceived much differently by professors than by the students in the traditional classroom (Feldman, 1986). Remaining ignorant of students' perceptions is not empowering, so enhancing mutual discussion and reflection is a most reasonable step toward true empowerment.

Conjectures that student teams would try to dilute course content or turn adversarial have proven to be completely unsupported. Smith (1993) found that even seventh graders, in a structured environment, can enter responsibly into collaborative decisions about curriculum. The team is the management entity, not the individuals within it, so if one member should initiate a self-serving or counter-quality agenda, the power of the group acts as the safety to control against this. The name, 'student management team,' emphasizes a managerial role for students, but it is important to realize that what is being managed is the teaching and learning environment; at no time is the professor being managed by students. It is the responsibility of the team to nurture the teaching and learning environment. Experience with over 200 teams shows that students can be trusted with this responsibility.

━━━━━ Tips for Successful Operation of ━━━━━ Student Management Teams

Student management teams are not for every professor. Those who reject the premise that we can learn anything of value from our students should not form a team. For those open to the possibility that there is something very important that we can learn, anticipate success! Student management teams have produced success for professors who have actually lived the worst-case scenario mentioned previously, and they have further improved professors who have already held prestigious teaching awards.

Forming a Team. Although continuous improvement is always desirable, the creation of a team should occur only if the faculty member wants it. It must not be formed in anyone's class because of external mandate from deans, chairs, or other administrators. The actual time one spends meeting with a team is small, on the order of about two hours a month, but improvement occurs only through making changes. Implementing good suggestions with these changes can involve more time. For this reason, form only a single team per term. Pick the course/class which is causing you the most trouble in terms of your own satisfaction or that expressed by students. Experience shows that the benefits that accrue from that one class will soon spill over into the other classes we teach. This is because the better management skills we learn travel with us; they don't stay in just one class.

Selecting a Team. All prospective student members for a team must also be willing participants; no one must be drafted. The basis for choosing team members depends upon what the professor wishes to accomplish. If the goal is general course improvement, one would ideally compose a generally representative group. If one wants to address a specific concern, such as low summative ratings in the area of treatment of women and minorities, then a team representative of the likely affected people could be formed to discover the reasons for such ratings and to suggest solutions. In all cases, one member of the team should be hand-picked by the professor on the basis of displayed enthusiasm, desire, and/or leadership; a spark plug is important to insure a productive team. Other members can be elected or chosen in a number of other ways. The concept of the teams and the opportunity to be on a team can be announced on the first day of class along with a standing call for volunteers, but team members should not be chosen until all have experienced the class for a few weeks.

Committing to the Project. The most common reason that quality circles fail is unresponsive management (Deming, 1986). As faculty, we continue to retain our academic freedom and with it the right to reject the team's suggestions. However, if we form a team, we must commit to meet regularly with it, to be open to enacting change, and to courteously explain to team members our reasons for rejecting their suggestions.

■■■ Principles for Student Management Teams ■■■

1. **The quality of a class seldom improves as a result of final inspection through student evaluations.** Improvement requires continuous attention by all participants through every step of the class.

2. **The primary purpose of the team is to improve the quality of the teaching and learning environment.** The team does not boss the professor. In a broader sense, the team works for all present & future occupants of the university.

3. **Good two-way communication must not be assumed.** Communication must be purposely built by students and the professor. The professor may need to help student members of the team to learn to work together.

4. **Responsibility and leadership are not reserved for the few.** Everyone should contribute to and receive credit for their contributions. The team must not be seen as elitist. It should be kept visible to the class by being introduced when formed, by having meeting times announced to which members of the class have an open invitation to attend, and by giving the team time to poll the class with a survey or classroom assessment at the start or end of some class meetings.

5. **Getting input from the entire class and the professor is a good way to set an agenda for improvement.** Brief, written summaries of results from whole-class formative surveys and classroom assessments are a basis from which to locate critical opportunities for improvement.

6. **Spirit is more than a warm, fuzzy ideal—its presence distinguishes the merely good class from the exceptional one that provides life-long inspiration.** Once you commit to a team give your best effort to producing an effective environment that is effective and supportive for all. Spirit is largely the responsibility of students. It cannot be created by the faculty member alone, nor by deans, faculty developers, *etc.*

7. **When an issue for improvement has been identified, action must follow and the results of these actions should be tracked.** The team goes beyond mere surveys and classroom assessment techniques to recommend suitable changes, to help when feasible in their implementation, and to evaluate the results. A written record of these activities must be maintained.

8. **Any compensation for team members must be completely separated from grades and credit.** Grades are measures of content mastery, not compensation. The two must not be confused.

Formal training in participatory management is not required in order to obtain benefits from a student management team, although some training from experienced faculty or development staff will help a team get off to an earlier start. The handbook of Nuhfer and others (1990-1996) was written to permit teams to achieve success without additional training. Any student management team composed of people who (a) recognize the need for courtesy and (b) can commit to action for a beneficial purpose will produce worthwhile results.

Start with a simple task like gaining some basic awareness. What are the fears or expectations about the team that students are bringing into it? Ask! Did your team members have any particular prejudices before they entered the class? Ask! Ask members to list the most difficult or exasperating part of the class they've experienced to date and get them to discuss what made the experience(s) difficult. Could the room's seating arrangement be better? What is the view and sound like at the back of the classroom? Get a team member or two to go back there and let you know. These are all simple tasks that can produce immediate and visible changes.

A final word of advice: ask your students for their help. Like the frustrated workers who were told to leave their creativity at home, students really do want to contribute to better teaching, to improve their learning environment, and to be part of a true learning community. Colleges and universities rarely provide the structure to allow them to do so. Asking students to fill out an evaluation form is not a legitimate substitute for participatory management. Instead, it can be an excuse to disempower the parties involved.

Sample Experiences with Student Management Teams

An engineering professor who wished to know about the attrition of women from the engineering program drafted a team consisting of four undergraduate women from differing engineering areas. He soon learned that the women students felt the college atmosphere was "cold." Providing more encouragement and positive recognition were proposed solutions.

A professor in business for whom English was a second language had low class ratings because of his thick accent. He asked his team to help him with communication. The team helped with pronunciation, encouraged use of overhead transparencies and handouts of lecture outlines, and called attention during class to terms that were difficult to understand so that they could be written on the chalkboard. His evaluations improved greatly, and one of his student team members was hired by an interviewer who was impressed by the student's experience in using quality management to solve real problems. (This student's experience fits well with the "seven skills employers want" compiled by the American Society for Training and Development and U.S. Dept. of Labor in 1988. Five of these skills are gained in a student management team experience but not in content lecture classes.)

When a professor of English found herself in an over-enrolled literature course in a room badly designed for discussion teaching, her team investigated several alternative seating arrangements and prepared the room before each class until an arrangement was found that promoted the best class discussion.

Another professor was troubled by overt hostility to the material he taught in a race and gender course, and particularly by hecklers who sat together in a part of the auditorium. His team simply suggested, "Tell 'em to "Shut up!"—which in fact he did after acknowledging the student source for the suggestion. The shock kept the hecklers at bay for about two weeks. When they again started, the instructor's "Shut up!" was echoed from the team members. When the hecklers tried once again, about 80% of the class turned toward the hecklers with a "SHUT UP!" that carried the weight of peer anger and disapproval. The class was reclaimed for learning the rest of the term. When students internalize their responsibility for success of a class, their empowerment often inspires unaccustomed support.

A nursing professor had often taught interviewing through videotaped interviews. Her team suggested instead that a live interview be staged in class as a role play exercise, so that dialogue could be questioned and examined. It worked so beautifully that it became a permanent addition to the course schedule (Cunningham, 1993; Cunningham and others, 1993).

One team from a night business class chose to address a phenomenon they termed "disconnect," which occurred when students' attention wandered from the faculty member's presentation. Their original assumption was that the phenomenon took place because students in night classes were exhausted after a full day's work. Through a very well-planned collection of data and statistical analyses, the team discovered instead that the dominant cause of "disconnect" was other students' irrelevant comments.

Several faculty have reported having a class saved by a team, which usually meant that the team dealt with a problem of hostility and solved it, thus keeping the faculty member out of a potentially destructive "him/her vs us" contest. Student members of teams have shown up, of their own volition, in the offices of deans or at open reviews to refute less-than-truthful complaints about their class.

Teams can do much processing of information and explain it from the students' viewpoint. Do you give "One-minute Paper" or "Muddiest Point" surveys? Give them to the team and ask them for prioritized recommendations based on the responses. Do you get approval texts from companies wanting you to adopt their books? Toss these books to your team! Ask the students if these books are really any better than the one you're using. Get their views before you adopt. Do you give a mid-term formative survey? Go over the results with your team and pick one area to work on.

The teams have proven to be remarkably resilient to small disasters. One professor ended up with a failing student on the team; another had to give a team member a failing grade due to plagiarism (though the student stayed on the team for the rest of the term). These teams still were successful and produced marked improvements. Teams that produce marginal results usually suffer from apathy and low energy; that's why instructors should hand-pick one of the student members solely on the basis of desire and energy.

Teams fail occasionally. On the basis of about 200 teams for which I have records, 2% of teams have been dismal failures. These failures occurred when faculty formed teams but then did not follow up by meeting with students, or inexplicably recruited a student to the team who was overtly hostile to the whole concept of quality circles and subverted every meeting. To date, no faculty member has been damaged by a team, but the failures resulted in wasted time.

About 80% of all the improvements attributed to student management teams fall under the category of "communication," which is in accord with formative evaluation data that also shows that the dominance of teaching problems are attributable to communication issues. Solutions to these problems are course-specific and range from producing handouts and improving visual aids through providing field trips and guest speakers to selecting new texts and revising syllabi.

Student management teams should limit themselves to considering topics centered on academic content and delivery; teams should not deal with problems which an institution has already developed structures to deal with. An example would be a sexual harassment charge brought by a student or teacher. This would be an inappropriate topic for a student management team to consider.

▬▬▬ "The Students Are Our Customers:" ▬▬▬ Management Perverted

Use of student management teams is a technology transfer of participatory management from the business world into the college classroom. Some academicians express suspicion of the wisdom of such transfers; they point out that colleges are not businesses or corporations, and should not be managed as businesses. They are often proven correct, not simply because universities and colleges are different from businesses (they are), but also because the transfer is performed ineptly. Customer satisfaction was obviously related to the quality of a product or service, and it became a central goal for some of the best known corporations (Peters & Waterman, 1982). It wasn't long before "The student-is-our-customer" jingle began to be heard with increasing frequency within the ivory towers. Those who mouthed the jingle were scarcely aware that they were participants in a classic example of inept technology transfer. Corporations focus on customers and products; in higher education students should not be considered as customers or products.

It is more useful to consider students as *colleagues* (Langford, 1993; Nuhfer, 1994). Corporations exist because of customer demand and are supported by profits from customers. Universities exist because of societal demand and are supported by a society that desires skilled, educated participants. The tuition and fees students pay to a university are minuscule contributions compared to society's cumulative investments in the institution. Customers usually have little vested interest in the ethics or atmosphere inside the corporate environment, and certainly do not form quality circles to address these issues. Students, like faculty and unlike customers, are inside the teaching-learning environment. They have an inherent interest in the processes that occur there. The true customer of the university is society in general, including employers, alumni, and future students. There are rarely consequences to customers if they reject a product. On the other hand, if students reject the product by cutting classes or by not giving sufficient effort, then society is harmed through having to absorb poorly prepared participants. When students abrogate their responsibilities, the same harm occurs to society as occurs when professors give only half-hearted efforts to teach effectively. We are colleagues in more ways than we realize.

Individual student responsibility has been outlined eloquently and in detail by Ellis (1994), but the popular concept of individual responsibility (Davis and Murrell, 1993) is understood as assuring one's own success in procuring skills and knowledge. Students' social responsibility for improving their own institution's teaching and learning environment is a concept that most college administrators have failed to grasp, let alone promote. Student management teams stress student responsibility. They enable an understanding of responsibility, both personal and social, through experience of both the labor and benefits.

Can We See Our Own Progress?

There are three easy ways to examine your own growth as a stronger teacher through working with student management teams. The simplest is to keep a list of beneficial changes and modifications that you make as a result of working with your team(s). Another is to draft a one page summary of your own teaching philosophy in your word processor and save it in two files. As you gain insights and skills by working with your students, see if your teaching philosophy has been expanded or modified. If so, make regular additions/revisions in one of your files and, after one year, compare the revised version to your initial draft. Everyone should write his/her teaching philosophy, whether or not one forms a team. It allows us to check to see if the practice we do is actually what we subscribe to in our philosophies.

A third way to measure growth is more quantifiable and measures changes in the use of teaching practices: use a good formative evaluation tool. If your campus has a faculty development unit, they will have such a tool; if not, you can write or call the author of this chapter to obtain one. Run the tool in your class before you start the team, and again the next time you teach the class and have incorporated the improvements suggested. At University of Colorado-Denver, we find that significant improvement appears in the areas of "clarity and organization" and "fair exams and grading."

Conclusions

For a teacher, there are few situations more enviable than being in a classroom with students who have made a formal commitment to seeing their class succeed. When students join with us in this way, it sets the cornerstone of true academic community and inspires us to go to extremes to give our very best to them. In such an environment, even embarrassing mistakes become vehicles for significant progress. As long as we are sincere about improving and learning from mistakes and are supported in our efforts by our students, we simply cannot lose in such a class. When the excitement for learning together becomes kindled in student and professor alike, we are all renewed.

References

Angelo, T. A., and Cross, K. P. *Classroom Assessment Techniques* (second edition). Jossey-Bass, 1983.

Baugher, K. 1996 "Using student teams in course evaluation," in T. W. Banta and others, eds. *Assessment in Practice.* Jossey-Bass, 1966.

Cunningham, M. E. "Improving a course using a student management team," Nov., 1993, *Imprint, Journal of the National Student Nurses' Assoc.,* 41:5.

Cunningham, M. E., Chambers, J., Howard, L., and Schenk, S. "The student management team: a vehicle for student empowerment," *Revolution, the Journal of Nurse Empowerment,* Oct., 1993.

Davis, T. M., and Murrell, P. H. *Turning Teaching Into Learning: The Role of Student Responsibility in the Collegiate Experience:* ASHE-ERIC Higher Education Reports - Report Eight, 1993.

Deming, E. *Out of the Crisis*. Massachusetts Institute of Technology Center for Advanced Engineering Study, 1986.

Ellis, D. *Becoming a Master Student* (7th ed.). Houghton Mifflin, 1994.

Fink, L. D."Monitoring: A method of diagnostic course evaluation," *Journal of Geography*, 72:5, 1973.

Feldman, K. A., 1986, "Correlation between personality traits as perceived by self, students, and peers," *Research in Higher Education*, vol. 24, 1986.

Glasser, W. *The Quality School*. Harper & Row, 1990.

Johnson, D. W., Johnson, R. T., and Smith, K. A. *Active Learning: Cooperation in the College Classroom:* Interaction Book Co., 1991.

Langford, D. P. "A day of total quality learning," PBS/MSU Videoconference, June 7, 1993.

Murray, H. G. "The impact of formative and summative evaluation of teaching in North American universities," *Assessment and evaluation in higher education*, vol. 9, 1984.

Nuhfer, E. B. "Students as colleagues: the case for student management teams," *The Department Chair*, 4:3, 1994. Also in *The New Academic*.

Nuhfer, E. B., and others. *A Handbook for Student Management Teams*. 1990-1996. The original 1990 manual is updated on a regular basis. Copies of the current edition are available at $7.00 from The Office of Teaching Effectiveness, Campus Box 137, University of Colorado at Denver, P.O. Box 173364, Denver, CO, 80217 - 3364. Only one manual per campus need be ordered; the book contains a copyright release allowing it to be reproduced for on-campus use.

Peters, T., & Waterman, R.H., jr. *In Search of Excellence: Lessons from America's Best Run Companies*. Harper & Row, 1982.

Rhem, J. "Paying students to observe teaching," *National Teaching and Learning Forum*, 3:2, 1993. (This is a condensed report of the same work described by Sorenson, 1994).

Schwartz, R. A. "Improving course quality with student management teams," *Prism: American Society for Engineering Education*, 5:5, January, 1996.

Smith, J. L. "Negotiation: student-teacher collaborative decision making in an integrative curriculum," *Proc. Annual Meeting of American Educational Research Association,* Atlanta, GA, April 12-16, 1993.

Sorenson, D. L. "Valuing the student voice: student observer/consultant programs," *To Improve the Academy,* vol. 13, 1994.

Walton, M. *The Deming Management Method.* Putnam Perigree, 1986.

Using Knowledge Maps to Enhance Teaching

Donald F. Dansereau & Dianna Newbern

Donald F. Dansereau became interested in knowledge maps as a graduate student, when one of his colleagues filled his office with models of human long-term memory constructed from Tinker toys™. Dansereau was struck by the possibilities these non-linguistic, graphical means of depicting a complex structure hold for teaching. A few years later, he began employing knowledge maps in his classes. His recent work has involved using mapping to enhance the communication between drug abuse counselors and their clients. It seems to be helping; a series of controlled studies has shown that heroin and cocaine addicted clients exposed to mapping versus standard counseling are more likely to stay drug-free during and following treatment. Dansereau is Professor of Psychology at Texas Christian University. His e-mail address is <d.dansereau@tcu.edu>.

Dianna Newbern's interest in knowledge maps was stimulated by a scene in *Close Encounters of the Third Kind*. When the spaceship finally descends on the Devil's Tower and plays its five note sequence, a scientist plays the same sequence back on a keyboard. The aliens respond with a more complicated version, the scientist embellishes, and they conclude with an impromptu composition; variations on the original five note theme. Newbern was impressed by the ability of the scientist and the aliens to communicate nonverbally. She sees knowledge maps as another way to communicate when words fail us. She currently is Associate Research Scientist with the Institute of Behavioral Research at Texas Christian University. Her e-mail address is <d.newbern@tcu.edu>.

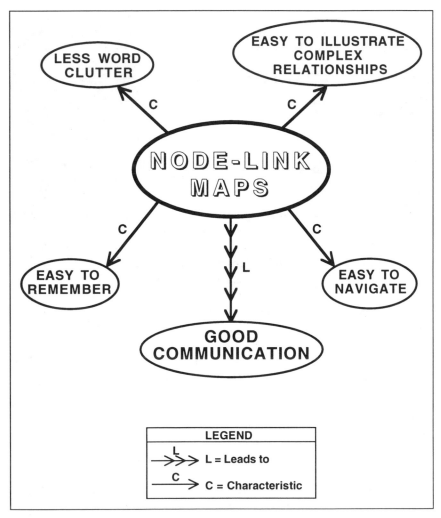

Figure 1. Map of maps.

Figure 1 is an example of a node-link map. The nodes (ovals in this case) contain ideas and the links (lines) show relationships between the nodes (note that the legend describes the nature of the relationships). Researchers and educators have written enthusiastically about the potential of this type of graphic device in teaching-learning situations (e.g., Alvermann, 1986; Buzan, 1994; Lambiotte & Dansereau, 1992; Novak & Gowin, 1984). The purpose of this chapter is to introduce you to a specific node-link approach called

knowledge mapping. It is a close relative to a number of other approaches (e.g., mind mapping, concept mapping, and graphic organizers), but, as we will see, it has some important and unique characteristics. When you finish this chapter, you will be able to use knowledge maps (K-maps) in your courses.

▬▬▬ *Reasons to Consider Using K-Maps* ▬▬▬ *in Your Teaching*

By far the most common way we express ideas to ourselves and others is through natural language (i.e., conversation and writing). Its pervasiveness is at least partly due to the early effectiveness of the printing press. Until very recently, the printing of lines of type was the only economical method for recording ideas. The emergence of computer graphics capabilities and laser printers has given us other options, but most of us still remain highly dependent on word sequences.

Although natural language is a powerful tool, it can be greatly limited by its linearity. Words in sentences need to be spoken, heard, or read one after another, resulting in a sequence that is fixed and one-dimensional. This strong commitment to linear order often conflicts with our own thinking experiences, which tend to be marked by non-linear shifts as we move from idea to idea.

A common communication dilemma is reflected in Figure 2. The communicator on the left side of the picture (the teacher or author) has stored experiences in the form of images and feelings. These are represented by cartoons on the lower level in his head. The upper level is a node-link map of these experiences. Recent theories of memory suggest that this is a reasonable model of the way things are stored (e.g., Anderson, 1995).

The communicator has the problem of transmitting the stored map and accompanying images to a receiver. Unfortunately, the usual way this has been done is through natural language. The communicator has to describe his or her map in words. The receiver (e.g., a student) then has the difficult task of trying to understand this description and discover the spatial and temporal relationships being implied. One way communication might be improved is by having either the communicator or the receiver draw a node link map.

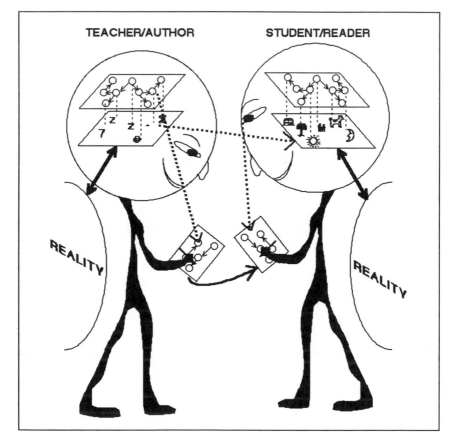

Figure 2. Communication process.

Maps, in addition to being more similar to our memory structures than is language, also have some other advantages that make them good thinking and communication tools.

Maps have less word clutter. Many of the words in written and spoken language are there just to maintain the flow of ideas. These words typically don't communicate any new information and are consequently superfluous to a deep understanding of what is being presented. Because node-link maps use lines and space to replace some of these maintenance words, there is less superfluous information to be processed. This may be a particularly important advantage in communicating with someone who is a novice in a subject or someone whose language skills are not very strong.

Maps can easily show complex relationships. One of the major dilemmas experienced by most teachers and writers is their desire to express two sets of ideas at the same time and to show their relationships. Although almost impossible in language, this is easy to do in maps because of their two-dimensionality. Many complicated domains are multilayered. In maps, these layers can be shown side-by-side or on top of one another, and connections between them can be indicated. Conceptual parallelisms between two sub-domains can be illustrated by creating visual parallelisms in a map (e.g., two competing theories can be laid out side by side).

Information in maps can be located quickly. Because of the lack of word clutter and a map's use of two-dimensional space, it is easy to find your place and move from idea to idea. This ability to navigate is very useful in keeping yourself and your students on track. A map of a knowledge domain provides landmarks that can be used to guide thinking from topic to topic.

Maps Are Experimentally Supported

There have been many published studies on knowledge mapping that support its effectiveness (e.g., Dansereau, 1995; Evans & Dansereau, 1991; Lambiotte & Dansereau, 1992; Rewey, Dansereau, & Peel, 1991; Wiegmann, Dansereau, McCagg, Rewey, & Pitre, 1992).

Selected results of these experiments are as follows:

- Individuals are able to acquire more effective metaknowledge (e.g., awareness of areas of complexity and parallelism) about a domain of information from a brief exposure to a map than from a brief exposure to text.

- Maps are generally more effective than their text counterparts for the recall of central ideas. No differences are found between maps and text on the recall of details.

- College students with relatively low verbal ability and/or low prior knowledge appear to benefit most from map presentations.

- Information is recalled better when presented in maps that are well-structured (e.g., symmetrical, uncluttered). The visually salient parts of the maps appear to be recalled better.

- Maps are more effective than pure text when used to guide performance (e.g., performance of laboratory procedures) and when used as reference aids (e.g., to answer questions about a domain).

- Participants in cooperative (e.g., peer tutoring and collaborative learning) activities benefit more from map communication aids than from text-based aids.

Maps Have Pragmatic Advantages

In addition to the empirical findings, knowledge maps have a number of pragmatic advantages.

- They can be introduced and used as easily as other materials, such as texts, handouts, overhead transparencies, self-tests, or student notes, and don't require heavy reliance on expensive technology.

- They are content-flexible. Knowledge maps can be made to communicate a wide variety of content domains. We have developed maps to cover topics in medicine, biology, probability and statistics, psychology, engineering, computer science, and education. Instructors and students can tailor their maps to fit their own needs; thus, while maps have direct pedagogical value, they also give instructors and students a sense of ownership of whatever material is mapped.

- They are multipurpose. Maps can serve a variety of purposes in the teaching/learning process; for example, maps can be

  ◆ used as lecture aids in the form of an overhead;
    made into handouts for notes, reference materials, and as aids to cooperative learning;

♦ made into posters for topic orientation and for showing progress through a semester course;

♦ designed for homework assignments and tests by leaving out important nodes or links that require student completion; and

♦ produced by students to review content or to facilitate self- or instructor-diagnosis of learning difficulties.

• They are easy to understand and produce. Although map "literacy" improves with experience, individuals can understand and create coherent maps after about two hours of instruction and practice.

• Knowledge maps can be merged easily with existing instructional practices. Since there are no rigid conditions associated with inserting mapping activities into a course, map activities can supplement or substitute for current approaches throughout a curriculum, to provide a change of pace or shift in perspective.

• They are low-cost. Given computer graphics capabilities, they are no more expensive than text. Even without computers, handmade maps are easy to produce.

Hopefully, you are now convinced that knowledge mapping may be worth a closer look. Toward this end, in the next sections, we will present the system in some detail, describe how to make maps, and discuss how to use them in teaching.

The Knowledge Mapping System

Nodes, links, spatial configuration, and unit organization are the major components of the knowledge mapping system.

Nodes

A node is a shaped line drawing such as a rectangle, square, or oval, which contains a single idea or proposition. The two important aspects of nodes are their visual appearance and the their verbal content. The shape, shading, and (sometimes) color of the node is used to signal levels of importance and to indicate the type of content they contain. In a standard sentence, key concepts are embedded within a group of words (e.g., propositions) that are employed to guide the reading process. However, with knowledge maps, the salient ideas are extracted from the body of verbiage and appear in their essential, propositional node-link-node form. The features of nodes are perceptual boundaries that isolate the node content. The verbal feature of the nodes is the meaningful idea that is related to other nodes via the links. Pictorial information can be included within nodes as well.

The reduced verbiage, propositional node format obviously allows much faster reading time than typical text. Although the majority of nodes contain domain-specific information, some nodes are designed to serve placekeeping, encoding, and pointing functions. Nodes of this latter type have the same function as headings, footnotes, and references in traditional text.

Labeled Links

Links are the directional arrows that connect the nodes, while **labels** describe or name the links. Arrowhead lines indicate the relationships of mapped information and offer routes through which one can read or study the information. Links are labeled by means of a standard, canonical set of symbols (e.g., P = part; L = leads to; see Figure 3). Labels indicate how the propositions contained in nodes are related or linked to one another.

The style of the link line itself also varies. The three categories of link styles consist of dotted lines, solid lines, and barbed lines. Dotted lines indicate analogies, examples, or comments (e.g., "In most cases"). Solid lines demonstrate a descriptive relationship between nodes such as characteristics, parts, and types. Finally, barbed lines show that a dynamic relationship is involved (such as "next," "leads to," or "influences").

The labeled links provide the relationship information which is typically conveyed in a regular text sentence. However, the information is communicated using a unique combination of visual and verbal features. Link labels can be customized by including links that are idiosyncratic to particular knowledge domains (e.g., "function,"

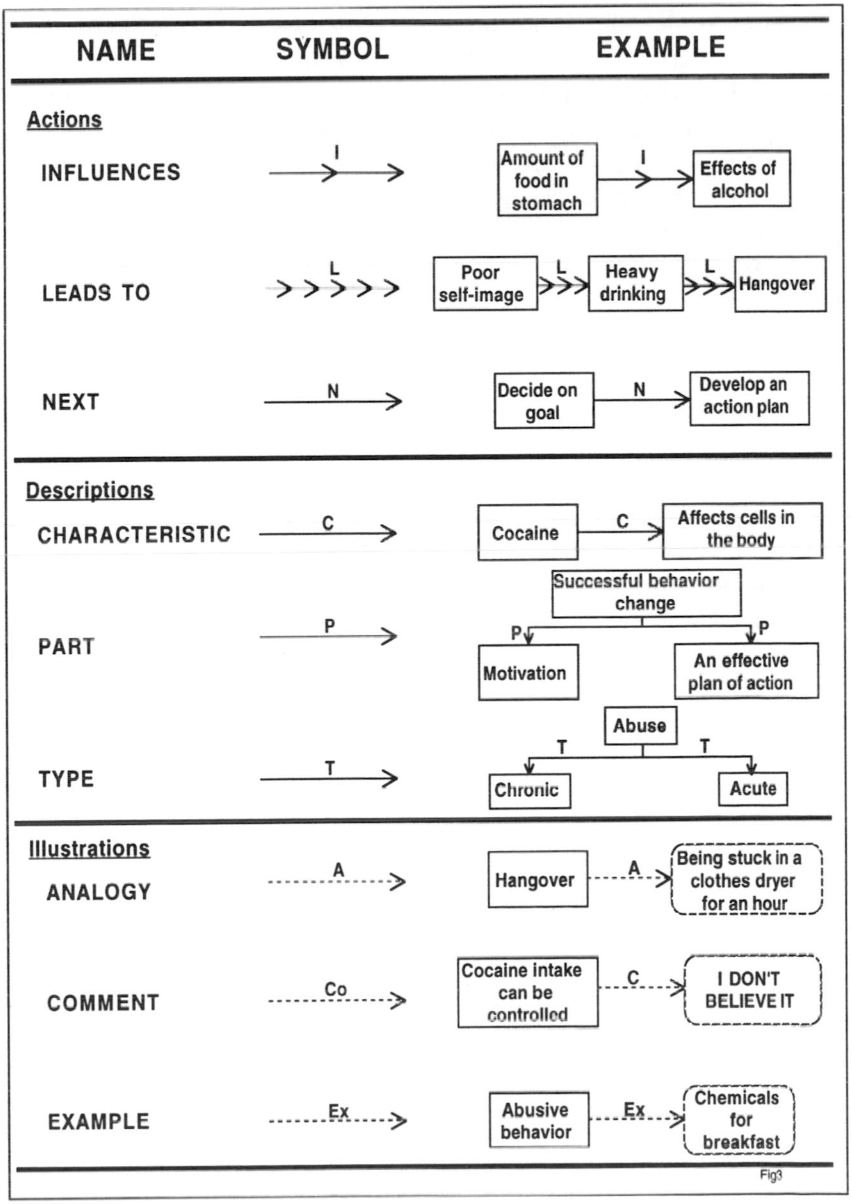
NAME
SYMBOL
EXAMPLE
Actions
INFLUENCES
I
Amount of food in stomach
I
Effects of alcohol
LEADS TO
L
Poor self-image
L
Heavy drinking
L
Hangover
NEXT
N
Decide on goal
N
Develop an action plan
Descriptions
CHARACTERISTIC
C
Cocaine
C
Affects cells in the body
PART
P
Successful behavior change
P
P
Motivation
An effective plan of action
TYPE
T
Abuse
T
T
Chronic
Acute
Illustrations
ANALOGY
A
Hangover
A
Being stuck in a clothes dryer for an hour
COMMENT
Co
Cocaine intake can be controlled
C
I DON'T BELIEVE IT
EXAMPLE
Ex
Abusive behavior
Ex
Chemicals for breakfast
Fig3

Figure 3. Standard link types.

"definition," and "results in" links are very useful in some topic areas); however, part of the elegance of the mapping system is the general applicability of a relatively small set of nine link labels.

The simple node-link-node grammar leads to a consistent communication style across domains and knowledge "mappers" (those who make maps). Since completed maps do not contain as much "word clutter" as text, they can be more efficiently read and processed. In addition, the link types provide the basis for a series of questions (e.g., What "leads to" X?), which can be used by the map maker in conducting a thorough search for all relevant information in a knowledge domain.

Spatial Configuration

The mapping system uses spatial properties to clarify the organization of a domain. For example, "gestalt" perceptual organizing principles (see Figure 4) are used to indicate continuation, proximity, similarity, symmetry, parallelism, and information gaps. Knowledge prototypes (that is, structural schemas or superstructures) are also used to organize the domain. These prototypes include descriptive hierarchies, logic and action chains, and concept clusters. The prototypes are emphasized by the arrangement of nodes and links.

Map Units

A map unit is similar to a book chapter or a lecture. A map unit of a knowledge domain can be presented as a single, large map or as a hierarchical set of interlocked maps (i.e., hypermaps, see Figure 5). Hierarchical or hypermap sets refer to interlocking maps of increasingly detailed information. Numbers, letters, or colors in nodes refer to more detailed maps. The resulting set is very much like an atlas of country, state, and city maps. We recommend an organization consisting of an overview map where the main topic nodes indicate what is covered in the entire unit, followed by the detail maps in a hierarchical fashion.

Making Maps to Organize Your Thoughts and Lectures

Even if you don't present maps to your classes, making your own maps can help you organize your thinking about a domain, help you

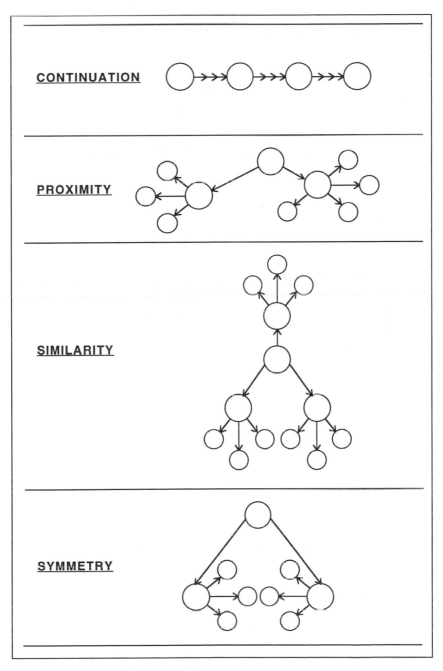

Figure 4. Gestalt mapping principles.

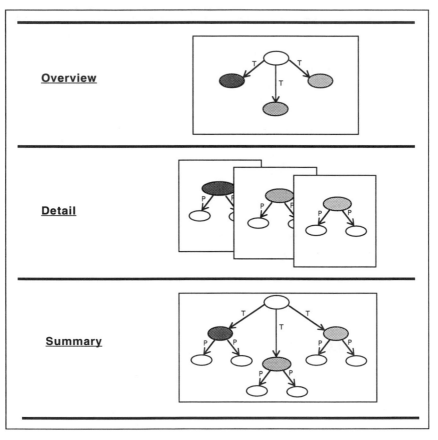

Figure 5. Hypermap unit.

see new conceptual connections, and even provide an alternative set of lecture notes. Below are two methods for making maps.

Link-Guided Mapping

When you're not sure what information should be included in the map and/or how it should be organized, you can start with a few key ideas and develop the map by asking yourself about relationships (or links) between ideas (e.g., "What does this idea **lead to**?" or "What are some **characteristics** of this idea?"). After the map has been "grown" into a first draft, you can then organize it to make it easier to understand.

We call this approach **"link-guided"** because it uses the link labels to develop information for inclusion in the map. For example, we could use this technique to develop a map of the common cold. In doing this, use "common cold" as the starting node, ask a series of link questions, and attach the answers using a "Tinker-toy"™ style. Here is a possible scenario (see Figure 6 Common Cold).

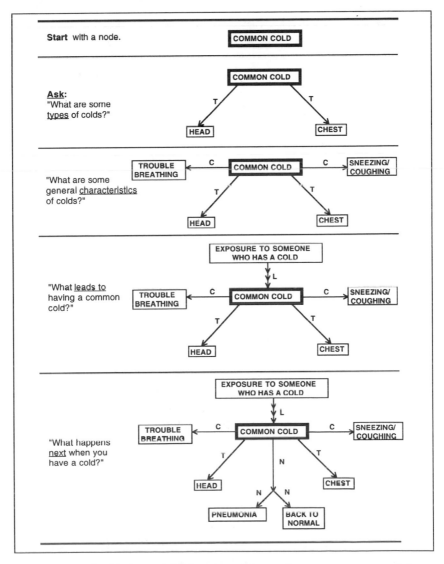

Figure 6. Link-guided search on the common cold.

We could use the rest of the **link types** to ask additional questions about the common cold and expand our map. It could be elaborated even further by asking **link questions** about some of the other nodes we have added. Our research (McCagg & Dansereau, 1990) with this technique indicates that it is an excellent method for developing ideas about a topic prior to writing or speaking. It also is an effective discussion aid. It's often better than simple "brainstorming" because the link questions help you search for information more systematically and thoroughly. It also helps to jog your memory and helps guide the direction and focus of class discussions.

A plan for developing a link-guided map is illustrated in Figure 7. It is important **not** to follow this plan robotically. The order in which link questions are asked is not magical. You may skip around and ask the questions in any order. Intuitive leaps are encouraged. Sometimes ideas emerge that do not seem to have a direct link with the node you are working on. Jot down these associated ideas and use them as possible starting nodes for other sections of the map. Use this technique as a rough guideline; this type of mapping does not have rigid production rules!

Structure-Guided Mapping

When you have a good grasp of the information you are intending to map, you will probably first want to develop an overview structure that lays out the major topics to be covered. For example, we could use our general knowledge of diseases to lay out the following overview of the common cold (see Figure 8).

We could then fill in specific information. If we wanted to show relationships between different sections of the map, we could use the link-guided technique to make interconnections. For example: "Which symptoms lead to which treatments?" The answer to this question could produce connections between the symptoms and treatment sections of the map, as illustrated in Figure 9.

Additional link questions can be answered to "flesh out" the remainder of the map. The map can then be redone to create relevant symmetries, and so forth. As you gain expertise in using various map structures in your classes, you might develop a set of your own schematic structures to help guide the thinking of your students (e.g., your version of cycles and hierarchies).

1. Create a starting node. Put node in a central location on your map.
2. Ask the following questions and draw the arrows on the map:
   - Can this node be broken down into different types?

   - What are the characteristics of each type?

   - What are the important parts of each type?

   - What led to the starting node? (What does it lead to?)

   - What things influence the starting idea or concept? (What does it influence?)

   - What happens NEXT?

   Elaborate the map by using analogy links or example links

   IMPORTANT: Be flexible in asking and answering the above questions; there is no one way of doing it. You need to tailor your maps to the specific topic, your purpose, and your students.

3. Pick another important concept or idea.
   NOTE: New ideas may emerge as you ask and answer the above concepts.
4. Repeat STEP 2 on the same or different sheet of paper.

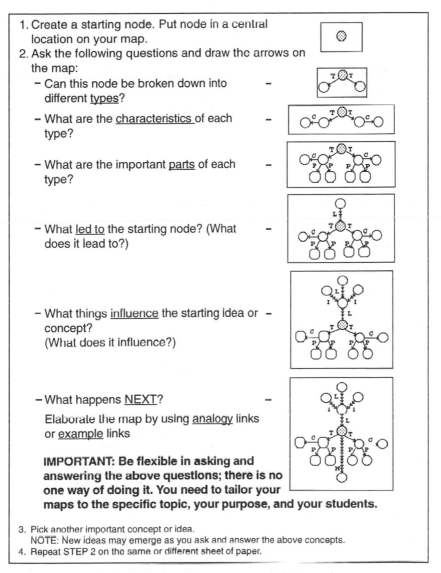

Figure 7. General procedure for link-guided search.

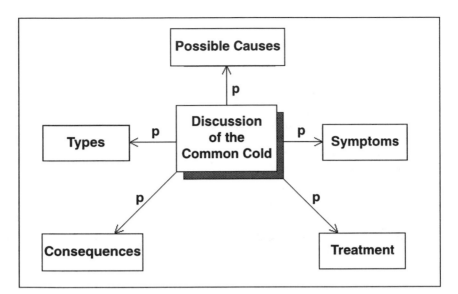

Figure 8. Structure-guided mapping: Overview.

Overheads and Handouts ────────────────────

We have used knowledge maps projected in a corner or in the front of the classroom to guide lecture and discussion in college courses. These maps help both students and instructors to keep track of the "forest" as the instructor presents the specific details orally and on the chalkboard. The overhead maps serve as a reference (something like a shopping mall map) that allows the instructor to show the students "where they have been" and "where they are going" as they move through the knowledge domain. Hard copies of the overhead maps can be provided to the students to serve as notetaking templates and for use as communication aids during peer collaborations (see next section).

Maps and Peer Collaboration ────────────────────

Peer collaboration can be used part way into a class as a way of "shifting gears," reviving attention, consolidating what has been

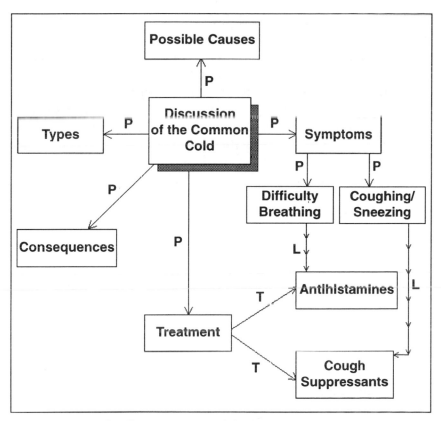

Figure 9. Structure-guided mapping: Details.

presented, and eliciting additional questions. College students taking complex subjects are particularly reluctant to ask questions, and the questions they do ask are often ill-formed. Since "good" questions serve a crucial role in learning and teaching, it is important to provide experiences that improve questioning. Our teaching experiences and our research (e.g., O' Donnell & Dansereau, 1992) suggest that intermittent peer collaboration using map overheads and handouts effectively serves this purpose.

We have found that relatively brief (3-5 min) map-guided collaborative episodes during lectures can be beneficial in a number of ways. In one type of collaboration, pairs of students alternate roles in cooperating with the aid of an instructor-provided knowledge map. For example, using material just covered in the lecture, student A will recall/summarize the first part of the information (referring to the map handout as little as possible), while student B will serve as a listener/facilitator, identifying and correcting errors, gaps, and misconceptions (again, with minimal reference to the map handouts). Then both students refer directly to their maps for complete verification. Next, the students attempt to integrate the new material with previously learned information and personal experiences. They also develop potential questions to ask the instructor. The students then switch roles and go through the second half of the target information.

The map-based scripts we have developed can be used at the beginning of a class to review information from the previous class, forming a "bridge" to new material and serving as an advance organizer for the current presentation. Peer collaborations can also be used to implement brief mapping assignments in which students collaborate on constructing their own maps. Finally, the map-based scripts can be used to put closure on a subject before moving on to a new one. Students have reported the use of these map-based, collaborative, learning strategies when the prepare for tests as well.

Link-Guided Mapping in the Classroom

The link-guided mapping approach described previously can be used to stimulate class discussion and to diagnose misconceptions. The instructor puts an important concept in a node on the chalkboard and asks the class a series of link-based questions to grow a map (e.g., "name the types . . .;" "what are the characteristics . . ."). A student can be assigned to serve as a recording secretary to record the map for photocopying and later distribution to the class.

Map Assignments

College students can be easily trained to generate their own maps, thus attempting to discover or clarify for themselves the underlying structural organization of a body of knowledge. Student maps can then replace or supplement their conventional notes or serve as review guides. Although precautions must be observed to prevent student frustration during training, it has been found that student mapping facilitates both multiple-choice and essay test performance (e.g., McCagg & Dansereau, 1990).

A team mapping project appears to be a good alternative to the traditional term paper. Students are assigned to teams of 2-4 members and are instructed to produce a comprehensive, creative poster map or set of maps on a course topic of their choosing. In other cases, teams are told to produce maps that synthesize the major themes of the course. A study was recently conducted to examine the effectiveness of such a project (Czuchry & Dansereau, in press). Students in an introductory psychology course and a memory and cognition course completed a team mapping assignment and were then asked to complete an anonymous survey that compared the mapping assignment to their perceptions of traditional writing assignments.

The mapping assignment was rated as more interesting and involving more learning than a traditional paper assignment, regardless of gender or course level. Students also preferred doing the mapping assignment over a traditional paper assignment. This was especially true for students in the introductory psychology course.

Most student-generated team maps are creative and informative. For example, one posterboard map developed in a memory and cognition class had detail topic information hidden behind a "pull-out" section attached to the back of the posterboard. The tabs were colored in corresponding shades used as the main topic nodes on the face of the map.

Some students created single, large, holistic maps. For example, a map on child development was made from posterboard cut into the shape of a human figure. Other students created stacked maps. Three introductory psychology students generated an overview map of drug effects on consciousness, with icons for the main topics: a yellow clock represented biological rhythms, a blue bed represented sleep, a pill represented drugs, and a green spiral represented hypnosis. Four submaps dealt with each topic in turn, such as two large posters that described the desirable and undesirable effects of cannabis, LSD, alcohol, and barbiturates.

In general, students' comments suggest that team mapping assignments enable them to be creative and expressive. For example, written comments include: "Making maps is a great alternative to writing papers. I believe it is much more interesting and more fun to do," and "The mapping project was very interesting and it was nice because it was something different than just a boring paper. I think I also learned a lot more through it."

Other comments suggested that the maps help students better organize and remember the information: "I usually like writing papers, but for this assignment, I think the map was very beneficial to me—it helped organize all the info in my head the same way I put it on paper," and "I think the mapping is more effective in that it causes one to study a broad amount of information and it is easier to remember when organizing it in map form."

Instructors and other students also gain benefits from the mapping assignment. The way that students organize and depict conceptual relations in their maps may allow the instructor to judge students' grasp of important concepts. Students can also view each others' maps in a classroom display, whereas a traditional paper assignment would require students to read each others' papers—a time-consuming and presumably less interesting task.

Fill-in-the-Blanks Maps

The instructor can create partial maps that have missing nodes and/or link information. Students can complete these maps for notetaking, homework, or testing. Scoring of these maps is similar to the scoring of traditional fill-in-the-blank and short-answer tests.

Chapter Summary

In this chapter we have presented the knowledge mapping system, rationale for its use in college teaching, and ways of implementing it in your courses. Many instructors at Texas Christian University and other universities over the country have been using knowledge mapping extensively. Their positive feedback and their continued use of the technique suggest that it's worth your attention.

References

Alvermann, D. (1986). Graphic organizers: Cuing devices for comprehending and remembering main ideas. In J. F. Baumann

(Ed.), *Teaching main idea comprehension*. Newark, DE: International Reading Association (pp. 210-226).

Anderson, J. R. (1995). *Cognitive psychology and its implications*. New York: W. H. Freeman & Co.

Buzan, T. (1994). *The mind map book*. New York: Penguin Books, Inc.

Czuchry, M., & Dansereau, D. F. (in press). Node-link mapping as an alternative to traditional writing assignments in undergraduate psychology courses. *Teaching of Psychology*.

Dansereau, D. F. (1995). Derived structural schemas and the transfer of knowledge (pp. 93-121). In A. McKeough, J. Lupart, & A. Marini (Eds.), *Teaching for transfer: Fostering generalization in learning*. Hillsdale, NJ: Lawrence Erlbaum Associates, Inc.

Evans, S. H., & Dansereau, D. F. (1991). Knowledge maps as tools for thinking and communication. In R. F. Mulcahy, R. Short, & J. Andrews (Eds.), *Enhancing learning and thinking* (pp. 97-120). New York: Praeger.

Lambiotte, J. G., & Dansereau, D. F. (1992). Effects of knowledge maps and prior knowledge on recall of science lecture content. *Journal of Experimental Education*, 60(3), 189-201.

McCagg, E.C., & Dansereau, D.F. (1990, April). A convergent paradigm for examining knowledge mapping as a learning strategy. Paper presented at the Annual Meeting of the American Educational Research Association, Boston, MA.

Novak, J. D., & Gowin, D. B. (1984). *Learning how to learn*. New York: Cambridge University Press.

O'Donnell, A. M., & Dansereau, D. F. (1992). Scripted cooperation in student dyads: A method for analyzing and enhancing academic learning and performance. In R. Hertz-Lazarowitz & N. Miller (Eds.), *Interaction in cooperative groups: The theoretical anatomy of group learning*. Cambridge, MA: Cambridge University Press.

Rewey, K. L., Dansereau, D. F., & Peel, J. L. (1991). Knowledge maps and information processing strategies. *Contemporary Educational Psychology*, 16, 203-214.

Wiegmann, D. A., Dansereau, D. F., McCagg, E. C., Rewey, K. L., & Pitre, U. (1992). Effects of knowledge map characteristics on information processing. *Contemporary Educational Psychology*, 17, 136-155.

Extending the Classroom Walls Electronically

Tom Creed

Tom Creed enjoys being at the cutting edge of information technology. Years ago he began accepting assignments via email; he noticed that, in many ways, the medium leveled the playing field for his students. As he began to incorporate electronic communication more extensively into his courses, he realized that it erased the limitations of time and place in interacting with students. He is Professor of Psychology at St. John's University and the College of St. Benedict, Collegeville, Minnesota. He founded the Learning Enhancement Service there and serves as its director. He writes about and gives workshops on active learning strategies, classroom assessment, and collaborative learning, and has consulted with several colleges on programs to promote enhanced student learning. Most recently, he co-wrote and produced *Opening Doors: Two Cases of Formative Assessment,* a videotape distributed by The Collaboration for the Advancement of College Teaching and Learning. His E-mail address is <TCREED@CSBSJU.EDU>.

We are bombarded daily with hype about the coming technological revolution in higher education. Technology is touted as the most recent panacea; the cure for what ails us. Certainly, technology is transforming our lives, and will continue to do so. But will it impact our teaching? And if so, how? The question that we need to ask is, "What do we want to accomplish in our courses, and can technology advance our teaching goals?" rather than "What can we do with technology?"

This chapter isn't about increased productivity, or the fears that we will all be replaced by machines, or any of the *Really Big Issues*, but about how electronic communication has the potential to help us extend and enhance the conversation that goes on within the classroom. The technology is available now, does not require great sophistication to use, and is generally available to faculty and students. But electronic communication involves compromises and trade-offs; I'll discuss the downside as well.

This chapter assumes the faculty member still meets students in a normal classroom and is hoping to extend, rather than remove, the classroom walls. No matter what the medium, we communicate with our students in different ways at different times for different purposes. Some of the information that we exchange in a course should be private. Much of a student's graded work should be private: it should be privately communicated to the instructor and the instructor's assessment of it should be privately communicated to the student. Also, the concerns of individual students about aspects of the course (e.g., expressing some dissatisfaction with an assignment, asking for clarification of the grading system, elaboration of a point raised in class, etc.) are probably best handled privately. Other types of information, such as discussions about the controversial issues of the class, should be public and dynamic (interactive)—we can all gain from sharing ideas and hearing the informed opinions of others. Still other forms of information, such as course syllabi, handouts, and other resources, should be publicly available but static (noninteractive).

Briefly, I see my use of electronic communication as falling into three distinct categories:

- **Private Discourse.** My use of private discourse falls into two subcategories: my students submit their writing assignments through E-mail and we carry on personal conversations, such as setting up appointments and holding brief discussions of routine questions about the course through E-mail.

- **Public forum.** Through an electronic conference set up specifically for my class, we discuss topics of general interest in the course. Issues raised during class discussions and discussions of questions raised by individual class members are the main subjects discussed.

- **Repository of information.** The major course materials—the syllabus, writing and reading assignments, and some of the textual content of the course (handouts, explanations, etc.)—are available through the World Wide Web on the Internet. Those interested can see how I use the web in my classes by visiting my web site at:
  <http://bingen.cs.csbsju.edu/~tcreed>

Each of these three broad categories uses a specific computer program. In the table below, I've summarized several parameters of communication and how these three categories compare, as well as typical uses and programs for each. This table should help you think about how you want to communicate with your students, and then pick the most appropriate technology. For example, if you want to communicate with an individual, E-mail would be preferable. It's private, quick, and easily created. But if you have a large amount of relatively unchanging information that you want available to many others, a World Wide Web site would be the way to go. It's public, it's organized, and while it's more difficult to construct (you need to use a special programming language, Hypertext Markup Language, or HTML), it is permanent. As with traditional communication, we need to be cognizant of how best to communicate with each other when we communicate electronically.

Three Categories of Electronic Information

	Repositories	Public Forums	Private Discourse
Description	Information stored by a (usually) large entity (schools, museums, government agencies) and retrieved by individuals.	Information from others is available and can be retrieved; the information is a collective knowledge base.	Two-way communication between individuals. The communicators control what information is available to each other.
Use	Efficient gathering and storage of collected knowledge that an individual or small group would be unable to compile and maintain on their own.	Small groups of individuals with a common purpose come together to share information, create a body of knowledge on a limited topic.	Two (or more) people share information that is of importance to themselves but of little value to others, or needs to be confidential.
Organization of information	Hierarchical --------------------------------Non-hierarchical		
Persistence	Permanent--Ephemeral		
User input of information	Little--Considerable		
Modifiability by user	Unmodifiable by user Highly modifiable by user		
Audience	Large, Public----------------------------------Small, Private		
Amount of information	Mass quantities---------------------------------Small amounts		
Ease of creating information	Fairly difficult--Easy		
Intrusiveness	Not intrusive ----------------------------------Very intrusive		
Conventional examples	Libraries	Roundtable Discussions, Town Hall meetings	Letters, conversation
Educational examples	Lecture	Cooperative Learning	Tutorial
Electronic forms	World Wide Web	Electronic Conferencing	E-Mail

My class, *Principles of Learning and Behavior,* an upper-division (junior and senior) course within the psychology major, is typical of how courses can use electronic communication. The structure of my course is driven by my goals for my students. I want them to:

- learn the basic principles of conditioning,
- come to appreciate that these principles can be used to explain, predict, and control human actions,
- "automatically" use these principles in analyzing situations they encounter,
- use these principles to improve their own lives, and
- have this ability five years from now.

The kind of learning that is important to me requires active rehearsal, and one of the best forms of active rehearsal is to talk to someone else about what you know. While learning is based on what we have individually acquired, the consolidation comes about best when we discuss our ideas with others—I think learning is primarily a communal event. I rely heavily on cooperative learning in my courses to meet this communal sharing of knowledge (Johnson, Johnson and Smith, 1991). I view my role in the course, then, as setting up the environment so that my students will most likely learn the material as well as possible, but I do spend some time playing expert and transmitting information.

Principles of Learning and Behavior meets twice a week for 70 minutes. I structure my courses in functional units (e.g., Pavlovian conditioning). Class periods are a combination of some lecture and class discussion, and a lot of small group cooperative learning. The way I assure that students have a solid knowledge base at the beginning of the unit is by having them write out answers to unit guide questions prior to starting the unit. So, every third or fourth class meeting my students are required to do some reading in the textbook and answer some questions that are designed to help personalize the material and to get them to think about the more complex aspects of the topic.

The unit on Pavlovian conditioning is an example. Before we begin our classroom discussion of Pavlovian conditioning, students read a chapter from the text, plus some short ancillary readings, then complete a writing assignment, consisting of three parts:

- the first part asks them to describe three examples in which they have been Pavlovianly conditioned. I ask them to come up with fairly unique and significant examples and to label the components of their example and to explain why they think their examples are Pavlovian conditioning.
- the second part asks them to write the one page text of a speech they would give to a seventh grade class explaining what Pavlovian Conditioning is all about.
- the third part asks them to make up their own question about the chapter and explain why this question is important to them.

The first part of the writing assignment helps them to personalize the material, while the second helps them to structure an overall picture of the phenomenon, determine what's important, and put it in their own words. The third part gives them some ownership of the material, in that we are likely to address their question in class or on our electronic conference.

Their written responses essentially drive what happens during the next three class periods. When we first meet to discuss Pavlovian conditioning, I'll give a short demonstration, make sure we are all using the same terminology, and provide a little clarifying information that I think was either missed, poorly explained or glossed over in the text. Next comes the most important part of the first class meeting—my students get into cooperative learning groups of three or four students, and talk about their examples. As a group, they write up their most intriguing examples and any questions they have. Each group submits what they have written to me at the end of class. Their write-ups tell me what I need to address during the next couple of class periods, either through mini-lectures, more small group discussion, demonstrations, or whatever classroom procedure that seems most suitable.

The Limitations of My Course Without Electronic Communication

I think it's important to stress that I first structured my courses in this manner several years ago, before I used electronic communication with my students. While I've found this structure successful in producing good student learning, there were four distinct areas of my class with which I was concerned: 1) the quality of my students' writing on their assignments, 2) whether I was getting adequate feedback about the class, 3) my management of the volume of material for the class, and 4) several issues related to the temporal and spatial limitations imposed by the traditional class structure. More specifically—

1. Did they write it on the bus coming to class? My students' writing was not always as thoughtful and reflective as I would have wished. Students were reluctant to do multiple drafts of a pre-class writing assignment, and their work often looked like it was dashed off minutes (or seconds!) before class. Also, if they wrote it right before class, they didn't have the opportunity to reflect on what they wrote. And if they got to use their written homework in class, which I think is a good idea, how could I know they were not writing it during class rather than before? Finally, their pre-class writing assignments were often so messy that I had a difficult time deciphering what they had written.

A related concern was how, when, or even if, they were engaging the material outside of class. Since I didn't know what they were doing when they weren't in class, it was difficult to know how they were structuring their time with the course material.

2. What are they really thinking about the class? I use quite a few Classroom Assessment Techniques (Angelo and Cross, 1993), and these are invaluable for getting a sense of what students know and how they feel about the class. But a student might be reluctant to tell me something that she is really angry about, for fear that I'd be able to tell from her handwriting who wrote it. So, was I getting the honest feedback I needed?

3. When did they give it to me, and where did I put it? Frankly, I'm not the most organized guy in the world, and I had a problem keeping track of everything that was submitted and when it was submitted. Like many professors, I have deadlines for when work is due. Students often claim that they put their assignment under the office door in time, it's just that I wasn't there, or they gave it to another student who put it under the wrong door, etc. And when papers were handed in at times other than class time, I had a tendency to misplace them. The kiss of death for a paper was when a student handed it to me in the hallway when I was on my way somewhere else. They must be some place in an alternate universe where all of those papers have accumulated, along with all of my pens and Phillips screwdrivers.

4. And several problems resulting from time and place constraints—

- **Sorry, time's up!** Many times, we had to stop a class discussion before we had come to some resolution. Other times, there were people who wanted to speak and didn't get the chance. Too bad the discussion had to end at 12:30—we could have gone on productively for another 20 minutes.

- **Pack it in—you don't have much time, and you won't see them again for a while.** Class time may not be the best time, nor should it be the only time, for the transmission of information. Handouts help, but the transmission of information seems like a poor use of that most precious of commodities, our time with our students. Class time shouldn't be the only time to convey important information, such as a new assignment. A corollary of this for me was the "Oh, one more thing..." phenomenon—about 30 seconds after class, I would think of something really important that I wanted them to think about, some important housekeeping information, etc. The opportunity was lost if I didn't remember it while I had them in my grasp. This was a big problem in my evening class that met once a week.

- **Betty writes great papers. Why doesn't she talk more in class?** Class discussions tend to favor the verbally adept, extroverted student. But what about those quiet ones sitting over there? They seem attentive. Don't they have something to contribute to the conversation? A small group cooperative learning structure certainly helps get around this problem, but the groups and reports from the groups can be dominated by the same people.

- **Sorry, I work then. How about midnight after I get off work?** There is no reason why the classroom should be the only place where the interchange goes on, but, as most people who use cooperative learning know, arranging face-to-face interactions outside of class is difficult. Students have busy schedules, and often live quite a distance from each other. Even on my campus, which is primarily residential, students have a difficult time arranging meeting times.

- **Sometimes grandmothers really do die.** Students frequently have legitimate reasons for missing a class. A student who misses a class has clearly missed something important, but in addition to missing the conversation that went on that day, they have usually missed announcements, assignments, etc. that will prepare them for the next class meeting. There's a double jeopardy to missing class—you've missed what went on that day, and you may be ill prepared for the next class meeting. How many of our students drop a class because they aren't sure how to catch up and are embarrassed to go find out?

Electronic communication has helped me address (with greater to lesser degrees of success) each of these problems.

━━━ The Advantages of Electronic Communication ━━━

Most of the communication on the typical campus between teacher and student, or even between student and student, takes place during the prescribed classroom meeting times. We gather in the same place at the same time, information is transmitted almost entirely orally, and in real time. This puts severe constraints and extreme pressure on the communication—what is communicated has to "fit" within the allotted time period, and since that time period is fixed and inflexible, you can't waste valuable time ("we have to cover the material").

Two characteristics of electronic communication give it promise: The first is that the communication is not restricted to a specific time and place (i.e.—it is *asynchronous,* not occurring at the same time, and *asyntopic,* not occurring in the same place). Second, it is primarily visual and textual rather than oral. This is all pretty obvious, but these differences have enormous implications for student learning. These two characteristics provide benefits in several distinct areas in that they:

- allow for increased accessibility to the information relevant to the course and the ongoing dialogue about this information,

- provide for a more pedagogically sound interaction with the information by students,

- encourage more thoughtful discussion by students about the information in the class,

- provide more equal participation in the ongoing discussion (level the playing field) in several important ways,

- enhance student interaction outside of class,

- provide a unique classroom assessment technique,

- enhance my ability to archive and retrieve my students' work, and provide increased structure of information,

- and provide access to diverse sources of information.

Increased Accessibility

Clearly the major advantage of electronic communication is that it is asynchronous and asyntopic. My students can be anywhere and ask me a question when it is of concern to them; they can comment on each other's views on our electronic conference when they have the time and inclination; and, through the World Wide Web, my students can get the important, static documentation for the class from a wide variety of locations and on demand. Their dog can't eat this syllabus. The web is always there and waiting for them—their electronic servant. Like the Wobblies, it never sleeps, it never forgets. If they miss a class, they know where to go to get the missing material.

In turn, these same advantages hold for me. I can address students' concerns from any place and when I have the time to devote to them, which is often while I'm at home after I've gotten my son to sleep. If I've forgotten to mention something important in class, I can contact them through a distribution list E-mailing, or post it on our electronic conference or our web site if I know they will be accessing either in the near future. I use the distribution list if it is something imperative, since it is more intrusive—it signals my students that it has arrived, so students are notified that I have sent them something. The electronic conference is more efficient (in terms of disk storage), but since it does not notify conference members that there is a new posting, they may not get the message before the next class meeting.

I'm off campus quite a bit, and I can log in from anywhere, access my account, and respond to my students requests, monitor the discussion on our electronic conference. I can easily update the material on my web site when I want (or need) to, from wherever I happen to be. And my most recent update is the version the students have—I can update the syllabus after it's in their notebooks. I can create and modify courselinks whenever I want. (A courselink is some information relevant to the class that I create and store locally in my account, such as a definition or description of a phenomenon. Examples of courselinks are definitions of terms, chapter outlines, diagrams, etc., the things that I would normally hand out on paper.) Courselinked material can be any size; the 8 1/2 x 11 size restriction paper handouts impose upon us is gone. A courselink can be as short as a sentence or two, or as long as it needs to be. How many of us feel like we have to use the whole page if we hand something out, or, if it is longer, feel like we have to trim it to fit on as few pages as possible? With courselinks, it's easy to embellish an on line syllabus, and it's easy to create links to new material that you've discovered after class starts.

The asynchronous and asyntopic nature of electronic communication provides the true extension of the classroom walls.

Pedagogically Sound Interaction with the Information ——

Electronic communication allows me to structure a more pedagogically sound way for students to complete outside writing assignments. For example, I ask my students to submit their written homework two hours before class begins. Since their E-mailings are time and date stamped, I know whether they've done it or not.

There are a couple of pedagogical advantages to this. First, they can't do their work on their way to class. Since they must do their work at a terminal, they are doing their work in a setting conducive to intellectual work. A computer terminal is a setting that has become associated with intellectual work for most students. Consequently, their work will be more thoughtful and they should be more efficient since the setting evokes scholarly work fairly immediately.

Second, they must do the assignment far enough in advance that they will be engaging the material twice—when they wrote it, and then again when they talk about it in class. The break of two or more hours between writing and discussing allows *incubation* to occur. Incubation occurs when we work on a problem, then leave it alone for a while. Even when we do not actively engage the material during the break, our thinking on the topic improves (Ellis, 1978).

One of the major concerns I've always had about my students is how they are spending their out-of-class time with respect to my class. Are they starting their reading with enough time to do a thorough job? How often are they engaging the material? This is even a bigger concern for me with my class that meets once a week. I don't want them to start thinking about it a couple of hours before class, with a week intervening since they last thought about it. Most of what was learned last week will be gone. I want them to reflect periodically on what happened last time, and prepare for next time. Our electronic conference was made for this purpose. For example, in my weekly class, I can ask them to post a response a day or two after the class meeting, either addressing a specific question that I post after class, or something more open-ended, such as "What did you find most interesting in class last night, and what interested you about it?" I might give them a day or two to respond, then ask them to rejoin the conference, read each others' postings, and respond to what others had to say. A couple of days later, I might post a new question that will get them thinking about the next class meeting, following the same format. The point is I've structured their interaction with the material so that they must think about the material, and in a thoughtful manner. They can do this when they have time, yet not too much time has gone by without their thinking about the class. Research conducted since the 1920's shows clearly that spaced practice—breaking the task into smaller, more frequent interaction with the material—produces stronger long-term learning than does the same amount of exposure to the material in one longer sitting (massed practice). In short, electronic communication allows me to structure their out-of-class interaction so they're not cramming.

The World Wide Web allows for some degree of hierarchical organization. The web author is like an architect. You structure the page, but students select their own path, very much like the relationship between the designer of a museum and one of its visitors. The better the designer has done her job, the less intrusive her presence is and the better the visitor gets to profit from the experience. The same is true for the design of the web page. Your organization of the information is evident, and student notes will be better organized than the chaos we frequently see.

On my web page, I can structure how my students get their writing assignments. I used to give them the option of first reading a short description of their reading assignment—what I wanted them to look for, etc.—or going straight to the questions. It became clear that they were not reading the introductory material, so I rearranged the site so that they must first click on the description; from there they can get to the questions. This method doesn't assure that they will read the description first (you can lead a horse to water . . .), but does make it more likely since it is right there in front of them. Also, I opted against direct submission of answers through the web. They must download the questions into their personal accounts, then edit the file with the questions, then submit the file. I chose this route since my goal is reflective answers. Editing a file, with the possibility of redrafting, leads to more reflective work than the one-pass submission that occurs when people respond directly to a website.

Perhaps more importantly, the native structure of the web is hypertext. Hypertext has the potential to be a pedagogically superior format. The student is in control of what information comes her way, and at what pace. Such a technology has always been the goal of designers of teaching machines (Skinner, 1957) and the web provides it. For example, my assignments on the web may have links to further explanations, definitions of terms, etc. If the student is familiar with a term, she can pass by the link, but if she is uncertain about what a particular term means, she can click on that link and find out more. That next link may lead to some small courselink I've created or may open up a vast array of new information through additional links. It may take the student in unexpected directions, very much like a good open-ended conversation. By selecting her own path through the web, the student creates her own unique learning. And she has some control over how she structures the web for her own use—once she finds a web site that is of value to her, she can mark it and always get back easily. The web is particularly suited to the independent, motivated learner, which is what most of us want our students to become.

However, hypertext's potential as a pedagogically superior format can only be realized if course pages are designed with effective pedagogy in mind. Anyone who has surfed the web quickly realizes that the typical homepage is a jumble of independent links interspersed with some personal opinion. Setting up a course page that is pedagogically sound is time consuming, and needs to be driven by the goals one has for the course. For example, one of the writing assignments for my Principles of Learning and Behavior class (UGLI 5, for those clicking along as you're reading) asks my students to give examples from their own lives of the four basic forms of operant conditioning. The assignment includes a course link to a table I created, showing the four types. There are some terms in the table that may be unfamiliar to my students, so each of these includes another link that explains the term and gives a brief example. For the student who is quite familiar with the basic concepts, all she has to do is download the assignment and start in. For those who are less familiar with the concepts, however, the information is there to help them. The student is in control of how much or how little information she accesses, based on her own assessment of what she needs.

More Thoughtful Discussion

Since the construction of our electronic correspondence is not limited by time, we can both compose what we have to say and take as much time as we need. This breaking of real-time constraints allows for a more thoughtful conversation, since we can ponder what we have to say and use the full editing power of a word processor. When I get a request from a student, say for an exemption from a class assignment, I have the opportunity to reflect on how to handle it. I have a tendency to feel rushed to judgment in face-to-face requests, and my response is often more moderated by my current mood than by the merits of the request. By having the opportunity to reflect (and edit!), my response is more likely to be well reasoned. I've been so pleased with the effects of this procedure that I ask students to submit requests by E-mail. My sense is that student requests are better reasoned and less frequent because they've had to think it through in order to put it in writing. The availability of E-mail doesn't preclude a student coming to see me. She may have some very personal matter to discuss, and would be uncomfortable committing it to text, or simply be uncomfortable with the fairly sterile medium of electronic communication.

Students' written assignments are more thoughtful for the same reasons. They work on them when they are ready, they can take as much time as they want, and I encourage multiple drafts, which computers were made for. In a similar vein, their electronic discussions can be as thoughtful as they wish. In fact, the medium commands thoughtfulness—what can be tossed off verbally comes off badly textually. But by using E-mail, students can quickly clean up the conversation. I find the general tenor of postings on our electronic conference getting more thoughtful as the semester goes along. And since there's a persistence to students' writings (they can see what they and other students wrote, and make comparisons), the flippant ones show the most marked improvement. I've had more than one flippant student come and tell me they felt embarrassed by what they had said when they saw what the other students had written.

Leveling the Playing Field

Since students' electronic work is formatted identically (80 characters to the line, 25 lines per screen), the electronic submission of assignments levels the playing field—the vagaries of handwriting and penmanship are eliminated. When I first asked students to submit their homework through E-mail, it was mid-semester, so I already knew a fair amount about their writing. I was amazed to discover that I read the work of several of them differently—the volume of those with BIG handwriting shrunk, those with tiny handwriting grew, and the bias of good vs. bad penmanship disappeared. It was immediately obvious to me that I was reading their work in a less biased fashion—I could much more easily see how well students knew the material. I could much more easily give them feedback on the mechanics of their writing as well, since the similar format allowed me to focus on what they said, not the clarity of their handwriting.

A further, and more important, leveling of the playing field derives from the fact that asynchronous communication is not bound by the "real-time" constraints that exist in the classroom, allowing the quieter, more reflective student the opportunity to participate in the discussion at his or her own pace. I have several students every semester who are quiet during entire class discussions who are "E-mail bloomers"—they come alive when they have the time to reflect on what they want to say and have the opportunity to edit and make sure that it is right. Another way of looking at this is to say that the electronic component of the course allows for the student with a different "learning style" to come forth—the reflective, contemplative student.

Breaking through the power differential. Electronic communication can be customized to level the playing field between students and the professor. For example, our system manager has set up a virtual member of my class—IPAVLOV. IPAVLOV has a single role in life—to provide me with anonymous feedback from my students, a task that is somewhat difficult electronically since everything we send is tagged with our names. IPAVLOV is set up so that, if a student types IPAVLOV at the 'USERNAME:' prompt, no password is needed and they are automatically thrown into the text editor for MAIL. After they have finished writing what they have to say, they close the file, it is automatically sent to me, and the account is closed. This assures anonymity (anyone can log on as IPAVLOV and there is no way to trace who has done so), yet protects against abuse (e.g., sending someone, other than me, a threatening note) since IPAVLOV can do only one thing—send me a message.

The web also levels the playing field since any site can be accessed by anyone. This essentially means that the web is, in some respects, uncontrollable—despite the wishes of the US Congress. While there is some level of control, the control that exists tends to be mutual. This semester, for example, I'm teaching a Senior Seminar, *Popular Delusions,* that explores the widespread belief in unsupported phenomena such as ESP and Creationism. One of my students, who is a real web surfer, has set up a page with lots and lots of links to various paranormal belief sites. As we were discussing his site, he wanted artistic control over it. Well, it's his page, I can't control what he puts on it. On the other hand, if I don't like what he's doing, I can always remove the link from my class's page to his page. Since we can not control what each other does, we had to negotiate an understanding.

This is the true power of the web—everyone becomes a master of their own material, and no one is compelled to visit a site if they don't like it. It is the true example of a democracy voting with its feet.

Enhanced Student Interaction Outside of Class ——————

One way that I extend the classroom walls electronically is by having my students respond to questions generated by other members of the class and posted on the electronic conference. The next class meeting, I have those who responded to particular questions discuss them in cooperative learning groups. They arrive at a group response to the question, then present it to the rest of the class.

Also, groups are assigned topics to research. They quickly learn to divide up the topic and E-mail each other the part they've done. (In cooperative learningese, this is known as a jigsaw technique—each student has part of the puzzle, and the solution only becomes apparent when each fits their part with that of the other students. This technique loads heavily on the "Positive Interdependence" component of cooperative learning, cf. Johnson, Johnson and Smith, 1991.) When the members of the group get together in class, they've already shared their knowledge and are ready to hit the ground running.

Many of my students have adapted the pedagogy and technology of the class to meet their own needs. For example, when they are preparing for the final exam, many groups break the task up into components, then each works on a part and E mails their answers to the others in their group (another example of the jigsaw procedure). I find their spontaneous adaptation of both techniques to their own needs very exciting, in that a tool I taught them, E-mail, and a pedagogical technique, cooperative learning, have quickly become adapted to their own uses. Part of my goal for the course is to have students learn skills that will be of value when they leave college. Learning to work cooperatively and to communicate electronically are two skills they are likely to need to be successful in the future.

A Unique Classroom Assessment Technique ───────────

As mentioned earlier, my students E-mail me their written homework assignments two hours before class. Not only does this allow for incubation for them, but it provides a unique and invaluable classroom assessment technique for me. I can read my students' submissions before class, which allows me to assess what they know BEFORE class begins—I go to class having a good idea what they know and where the problems with their understanding are. This allows me to skip material that they seem to know well already and concentrate on the areas where there are widespread weaknesses. My homework assignments usually include a *Make Up Your Own Questions* section; by reading these in advance, I can address in class the topics that they have already identified as being of interest to them. Similarly, the ongoing discussion on our electronic conference gives me vast insight into how they are viewing the more controversial areas of the course. Our discussions are enhanced since we all have an enlarged shared cognitive set—we all know what the others are thinking about the topic.

An unexpected benefit that E-mail and electronic conferencing provide is that I have a much more accurate assessment of my students' work habits. Since postings are time and date stamped, I've been amazed at how many of them do their work very late at night (a good percentage of the postings are after midnight). I know they are in fact more organized than I had thought (most of them start their work in a timely manner, usually a day or two before it is due). Consistent patterns show up, and I've been able to point out to some students whose work is poor (and usually comes in right at the deadline) how they might do better work if they started earlier.

Enhanced Ability to Archive and Retrieve My ───────────
Students' Work, and Provide Increased
Structure of Information

Electronic submission of assignments has considerable organizational advantages for me. I know when the student's papers were submittcd, and I know where I can find them. They submit their assignments to BFSKINNER, the other virtual member of our class, rather than directly to me. The advantage is that their assignments don't get mixed in with all the rest of the virtual clutter in my account. The only mail BFSKINNER gets is my students' assignments, so I know where they are, and since there's nothing else in his account, it's easy to find my students' work. Further, I can file their assignments with a uniform notation— their initials, the assignment, and as an extension, the semester, which allows me to find easily any particular student's assignment, from any semester. Another advantage of this separate account is my Teaching Assistants can have access to it, do an initial read-through of the class's submissions, yet my personal account remains secure.

Not to be overlooked is the fact that electronic communication also allows students to keep systematic records of their own work as well. I encourage them to keep copies of anything they send me, just in case mine happens to get deleted (it has happened).

Provides Access to Diverse Sources of Information ───────

I can't keep up with everything in my field, but there are repositories of information out there that can be of great value to my students. For example, several schools have established large electronic repositories of information on conditioning—on-line abstracts of journals, compilations of annotated references, databases on active researchers in the field, etc—which have been of great value to students taking *Principles of Learning and Behavior*. The World Wide Web is a democratically distributed network of resources that is constantly changing and being updated. For a class like *Popular Delusions*, where we look at current beliefs, the web is a bonanza—it seems like every possible world view (including craziness not available in the library) is available on the web.

Our electronic conference provides more restricted access to diverse opinions — the diverse opinions of the members of the class. I think students generally are not aware of the diversity of opinion in a typical class, and our electronic conference brings that diversity to the fore.

The table below briefly summarizes which forms of electronic communication provide what sort of benefits:

Advantages of Electronic Communication

Advantage	Repository	Public Forum	Private Discourse
Increases Accessibility	very high	very high	very high
A pedagogically better technique	-	high	high
More thoughtful communication	-	high	high
Levels the playing field	-	high	high
Enhances student interaction	-	high	high
A unique classroom assessment technique	-	very high	very high
Enhances record keeping and structure	very high	high	very high
Access to diverse sources of information	high	moderate	-

Not all forms of electronic communication are both asynchronous and asyntopic. For example, one can "talk" electronically with another person in a different location via computer—each types what they want to say, in real time, and it immediately appears on the screen of the other person. Such a program is asyntopic but not asynchronous. While it is more interactive than E mail, anyone who has been in a talk session knows right away that it's of limited utility. People make lots of typos and take time to go back to correct them, etc., while the other person waits.

Generally speaking, the most advantageous forms of electronic communication are those which take advantage of both asynchronicity and asyntopicality. We all know how difficult it is to get a group of people together, and once we have, the time constraints we have in getting anything accomplished. How nice not to have to go out on a frigid Minnesota February morning (which it is as I write these words), but E-mail my chapter outline to a colleague for critique. On the other hand, we still put a lot of effort into arranging to come together to meet, so there may be something about the face to face interaction that is important, and important parts of the communication process may be lost with electronic communication.

▬▬▬ *Some Cautions and a Few Suggestions* ▬▬▬

In short, electronic communication has several advantages, offering the potential for enhanced learning for students and organizational advantages for us. So, sign me up, Doc, right? Not so fast. Several factors need to be addressed if electronic communication is to be worth the effort. The first is that there are some cautions to be kept in mind about using electronic communication. Electronic communication will only live up to its potential in our courses if it is employed in a rational, well thought-out manner. Ignoring these cautions can lead to electronic communication being a frustrating and counterproductive experience for everyone. Second, there are things we can do to make it serve us better. Third, there are costs associated with electronic communication. I want to turn my attention to these, and discuss ways that many of these costs can at least be minimized, if not eliminated, with some planning. Before employing electronic communication, you should address the following issues.

Have a Rational Plan in Mind ▬▬▬▬▬▬▬▬▬▬▬

Electronic communication should meet a need. A little confession at this point may be in order. I like technology, and much of my early use of it in my classes was driven by my desire to use it because I liked it. Much of my early frustration resulted from many of my students not being nearly so enamored with it. When I started thinking first of what needs I had in my class and whether technology could meet that need, rather than how I could use these wonderful toys, I had fewer problems. From that point, technology started meeting my students' learning needs as well as satisfying my own interests.

Electronic communication should be driven by effective pedagogy. Roger Johnson, one of the gurus of cooperative learning, frequently says that cooperative learning without a well thought out structure is just another seating plan. Electronic communication without student learning in mind can be just one more technological hoop for students to jump through. The reason that I have not used multimedia in my classes is because it doesn't meet a particular need I have, and I am concerned that a multi-media presentation won't actively engage the students. If my subject matter were more visual, such as Anatomy and Physiology, it would probably be more useful. But even then, I would want to put the control of the mouse in the hands of the students—it's too easy for the instructor to get wrapped up in the presentation, in which case the "high-tech classroom of the future" becomes just another chalk-and-talk, minus the chalk dust on the back of the professor's coat at the end of class.

One of the forces working against effective pedagogy is the fact that campus electronic communication systems have not been designed with effective pedagogy in mind. Most computing staff are not trained in effective pedagogy and tend to encourage a usage of the system that is not pedagogically sound. Structuring a pedagogically effective use of electronic communication may require extra steps, but the extra effort is worth it. For example, electronic communication is designed to encourage simple, immediate communication. Creating, editing and finally sending a file is more cumbersome than dashing off a quick E-mail, which is what the system promotes. I gave an earlier draft of this chapter to a friend who teaches on another campus who uses many of the same programs as I do. One of her comments was, "Is my VAX system idiosyncratic, or do you think others also have the problem of not being able to save a message and go back later to edit it? We have to send it right away, so we don't get the reflective time." The fact is, I use the system she does quite often, and more reflective practice is possible, it's just that most faculty aren't aware of it because it is not promoted by computing staff.

Start with what you already use and know well. Even seemingly simple techniques have subtle nuances; mastering them can mean the difference between success and failure. So the best insurance for successfully using electronic communication is to start small, with a technique that you are already fairly comfortable with. Master it, then add other components when they seem to meet a need. A brief description of my use of electronic communication as a case study may be instructive. I've been using electronic communication with my students for six years. Each year, I've modified what I'm doing or added a little more that's done electronically, so that at this point in my class, much of the course—essentially, that part of it that is best conducted outside of the classroom—is conducted electronically. My use of electronic communication has changed over the years as I've thought about when it's worked well and when it hasn't.

Like many of my colleagues, my introduction to electronic communication was through E-mail. I loved it, and quickly adopted it to my classes. Some of my uses of E-mail worked fine, and others not so well. Like most things I do, I jumped into it with both feet and was sending out lots and lots of E-mail to my students. I was kind of like a little kid who first discovers hammers—I used it for everything, even when it wasn't the most appropriate tool. We liked the opportunity to communicate individually over this new medium, but my students quickly became overwhelmed by all of the E-mail I was sending them, and the system manager wasn't thrilled with my clogging his precious hard drives, either.

Add a new electronic communication technology when it better serves your needs. Discovering the electronic conference solved some of my problems and first got me to thinking about different types of electronic communication. Why did the conference work better than E-mail for some things but not others? It was clear to me from the outset that since it was more public, was organized hierarchically, and had more permanence, it was advantageous for material like syllabi and handouts. The electronic conference also allowed my students to carry on public discourse on issues raised in the course, which I thought was really neat. It turns out, this is the only part of the conference that I've retained.

If the conference was an advantage for syllabi and handouts, why did I abandon it for this use? The start of the next semester presented me with a problem—should I start a new conference, or keep the old one? Starting a new one meant copying all of the permanent stuff to the new one, keeping the old one meant I had lots of conversations that I either needed to delete or have an unwieldy huge conference. Worse, electronic conferences are designed to keep an historical record of the discussion, which means that it's difficult to replace an old syllabus with a new one. But if I wanted to make even slight modifications, that's what I had to do. Quite the dilemma.

Then I discovered the World Wide Web. The web provided me with the last piece of the puzzle I needed for efficient communication with my students, since it had all of the advantages of the conference for my more permanent material, but without the disadvantages. Material placed on the web is permanent, but unlike an electronic conference, it is easily modifiable. So by using the technology I first knew, then adding new techniques as I became familiar with them, I was able to use each technique most effectively by using each for what it was best designed to do.

Choose the electronic communication technology that best meets your needs. What you need should drive which mode of electronic communication you choose. Many of the problems we have with electronic communication result from the inappropriate use of an electronic tool when a different one would be more appropriate. I ran into trouble when I used a technique inappropriately— trying to use E-mail, which is designed for small quantities of private communication, for a repository.

There are lots of inappropriate uses of electronic communication. A listserve is a derivative of distributed E-mail[1], but is being used primarily for public discourse—an inappropriate use of the technology. Anyone who is on a listserve will recognize that much of what gets posted should never have been—not all 4,000 people

---

[1] An E-mail can be arranged to reach many people simultaneously by sending it to a distribution list—a listing of many people who share something in common (e.g.-all members of a professional organization.)

on the listserve need to know that Fred wants to know if Bob is ready for lunch yet, or that Mary thinks Mike is a jerk. Since listserves mimic E-mail, they are intrusive—they notify you that a new posting has arrived. Some people like listserves for this reason, but it's also a prime reason that they can be so irritating. In comparison, electronic conferences must be intentionally accessed, and people have a tendency to forget to do so, so the postings may fall on deaf ears.

Electronic communication has a steep learning curve, and can be frustrating for students. Technology does not come easily to all. Many of your students are going to experience the deer-in-the-headlights effect when they first try to learn a program with which they are unfamiliar. Computers just spook some people, and you need to be prepared to be patient with them. It's easy to see where their lack of confidence comes from. Both you and your students need to understand that you have to play strictly by the machine's rules. Electronic communication technology is like an idiot savant—it is very fast and very good at doing one thing. But if you try to get it to do something other than what it wants to do, or if you do not do things precisely as it wants them done, it will simply refuse to work and become uncommunicative. And the task of the user is to figure out what they did wrong, and not do that again. For the neophyte, this can be both frightening and frustrating (every semester someone says, during our first training session, "I think I broke it!"). Electronic Communication may be a real transition in how your students approach their work. They not only need to learn how to use the technology, but they need to make a cognitive switch in terms of how they see their roles.

To cope with this potential problem, it is important to make sure your students have lots of instruction, that you be patient with their initial attempts to use it, and provide lots of support and encouragement. Our task is to get everyone up to speed as quickly as possible so that those who are technologically challenged are not put at a disadvantage by using this form of communication. I have some real technophobes in my classes, but they all get there eventually, and most all of them like it after a while.

Asynchronous and asyntopic does not mean anytime, anyplace. One of the positive points of electronic submission of assignments is that the students' work is done in a setting that is conducive to academic work—in front of a terminal rather than on the bus right before class. But what if it's a nice day, and the student wants to be inspired by the great outdoors as they write? She could always haul her subnotebook out with her—if she owns one. Another potential unlevelling of the playing field. Students who do not live on campus or go home for the weekend, if they don't have access from home, can also be excluded.

The medium requires that participants in the communication access the system; people have to log on to find out if there's anything there. Anyone who has become a somewhat frequent user knows how frustrating it is to send an E-mail message to someone who isn't hooked on the technology. And some of our students simply are not. They log on when they have to, but if they are not frequently reminded, they just don't participate in the conversation.

Electronic communication can be a time sink. It takes a lot of time and effort to learn electronic communication technology well enough to use it effectively. And to be most effective, students need to learn how to use it effectively, also. Where does the time come from for both you and your students? Can we reasonably expect students in our courses (especially if this is the only course they have that uses the technology) to put in the extra hours that it takes to learn it?

The time commitment with technology doesn't end with learning it and thinking through how best to use it. Electronic conferences, and especially web pages, require maintenance and vigilance to remain effective. If you have your class schedule as part of your course page, it needs to be updated as changes are made, or at least every semester. Other material can get out of date even faster. Not only do you need to be vigilant about your own material, but hyperlinks sometimes disappear or go stale quickly.

One way of minimizing the problem of the increased time commitment is to use what you already know, or want to learn anyway. E-mail in particular is so ubiquitous at this point, and useful in so many ways, I highly recommend its use with students. Electronic conferences, since they have a look and feel similar to E-mail, are learned easily. If you are interested in encouraging your students to discuss course issues outside of class, conferences are the way to go.

Learning how to set up a course page on the World Wide Web, however, is a different issue. Frankly, at this point, I would only recommend it if it is something you really want to learn how to do. It has a steep learning curve, and in all likelihood is going to be very different from anything you've learned before. It has it's own programming language, Hypertext Markup Language (HTML), and getting hooked into the Internet requires assistance (at least it did for me). In other words, if you don't find the technology inherently interesting, I don't think that it's worth the time and trouble at this point. If you are interested in learning the technology, though, it has considerable benefits. If you do decide to take the plunge, find someone who already uses it to hold your hand through the first few steps. Also, look at the source code of sites that you like you can learn a lot from them. Like much else with computers, once you get past those first few bewildering steps, you will quickly get the hang of HTML and be off and running.

Electronic communication can be a time sink for students, also. One of the joys of the web is that the student is in control of how she navigates it. But that sense of control (and the intoxicating variety of places one can get to) can become addicting. A recent article in the *Chronicle of Higher Education* reported that many campus counseling centers have begun offering programs for students "addicted" to the web, and many students' grades are falling due to the amount of time they spend on the Internet, surfing web sites and on "chat lines."

Using electronic communication may also require some shifts in how we view our task as well. Since our students are writing more, does it mean we need to read more? Yes. But does it mean we need to correct more? Not necessarily. I have come to view my students' writing on our electronic conference as primarily for their benefit, so even though I read it and comment upon it in class, I don't spend time writing comments on their discussions. And I've also come to spend less time "correcting" their pre-class writing assignments. I do give them feedback, but since their writing primarily sets up their classroom discussions, I've found that they simply need less written comment from me. I save my commenting for complimenting the really good points made, and redirecting the submissions that are really off the mark.

Is it true, or is it bogus? Publishing books and magazines is an expensive process, so it makes sense for them to be well edited and well thought out. Because of this, we have a tendency in our society to equate professional-looking with accurate. But publishing on the web is virtually free, so almost anyone or any group can become an electronic publisher. This clearly allows for greater access to publishing—another leveling of the playing field. But with the decrease in the cost of admission to the playing field, the web becomes the place where any demented but HTML-sophisticated crackpot can have his electronic soapbox look as good as anyone else's. It's tough to separate the wheat from the chaff. For example, there are many more sites extolling the reality of UFOs than there are for serious skeptical inquiry of the existence of extraterrestrial life forms. Students can easily be confused by all of the misinformation.

On the positive side, developing a set of criteria for determining what's of value and what isn't is a valuable skill, and helping students to decipher what is of value on the web helps them build that skill in a fairly benign venue.

Much of the context is lost. For all of the advantages that electronic communication brings in terms of the transmission of ideas, much of the content of personal communication is expressed through tone, body language, etc., which is missing with electronic communication. One doesn't have to look far to find out where the loss is. Ideas are expressed well with electronic communication—in fact, probably better than in face-to-face exchanges. But the interchange, the personal relationship that is a part of communication is missing with electronic communication. Much of the context of a conversation is lost. And when the non-verbal component of the communication can't be detected because body language and voice inflections are absent, people can be hurt by a "playful" comment that is taken seriously. Users of E-mail have tried to replace the "non-verbal" element of communication by using emoticons; all of those irritating little smiley faces that pop up in messages. How do you tell irony? Is it :-), or is it ;-)?

Since this is a relatively new medium of communication, people are still trying to work out the rules—netiquette, if you will. Learning at least some of the basics of netiquette can save embarrassment and extra work.

Not everything is communicated well textually. Electronic communication works fine for students discussing ideas that are easily expressed alphanumerically, but some disciplines rely on symbols not contained on the typical QWERTY keyboard. For example, those in mathematics have difficulty with their students doing mathematical computations on the computer, although theory, discussion, hints, and explanations are still possible and useful. Foreign languages that have different character sets also pose a special problem, especially with the text-based programs that are most widely accessible. Again, another trade-off.

A Few Tips

The better you and your students understand the technology, the more useful it will be for you. The system you use no doubt has several subtle features; the better you know them, the more useful the system will be. I have several examples.

- Posting files rather than immediate mode postings (or what many E-mail programs call 'replies') make for more reflective practice. Learning how to use a mail directory efficiently makes the mail system a much more valuable filing system. Informative (and relevant) subject lines on E-mailings let you and the recipient find the right posting more easily. (This is especially important on a large electronic conference. A title for the posting such as "Posting #1" doesn't tell much, whereas "Why gambling is addictive" is not only more precise, but will entice more readers to read the posting carefully.) Knowing how to transfer, extract and modify files gives power to the word processing capacities of electronic communication.

- The immediate mode response that most systems encourage discourages reflective writing, as is evidenced by the large number of intemperate postings common with E-mail. It is so ubiquitous that the phenomenon even has a name—flaming.

- Most systems can give you feedback on what you've sent. A frequent question I get at the beginning of the semester, especially from students who are nervous about using the system, is "Did you get my homework?" I now show them how to make a simple modification so that they get copies of all of the E-mail they send.

- When replying, including the relevant text of what you're responding to helps the recipient—they may have been involved in lots of things since they sent you their posting, and a response that simply says, "OK" without a proper reference may be meaningless (or misleading!).

Know how to get help. Murphy's Law applies to electronic communication as well as to everything else. When using electronic communication, if things can possibly go wrong, they will, and at the worst time. Even fairly simple technology is pretty complicated and all kinds of things can easily go wrong. It's often very difficult to figure out why it's not working, even to those with some expertise. There must be some corollary of Murphy's Law to cover the use of electronic communication on the first day of class when you're all together in the new high tech computer public access area on campus. Everything that can go wrong will.

Anyone who has given a workshop on computer use, either to their students or to a group of faculty (worse yet!) has horror stories to tell. I gave a week-long workshop on cooperative learning last summer, and I wanted us to use an electronic conference to keep in touch with each other. We got over to the public access area, everyone sat down in front of the computer, we went through joining the conference step by step, and everyone was told the conference didn't exist. This is one of those points in your career where you really find out what you're made of. The error message was useless. So, we turned it into a cooperative learning exercise! One group finally asked me to look at the list of conferences in my directory and we figured out that I had named it slightly differently from what I had asked them to join. We tried the correct name and things worked. Another time, my class had just arrived at the public access area when the mainframe went down. We used the time to brainstorm about how we could use electronic communication, and it was a productive use of our time until the mainframe came back up.

Official support can be very helpful—our system manager has been of great help in customizing the system to meet my needs (such as setting up IPAVLOV). But it may not be everything you need, when you need it. I've gotten a lot of valuable assistance from my colleagues. They often best understand what I'm trying to do, and may have already worked out a solution to the problem I'm experiencing. This is even more important when I've started moving into the cutting-edge technologies, such as using the web in my classes. A couple of my colleagues in Physics and Computer Science have helped me set up my web site and make it do what I want it to do.

Choose the most widely accessible technology. Electronic communication has the potential for leveling the playing field for many students, but lack of access to the technology can shut some students out of the conversation. Assuring access is a considerable problem. Simply put, some of your students will have greater access than others. Those on campus will likely have greater access, as will those with computers at home. A case in point—I've been working with the Weekend College program at another college for the past three years, helping to develop a pedagogy that can make a program in which students attend classes every other weekend an effective learning experience. The research is pretty clear. Students need to interact with the material with some regularity, and electronic communication is ideal for that. So we've been working to "electronicize" the classes, but we keep running up against the problem of access. Since the students' learning is primarily an "off-campus" activity, what do you do about the students who do not have computers at home or at work? Can you require those students to make frequent trips to campus, especially if campus is a long drive? If you do, isn't that defeating the purpose of the program? And just those students whom you wish to serve are the ones who will be excluded. But if you don't require use of the electronic communication technology, aren't you missing one of the best tools you have at your disposal? The university could supply computers to everyone who needs one, but that may not be cost effective. This is precisely the sort of Hobson's choice into which technology can force us.

Access problems are exacerbated when you use the newest technology. There are some nice electronic communication programs that only run under a Local Area Network (LAN). The problem, though, is it excludes those not on the LAN. For example, if someone sends me an E-mail with a WordPerfect attachment, that's fine if I'm at school. I can't read it, though, if I'm at home using my old clunker 386 connected to the mainframe by a modem. Using a technology that is widely accessible, such as VAX Notes, is more inclusive, but the program doesn't have as many options, and is fairly idiosyncratic. Again, another trade-off. (I'm not sure that it's that much of a trade-off, though—not as many bells and whistles means simpler to learn and use.)

And there's another access issue that is becoming increasingly problematic—what happens when everyone discovers E-mail and the system can't keep up? I'm finding it harder and harder to access our mainframe from home; everyone wants to use it now. For me, one of the advantages of electronic communication was that I could do it from home. Every time I get shut out at home, I kick myself for all of those workshops we put on touting the marvels of electronic communication.

Towards the Brave New World

I'm an "early adopter" of electronic communication. I've used it in my classes for six years and my use has settled into a fairly stable pattern. I'm quite happy with how my students get their assignments off of the web, how they submit their assignments to me through E-mail, and how the electronic conference is getting my students to interact with each other outside of class. I do see some fine tuning needed with these, however. One trend I've noticed as I've thought about this chapter is that, over time, I've asked my students to take more control over their use of the electronic conference. I'll probably push them to take even more control in the future, especially as they become more sophisticated users of the system. Their spontaneous use is encouraging, but I can do more to get them to use electronic communication more and earlier, even for their own uses. For example, in my *Popular Delusions* course, students have a take-home final consisting of a single question that I give them the first day of class: "What do popular delusions tell us about human nature?" It strikes me that this is a question that they could be answering throughout the semester, publicly, with each of them working on their answer as a separate topic on the conference, and responding to each others' musings. Just a thought—I haven't worked out the details. It's just that this technology does open up other ways of doing business.

There are, however, some significant changes in my class down the road as a result of electronic communication. I want to address two of these:

I will lecture even less in the future. Currently, I spend less than half of my time in class "lecturing," but when I do, it is primarily to fill in what is missing, inaccurate, or confusing in the text. I believe more and more that transmission of information is not a good use of classroom time. Class time is such a precious commodity, I want us to use it talking to each other, students in their groups, me listening and responding to what they are saying, etc. I don't want to waste time in class simply conveying information. Transmitting information on the web is not only a better use of time, it may be better pedagogically, too. The web may be superior to class presentations, which are almost completely oral, since the information on the web can be any combination of textual, visual and aural, and the web allows me to present the information in hypertext as courselinks.

I probably won't have a text in the future. I've never been completely satisfied with any text I used in my classes. So if I'm not happy with my text, why didn't I just write my own? Like many professors, I have thought about it—for 25 years! But it has always seemed like such a massive undertaking and I'm never satisfied with what I have to say (this chapter will be much better six months from now!). A textbook is such a static thing; you have to get all of that stuff together, and once it's printed, you can't change it. The major advantage that the web provides for someone like me is that my site is a work in progress. I can put up what I have, add to it when I can, and modify it when I'm no longer satisfied with something I've said. Plus, the book-of-the-web is an endless set of links to other things that I don't have expertise in. In short, the web as a publishing vehicle meets my style. I can start where I am now, and tomorrow's homepage is better than today's. My web site, as a compendium of the things I want my class to know, as well as links to other sites that I can create, will (hopefully) become my text in the future.

For me, the answer, clearly, is "Yes." The flexibility electronic communications give me to interact with my students when I want, the opportunity to structure my students' interaction with the course material and each other better than I could before, the reflective interaction my students have with the material, and the opportunity to assess their learning better are all significant advantages to me. But these advantages come at some cost. I've had to put in the effort to learn how to use the technology effectively, devise an effective plan for its use, and be vigilant that I continue to use it to my students' advantage. I recommend its use to other faculty, but with the following caution.

Technology amplifies bad pedagogy. There's the old saying—to err is human, but it takes a computer to really screw up. Both the instructor and students need to have a solid understanding of how to use the technology, or electronic communication will be largely ineffective. Learning the technology well enough to use it effectively takes time, but simply learning the technology well is not enough. If its use is not grounded in a thorough understanding of cognitive development and a pedagogy that is driven by this understanding, the use of the technology will be frustrating to both instructor and students, will impede rather than enhance student learning, and will distance us from each other.

References

Angelo, T. A. and Cross, K. P. *Classroom Assessment Techniques: A Handbook for College Teachers.* (2nd ed.) Jossey-Bass, 1993.

Johnson, D. W., Johnson, R. T., and Smith, K. A. *Active Learning: Cooperation in the College Classroom.* Interaction Book Company, 1991.

Ellis, H. C. *Fundamentals of Human Learning, Memory, and Cognition* (2nd ed.). Wm. C. Brown, 1978.

I've included a few resources that might help you get started (or further advanced) in effectively using technology in the classroom. I've listed them in order of what I consider to be of most value.

- *The American Association for Higher Education.* AAHE (Suite 360, One Dupont Circle, NW, Washington, DC 20036) is probably the best single source for resources related to the effective use of technology in higher education. Among these resources are the AAHESGIT listserve, moderated by Steve Gilbert, Director of Technology Projects for AAHE, addresses issues of technology in higher education. Postings come at irregular intervals, but because it is a moderated listserve, they are of higher quality than is true of most listserves. It is probably the place to begin. It's free, and the discussions are insightful and current. Pre-prints of future *Change* articles on technology appear here first. To subscribe to the AAHESGIT listserve, send an E-mail message (with subject line left blank) to:

  <LISTPROC@LIST.CREN.NET>

  Then, send the following one line message

  <SUBSCRIBE AAHESGIT yourfirstname yourlastname>

- *Change, The Magazine of Higher Learning* (1319 18th St., NS, Washington, DC, 20036 1802). In addition to frequent articles on the role of technology in higher education, the March/April, 1996, issue is devoted exclusively to technological issues.

- *Teaching and Learning Technology Roundtable.* This program is designed to help colleges design a coherent strategy for using technology on their campuses. It's probably not of great value to the individual faculty member, but if you are part of a campus effort on technology, it's a valuable resource. For further information, contact Ellen Shortill at AAHE via E-mail at this address:

  <shortill@clark.net>

- *T. H. E. Journal* (Technological Horizons in Education, 150 El Camino Real, Suite 112, Tustin, CA 92680-3670) *T.H.E. Journal*, published monthly, focuses on issues of technology at all educational levels, but most of the articles are of relevance to higher education. Subscription is free to those who have some role in technology on their campus.

- *Syllabus* (Syllabus Press, 1307 S. Mary Ave., Suite 211, Sunnyvale, CA 94787-3018). *Syllabus*, published 10 times a year, features articles about the uses of technology in higher education. Subscription is $24/yr, but free to those who have some role in technology on their campus. Syllabus also sponsors an annual conference on technology/higher education each year.

- *Educom Review* (1112 16th St. NW, Suite 600, Washington, DC 20036). *Educom Review*, published bi-monthly, also addresses issues about the uses of technology in higher education. Subscription is $18/yr, but free to those who have some role in technology on their campus. Educom sponsors a large annual conference on technology/higher education each year.

Cooperative Learning for New College Teachers

Karl A. Smith & Alisha A. Waller

When Karl Smith started teaching engineering courses, he knew only one model to follow: stand up and lecture. He was the one with the knowledge, the students needed it; his job was to deliver the information to them. It didn't work very well. His students weren't getting it. He was very frustrated; jobs in industry began to look very attractive. But in seeking different ways to teach he took a course from one of David Johnson's students, where he was encouraged to work cooperatively with other students to learn the material. Cooperative learning brought back memories of work as an engineer, where teams of engineers (and others) divide complex problems into manageable parts for solutions, with everyone taking responsibility both for his/her own part and for the quality of the whole. Intrigued, he participated in Johnson Brother's cooperative learning workshops. Since then he has been practicing cooperative learning techniques in all of his courses. He currently serves as Associate Professor of Civil Engineering at the University of Minnesota and gives numerous workshops around the country on problem-based, cooperative learning, and creating supportive learning environments for all students. His email address is <ksmith@maroon.tc.umn.edu>.

Alisha Waller hated working in groups as an undergraduate. Instructors would assign group projects to be completed out of class. A perfectionist, Alisha would assume that no one else could do as well as she, so she would do all the work and share the credit. But she gradually realized that she works well with others—explaining herself to them, hearing their approaches, and working together to understand. Working with former colleague Karl Smith showed her that the group assignments she hated were fatally flawed: not enough structure, no training for participants, not enough accountability, not very cooperative. Since that realization, she has incorporated cooperative learning into her classes and has experienced tremendous increases in students' learning and in their positive feelings about working together. And she's having more fun. Today, Alisha is an Instructor in Mathematics and Computer Science at Macalester College, St. Paul, MN. Her email address is <WALLER@macalester.edu>.

Why bother actively engaging students?

Because it's easier for the teacher? Because it's the fad? Engaging students with the academic material and with other students is important for learning. Actively engaged students learn more! Cooperative learning is one very effective way of getting students involved.

We have been using cooperative learning for many years and offer our guidance on getting started. We also clarify the differences between cooperative learning and simply putting students in groups; provide background and rationale for cooperative learning; summarize specific cooperative learning strategies to start with; discuss the types of cooperative learning groups; suggest procedures for developing skills and confidence for implementing cooperative learning; and open up the bigger picture of active and cooperative learning in the college classroom.

Support for Cooperative Learning

How do you learn best? What conditions, environment, circumstances, etc. make is easiest for you to learn? Please reflect for a moment. We have asked this question of thousands of faculty around the world. Usually we ask it in an informal cooperative learning format: *Formulate* an answer individually, *Share* your answer with a partner, *Listen* carefully to your partner's answer, and *Create* a new answer through discussion (or, alternatively, *Learn* your partner's response well enough to present it if you're called on). Typical responses include: "I learn best when it's something I'm interested in," "When I'm motivated to learn either through interest or need," "Through reading on my own and making notes," "Through expressing it in my own words, such as by writing a summary," "Through explaining it to someone else," "Through preparing to teach," "By doing it." Our surveys indicate that faculty prefer to learn in a variety of ways, most of them active. Very few faculty have said, "I learn best by listening to a lecture."

Who learns the most in the typical college classroom? Who is organizing, summarizing, and presenting? Who is elaborating, and providing rationale and justification? In other words, Who is actively involved? Who is having the most fun in the typical college classroom? Perhaps no one. Most likely, however, the professor is learning the most and having the most fun!

During the past 90 years nearly 600 experimental and over 100 corelational studies have been conducted comparing the effectiveness of cooperative, competitive, and individualistic efforts. These studies have been conducted by a wide variety of researchers in different decades with different age subjects, in different subject areas, and in different settings. More is known about the efficacy of cooperative learning than about lecturing, departmentalization, the use of instructional technology, or almost any other aspect of education. The research reveals that the more students work in cooperative learning groups the more they will learn, the better they will understand what they are learning, the easier it will be to remember what they learn, and the better they will feel about themselves, the class, and their classmates.

The multiple outcomes studied can be classified into three major categories: achievement/productivity, positive relationships, and psychological health. Cooperation among students typically results in (a) higher achievement and greater productivity, (b) more caring, supportive, and committed relationships, and (c) greater psychological health, social competence, and self-esteem. A summary of the studies conducted at the higher education level may be found in Johnson, Johnson, & Smith (1991). A comprehensive review of all studies and meta-analyses of their results is available in Johnson & Johnson (1989).

McKeachie (1988) concludes that at least three elements of teaching make a difference in students' gains in thinking skills: (1) student discussion, (2) explicit emphasis on problem-solving procedures and methods using varied examples, and (3) verbalization of methods and strategies to encourage development of metacognition. He states, "Student participation, teacher encouragement, and student-to-student interaction positively relate to improved critical thinking. These three activities confirm other research and theory stressing the importance of active practice, motivation, and feedback in thinking skills as well as other skills. This confirms that discussions, especially in small classes, are superior to lectures in improving thinking and problem solving." (p. 81)

Cooperative learning researchers and practitioners have shown that positive peer relationships are essential to success in college. Isolation and alienation are the best predictors of failure. Two major reasons for dropping out of college are failure to establish a social network of friends and classmates and failure to become academically involved in classes (Tinto, 1994).

Alexander Astin (1993) recently addressed the question, "What environmental factors make the biggest difference in college students' academic development, personal development, and satisfaction"? A longitudinal study was conducted of 27,064 students at 309 baccalaureate-granting institutions. This work represents the first attempt to study the impact of different approaches to general education on student development using a large national sample of undergraduate institutions and a wide range of student outcomes. He was primarily interested in the *outcomes* and in particular how they are affected by *environments*. One hundred ninety two environmental factors were investigated to determine which factors influenced students' academic achievement, personal development, and satisfaction with college.

Astin found that the particular manner in which the general education curriculum is structured makes very little difference for most of the 82 outcomes. Instead, Astin found that two environmental factors were, by far, most predictive of positive change. These two factors—interaction among students and interaction between faculty and students—carried by far the largest weights and affected more general education outcomes than any other environmental variables studied, including the curriculum content factors. Student-student interaction produced significant effects on 18 of the top 22 outcomes and student-faculty interaction produced significant effects on 17 outcomes.

In short, Astin says it appears that how students *approach* their general education and how the faculty actually *deliver* the curriculum is far more important that the formal curricular structure. More specifically, the findings strongly support a growing body of research suggesting that one of the crucial factors in the educational development of the undergraduate is the degree to which the student is actively engaged or involved in the undergraduate experience. His research findings suggest that curricular planning efforts will reap much greater payoffs in terms of students' outcomes if we focus less on formal structure and content and put much more emphasis on pedagogy and other features of the *delivery system,* as well as on the broader interpersonal and institutional context in which learning takes place.

Intensive interviews with a randomly selected sample of Harvard undergraduates resulted in conclusions similar to Astin's. Richard Light (1992) wrote in the preface to the *Harvard Assessment Seminars: Second Report* (p. 6):

> The biggest challenge for me is to ask what the details all add up to. Do the many suggestions that interviewers get from their long conversations with undergraduates drive toward any broad, overarching principle? Is there any common theme that faculty members can use to help students, and indeed that students can use to help themselves? *The answer is a strong yes.* All the specific findings point to, and illustrate, one main idea. It is that students who get the most out of college, who grow the most academically, and who are the happiest, *organize their time to include interpersonal activities with faculty members, or with fellow students, built around substantive, academic work.*

Experience is another important source of support for cooperative learning. For example, Harry Pence (of SUNY Oneonta) recently posted the following note to a teaching forum on the Internet:

I've used cooperative learning for five years in a variety of classes ranging in size from a dozen to a hundred. The vast majority of students have been extremely enthusiastic, including the best students I've had in each of those classes... Judging from my experience, a major barrier to using cooperative methods is the instructor. I've spent most of my career in higher education with the assumption that I was getting paid to organize and present information to students. Unfortunately, I realized rather late in the game that the real goal is not for me to learn how to organize information better, but for my students to learn that skill. As long as I do most of the work, and they only have to memorize what I have already processed, they are missing the most important skill to be gained from higher education, learning how to learn. I use a mixture of lecture, multimedia, and cooperative learning, so I still do some of the organization, but I have succeeded in transferring much more responsibility to the students.

After teaching a senior level engineering class using cooperative learning, Alisha asked her class to write for two to three minutes how they felt about cooperative learning. A few of their thoughts:

Learning to interact and work with other people in class was a good experience for working in the "real" world.

Cooperative learning is a valuable tool in pursuing higher levels of learning and performance. It is a must when maximum efficiency is truly desired.

It's too bad cooperative learning is not used earlier in educational systems. It really gives the students a chance to develop their strengths and fix their weaknesses. Students know what they do and don't know, and this gives them a chance to really take a controlling aspect of their education.

"I've got so much to do! How can I write proposals to get my research program going, keep up with professional meetings, prepare my lectures, meet with students, and find time to learn how to do cooperative learning?" Concerns such as this are expressed by almost all beginning college faculty. You are not alone in feeling stressed. In the rest of this chapter, we will share some strategies for learning about and implementing cooperative learning in a series of small steps. The first step is to explore the meaning of cooperative learning a little further.

Cooperation is working together to accomplish shared goals. Within cooperative activities individuals seek outcomes that are beneficial to themselves and beneficial to all other group members. *Cooperative learning* is the instructional use of small groups so that students work together to maximize their own and each others' learning. Cooperative learning in college classes involves small groups of students working together to achieve the common goal of maximizing their own and each others' learning. Cooperative learning shares many features with collaborative learning (Bruffee, 1993) and team learning (Michaelson, Jones, Firestone, & Watson, 1993). Cooperative learning involves structured interaction among students within the college environment, especially within the classroom.

Many college faculty members have not had an opportunity to work as a member of a team either in the classroom or on the job. A team is *a small number of people with complementary skills who are committed to a common purpose, performance goals, and approach for which they hold themselves mutually accountable* (Katzenbach and Smith, 1993).

When they first hear about cooperative learning, many faculty tell us they already to that—they have students complete term projects together. Further exploration, however, reveals that although they do have students working in groups, the work is not cooperative learning. The table below summarizes some of the major differences between traditional learning groups and cooperative learning groups.

Comparison of Traditional and Cooperative Learning Groups

Traditional Learning Groups	Cooperative Learning Groups
Low interdependence. Members take responsibility only for themselves. Focus is on individual performance only.	High positive interdependence. Members are responsible for their own and each other's learning. Focus is on joint performance.
Individual accountability only.	Both group and individual accountability. Members hold themselves and others accountable for high quality work.
Little or no attention to group formation (students often select members). Groups typically large (5-10 members).	Deliberately formed groups (random, distribute knowledge/experience, interest). Groups are small (2-4 members).
Assignments are discussed with little commitment to each other's learning.	Members promote each other's success, doing real work together, helping and supporting each other's efforts to learn.
Teamwork skills are ignored. Leader is appointed to direct members' participation.	Teamwork skills are emphasized. Members are taught and expected to use collaborative skills. Leadership shared by all members.
No group processing of the quality of its work. Individual accomplishments are rewarded.	Group processes quality of work and how effectively members are working together. Continuous improvement is emphasized.

No doubt you're saying "Cooperative learning involves a lot of structure!" Working effectively as a member of a team is quite complex and there is a lot that faculty can do to help students succeed. Providing a supportive structure is one of the most important things we can do. Many students have had bad experiences with groups. For example, they've been told to go off and work on a joint project without any class time to help them get organized or even to meet the other members of their group. As students' skills and competencies grow with repeated group experiences, faculty can turn more of the responsibility over to the student. Initially, however, many students appreciate the guidance provided by a carefully structured cooperative learning group.

Key Concepts in Structuring Cooperative Learning Groups

Students working together to get a job done in a classroom where students are concerned about each other's learning in addition to their own is the heart of cooperative learning. The conceptual approach to cooperative learning is characterized by five basic elements:

Positive Interdependence exists when students believe that they are linked with others in a way that one cannot succeed unless the other members of the group succeed (and vice versa). Students are working together to get the job done. In other words, students must perceive that they sink or swim together. In a problem-solving session, positive interdependence is structured by group members (1) agreeing on the answer and solution strategies for each problem (goal interdependence) and (2) fulfilling assigned role responsibilities (role interdependence). Other ways of structuring positive interdependence include having common rewards, being dependent on each other's resources, or dividing labor.

Face-to-Face Promotive Interaction exists among students when students orally explain to each other how to solve problems, discuss with each other the nature of the concepts and strategies being learned, teach their knowledge to classmates, and explain to each other the connections between present and past learning. This face-to-face interaction is promotive in the sense that students help, assist, encourage, and support each other's efforts to learn.

Accountability/Personal Responsibility requires the teacher to ensure that the performance of each individual student is assessed and the results are given back to the group and the individual. The group needs to knows who needs more assistance in completing the assignment and group members need to know they cannot hitch-hike on the work of others. Common ways to structure individual accountability include giving an individual exam to each student, randomly calling on individual students to present their group's answer, and giving an individual oral exam while monitoring group work.

Teamwork Skills are necessary for effective group functioning. Students must have and use the needed leadership, decision-making, trust-building, communication, and conflict-management skills. These skills have to be taught just as purposefully and precisely as academic skills. Many students have never worked cooperatively in learning situations and, therefore, lack the needed teamwork skills for doing so.

Group Processing involves a group discussion of how well they are achieving their goals and how well they are maintaining effective working relationships among members. At the end of their working period the groups process their functioning by answering two questions: (1) What is something each member did that was helpful for the group and (2) What is something each member could do to make the group even better tomorrow? Such processing enables learning groups to focus on group maintenance, facilitates the learning of collaborative skills, ensures that members receive feedback on their participation, and reminds students to practice collaborative skills consistently.

Many educators who believe that they are using cooperative learning are, in fact, missing its essence. There is a crucial difference between simply putting students in groups to learn and in structuring cooperation among students. Cooperation is *not* having students sit side-by-side at the same table to talk with each other as they do their individual assignments. Cooperation is *not* assigning a report to a group of students where one student does all the work and the others put their names on the product as well. Cooperation is *not* having students do a task individually with instructions that the ones who finish first are to help the slower students. Cooperation is much more than being physically near other students, discussing material with other students, helping other students, or sharing material among students, although each of these is important in cooperative learning.

To be part of a genuine cooperative learning group, members must be committed to a common goal, must promote each other's learning and success face-to-face, hold each other personally and individually accountable to do a fair share of the work, use the interpersonal and small group skills needed for cooperative efforts to be successful, and process as a group how effectively members are working together. These five essential components must be present for small group learning to be truly cooperative.

Types of Cooperative Learning Groups

There are many ways to implement cooperative learning in college classrooms: informal cooperative learning groups that involve very little structure (typically small, short term, ad hoc groups); informal cooperative learning groups that contain more structure (such as the 'bookends on a lecture' format); formal cooperative learning groups that are highly structured and task oriented; and cooperative base groups that are long term formal groups created for student support and encouragement. Each has a place in providing opportunities for students to be intellectually active and personally interactive both in and outside the classroom.

Informal cooperative learning groups are commonly used in predominately lecture classes. Formal cooperative learning can be used in content intensive classes where the mastery of conceptual or procedural material is essential; however, many faculty find it easier to start in recitation or laboratory sections or design project courses. Base groups are long-term cooperative learning groups whose principal responsibility is to provide support and encouragement for all their members; that is, to ensure that each member gets the help he or she needs to be successful in the course and in college.

Informal groups are temporary, *ad hoc* groups that last for only one discussion or one class period. Their purposes are to focus student attention on the material to be learned, set a mood conducive to learning, help organize in advance the material to be covered in a class session, ensure that students cognitively process the material being taught, and provide closure to an instructional session. For example, you may begin class by asking the students to take two minutes to review their notes from the last class and then pair up with someone sitting nearby. Together the students should come up with a question about the material. Often, this is much more effective in focusing students' attention and identifying confusion than the typical "Does anyone have any questions from last time? No? Then let's begin today's class. . ."

Informal cooperative learning groups may be used at any time, but are especially useful during a lecture or direct teaching before the students' eyes begin to glaze over. Some estimates of the length of time that people can attend to a lecture is around 12 to 15 minutes; students then need to process what they are learning or their minds drift away. During lecture, the instructional challenge for the teacher is to ensure that students do the intellectual work of organizing material, explaining it, summarizing it, and integrating it into existing conceptual networks. For example, Eric Mazur, a physics professor at Harvard, uses multiple choice, conceptual questions after each lecture segment which require the students to apply the new concepts or theories to real world hypothetical situation (*Thinking Together,* 1991). Breaking up lectures with short cooperative processing times will give you slightly less lecture time, but will enhance what is learned and build relationships among the students in your class. It will help counter what is proclaimed as the main problem of lectures: "The information passes from the notes of the professor to the notes of the student without passing through the mind of either one."

Here is a specific example of how one would incorporate an informal cooperative learning activity. When Alisha teaches *Introduction to Operations Research* in engineering (a mathematical modeling course), one of the biggest challenges is to help students understand the assumptions underlying the models. For each model category, she gives a mini lecture on the assumptions and data requirements inherent in the model. The students pair up and develop a list of "real world" applications that fit the model requirements and a list of ones that *do not* fit the model. She then randomly calls on students (by drawing from a stack of index cards with their names) to share the lists they developed. This five minute activity helps the students develop a conceptual framework that is based on a comparative and network approach of a series of independent units of information.

When planning an informal cooperative learning exercise, answering the following questions will help you clarify your goals and structure.

- Who is interacting? Will students pair up with someone beside them? Or perhaps someone sitting behind/in front of them? Should they pair up with someone from a different background? Someone they don't yet know?

- When does the activity occur during the class? Beginning? Middle? End? How much time are you willing to spend on it?

- Will they write down their answers/ideas/questions? If they are asked to turn them in, should they put their names on them?

- Will you give individuals a minute or so to reflect on the answer before discussing it or will they just jump right into a discussion?

- Will you grade their responses or not?

- How will they share the paired work with the whole class?

- How will you share the feedback and insight you gain from their responses?

- If they are responding to a question you pose, how are you going to ensure that they leave with confidence in their understanding? (Often, if the various student answers are discussed without the instructor explicitly indicating which ones are right, students become frustrated. Even with a question that has no absolute right answer, students want to know the professor's stand on the question.)

- What preparation do you need to use the activity? What preparation do the students need in order to participate fully?

There are a variety of informal cooperative learning techniques professors can employ. We use these four regularly.

Book ends on a lecture. The book ends procedure begins with a question or task that students work on individually and then in pairs. The purpose of this initial task is to focus students' attention and to try to spark their curiosity and engage them in dialogue. A brief lecture that addresses the question follows. After lecturing 10 to 12 minutes, give each student a chance to process the lecture intellectually with another student. You might ask each pair to construct relationships, make predictions, or create explanations. Continue the lecture, if appropriate, or engage the class in a discussion. Close the class period with a focused concluding discussion wherein the students are asked to create a summary of the main points. This procedure will help you plan a lecture that keeps students actively engaged intellectually.

Focused Organizing Discussion. Plan your lecture around a series of questions that the lecture answers. Prepare the questions on an overhead transparency or write them on the board so that students can see them. Have students discuss the questions in pairs. The discussion task is aimed at promoting *advance organizing* of what the students know about the topic to be presented and *set expectations* about what the lecture will cover. For example, before the opening lecture on Shakespeare's Hamlet, ask students the following questions to be discussed in pairs. What does it do to your understanding of the play to read it through Ophelia's eyes? Do you agree with Hamlet's view of his mother's remarriage? Why or why not? How old does Hamlet seem to you as you read the play?

Turn-To-Your-Partner Discussions. Divide the lecture into 10 to 15 minute segments. This is about the length of time an adult can typically concentrate on a lecture. Plan a short discussion task to be given to pairs of students after each segment. The task needs to be short enough that students can complete it within three or four minutes. Its purpose is to ensure that students are actively thinking about the material being presented. The discussion task may be to:

- Summarize the answer to the question being discussed.

Example: In kinesiology, what is the role of a heart rate monitor in determining training schedules?

- Solve a problem. Example: Integrate an equation by parts.

- Give a reaction to the theory, concepts, or information being presented. Example: In a lecture on Toni Morrison's novel *Beloved*, ask students to share how each feels when reading the climactic scene in which the central female character tries to kill her children to prevent their being retaken into slavery.

- Elaborate on the material being presented or relate material to past learning so that it is integrated into existing conceptual frameworks. Example: In an early lecture on feminism in the 20th century ask these questions: How does the 20th century or second wave of feminist activity differ from the 19th century suffrage efforts? What are the chief issues around which feminist activism has organized itself? Who are the four leaders in the 20th century women's movement? To what extent has this movement been dominated by white, middle-class, heterosexual women and their issues? How can the 21st century effort be more inclusive?

- Predict or explain. Example: Conceptual questions in physics, such as "think about a ball that is spinning at the end of a string. If you release the string, what path does the ball follow? (a) curves in the direction it was spinning, (b) straight line, (c) curves in the opposite direction to the one it was spinning." (See Hestenes, *et. al.,* 1992, for more details).

- Attempt to resolve the conceptual conflict the presentation has aroused. Example: In the Pacific Northwest, should the government preserve the forests for endangered species or should they permit timber harvesting?

- Hypothesize answers to the question being posed. Example: In an economics class discussing price elasticity, ask students to predict the changes in demand for Coca-Cola products in a region where Pepsi products are introduced.

Each discussion task should have four components: *formulate* an answer to the question being asked, *share* your answer with your partner, *listen* carefully to his or her answer, and *create* a new answer that is superior to each member's initial formulation through the process of association, building on each other's thoughts, and synthesizing. Students will need to gain some experience with this procedure to become skilled in doing it within a short period of time. *It is important to call on students to share their answers after each discussion task.* Such individual accountability ensures that the pairs take the tasks seriously and check each other to ensure that both are prepared to answer.

Focused Concluding Discussion. Prepare an ending discussion task to summarize what students have learned from the lecture. The discussion should result in students integrating what they have just learned into existing conceptual frameworks. The task may also point students toward what the homework will cover or what will be presented in the next class session. This provides closure to the lecture.

Formal Cooperative Learning Groups ⎯⎯⎯⎯⎯⎯⎯⎯

Once you have some experience with informal cooperative learning groups, you may want to extend the use of cooperative learning in your classes. Formal cooperative learning groups allow your students to gain the benefits of cooperative learning throughout the course. Formal groups can be very successful in helping students master complex course material, solve problems and reach consensual decisions, and support each other through difficult learning experiences. (For more detail about establishing formal cooperative learning groups, see Johnson, Johnson, & Smith, 1991.)

Before choosing and implementing a formal cooperative learning strategy, there are several conditions that should be evaluated to determine whether or not it is the best approach for the situation. First, is there sufficient time available for students to work in groups both inside and outside the classroom? Second, are the students experienced and skillful enough to manage their work in formal cooperative learning groups? Third, is the task complex enough to warrant a formal group? Fourth, do other instructional goals (such as the development of students' critical thinking skills, higher level reasoning skills, or teamwork skills) warrant the use of formal cooperative learning groups? If several of these necessary conditions are met, then your class is probably ready for formal cooperative learning groups.

Formal cooperative learning groups may last from one class period to several weeks to complete specific tasks and assignments—e.g. learning new conceptual material, solving a specific problem or coming to a decision, writing a report, conducting a survey or experiment, preparing for an exam, or answering questions or homework problems. Any course requirement may be reformulated to be cooperative. In formal cooperative groups the professor should:

Specify the objectives for the lesson. In every lesson, there should be an academic objective specifying the concepts, strategies, procedures, etc. to be learned and a teamwork objective specifying the interpersonal or small group skill to be used and mastered during the lesson.

Make instructional decisions before the lesson commences. The professor should decide on the size of groups, the method of assigning students to groups, how long the groups stay together, the roles the students will be assigned, the materials needed to conduct the lesson, and the way the room will be arranged.

Although each of these decisions is complex, some general guidelines may be useful. First, keep groups small, especially at the beginning. Groups of two or three maximize members' involvement and help create a sense of interdependence and accountability. Second, choose the groups yourself. Random assignment works very well for many faculty. Stratify students along some relevant criterion, such as computing skills or experience, and then randomly assign student from each category to all the groups. Permitting students to choose their own groups often leads to students working with friends who have a lot of other things to talk about beside the work and to some students being left out. Third, keep the groups together until the task is completed, perhaps even longer. But not forever; changing groups periodically gives students a chance to meet more of their peers and helps them gain skills for quickly getting a group up and running. Fourth, choose roles that are consistent with the requirements of the task and are important for the smooth functioning of the group. Many faculty only assign a recorder for the first group assignment.

Explain the task and the learning strategies the group will employ. The professor should clearly define the assignment, teach the required concepts and strategies, specify the methods for positive interdependence and individual accountability, give the criteria for success, and explain the teamwork skill groups should employ.

To make a group project truly cooperative, positive interdependence and individual accountability must be structured in a variety of congruent ways. Positive interdependence is typically structured by asking the group to prepare a single product (goal interdependence), asking the students to make sure each person in the group can explain the groups' answer (learning goal interdependence), giving the group one copy of the assignment (resource interdependence), and assigning a special role to each member (role interdependence).

Individual and group accountability is typically structured by assigning specific functions to each role, randomly calling on individuals to explain their group's answer, monitoring the groups and occasionally asking a student to explain his or her group's answer or method (individual oral exam), asking each member to sign the group's report, and of course, by giving individual quizzes, exams and writing assignments. Courses with extensive formal cooperative learning usually use a combination of group assignments and individual assignments to determine each student's final grade. Typical distributions between individual and group are 95-5 to 70-30; that is, between 5 and 30 percent of an individual student's grade is based on group work. Some faculty use the groupwork as a base line or threshold that students must complete satisfactorily, but base grades on individual work only. A few faculty in project-based courses base 100 percent of each students grade on group work.

Monitor students' learning and intervene within the groups to provide task assistance or to increase students' teamwork skills. The professor systemically observes and collects data on each group as it works. When it is needed, the professor intervenes to assist students in working together and completing the task effectively. While students are working faculty can learn a great deal about what the students know about the material and can often identify problems students are having, either with the academic material or in working in the group. Typical things to look for are on-task interactions (what happens when someone says something?), involvement of group members, the strategy the group is using, how the groups deal with task or group functioning difficulties, etc.

Evaluate students' learning and help students process how well their group functioned. Students' learning is carefully assessed and their performances are evaluated. A criteria-referenced evaluation procedure must be used; that is, grading must not be curved. Individual student's learning is typically evaluated by written exams, quizzes, and papers. The professor provides time and a structure for members of each learning group to process how effectively they have been working together. A common method for processing is to ask the students to list things they did well while working in the group and things that they could improve. A quick process strategy is to ask each individual to list something they did to help the group accomplish its task and one that they could do even better next time.

Cooperative Jigsaw Strategy

The cooperative jigsaw strategy was described by Elliot Aronson in 1978. It is a strategy that highly effective student study groups in content-dense disciplines such as medicine and law have used on an ad hoc basis for many years. The professor's role in a jigsaw involves carefully choosing the material to be jigsawed; structuring the groups and providing a clear, cooperative context for the groups; monitoring the groups' work to ensure high quality learning and group functioning; and helping students summarize, synthesize, and integrate the conceptual material. The conceptual material you choose for the students to learn via a jigsaw strategy should be at a difficulty level that makes the materials accessible to the students, it should be easily divisible into sub-parts, and it should have some common overriding theme that can be used to integrate the sub-parts. Students need substantial guidance in working in a jigsaw format.

Suppose you are about to give a reading assignment. Divide the assignment into parts. Ask each member of each group to read a single part. Two readers of each part should meet to discuss the part they read to agree on its major points and plan how to teach them to other members of the group. Next, two readers of different parts should meet to practice teaching the major points of their respective readings to each other. Then the original groups meet and members teach each other the major points of all parts of the reading. Finally, the professor assesses the students' mastery of the material, through one or more means: reports by randomly selected groups, individual reports, quizes, etc. Once again, preset criteria of mastery should be used rather than a curve.

Cooperative Base Groups

Base groups are long-term, heterogeneous cooperative learning groups with stable membership whose primary responsibility is to provide each student the support, encouragement, and assistance he or she needs to make academic progress. Base groups personalize the work required and the course learning experiences. These base groups stay the same during the entire course and longer if possible. The members of base groups should exchange phone numbers and information about schedules as they may wish to meet outside of class. When students have successes, insights, questions or concerns they wish to discuss; they can contact other members of their base group. Base groups typically manage the daily paperwork of the course through the use of group folders.

Base groups can significantly affect student retention. Academic factors in retention are (1) students see the work as worthwhile, and (2) students experience success. Base groups contribute to both of these factors. Personal, peer support is essential in student retention as found in the Berkeley Mathematics Workshop Program (Fullilove & Treisman, 1990; Tresiman, 1992).

Getting Started with Cooperative Learning

Often faculty find it difficult to stop talking and give students an opportunity to talk with one another. Since many faculty have not experienced a cooperative classroom, you may lack an experiential model of how a cooperative classroom operates. Therefore, the most important advice we can give is to *start small and be brief.* Choose one simple informal cooperative learning structure that only takes a few minutes, use it and modify it until you and your students are confident and experienced. Remember that just as you are not accustomed to teaching this way, many students are not accustomed to learning this way. It may take a few weeks for the process to become smooth. Some additional keys to successful implementation of cooperative learning include:

- Develop a plan for a cooperative learning activity, try it out, collect feedback, then modify and try it again.

- Learn strategies for formulating questions, encouraging conversation among students, making smooth transitions between small group and whole class discussions, and working with students' contributions to the whole class discussions.

- Start from the first day of class. For example, have students pair up and write responses to questions about the course, such as their expectations or reasons for taking the course. Always try the question or task yourself before you assign it to your students. Whenever possible, try it on a colleague as well.

- Be explicit with students about why you are doing this and what you know about the learning process. Or ask students what helps them learn. Spending a few minutes at the beginning of the term discussing ways of learning in your discipline can be very beneficial to students.

- Use obvious means of timing, e.g. hourglass, class clock, etc., if students are reluctant to stop talking. Negotiate a transition signal, such as raising your hand or ringing a bell (preferably one with a pleasant tone).

- Learn students' names (and help them learn each other's names) to personalize classroom environment and to increase accountability. Walk among students as they work to increase accountability.

- Randomly call on pairs to share. To keep choices random, have each student write their names on cards, then shuffle the deck and pull out a card. Occasionally have the students turn in their questions or responses. Compile their questions/responses and work with them during the next class period.

- We recommend that you take a time-tested engineering approach to change as you implement cooperative learning: make many small changes, rather than one huge change. Start early in the term with short-term informal cooperative learning strategies; modify, drop, and add strategies as you find out what works for you in your setting; progressively refine what is working. Find a colleagues or two to plan (and perhaps teach) with while you're implementing cooperative learning. Two faculty working together progress more than twice as fast as one person working alone. Also, it's often a lot of fun working together.

When using cooperative learning, it is imperative that a criteria-referenced evaluation is used. Competitive grading, such as grading on a curve where only a fixed percentage of the student will earn an "A", is not compatible with cooperative learning. A student will not be able to wholeheartedly contribute to a classmate's learning if, on the exams, the classmate's improved performance lowers his or her own grade. This does not mean that students are graded on effort alone, because typically performance standards are set very high in cooperative learning classes. Instead, it simply means that the grading system is such that if I help you to learn more, my grade will not be reduced as a result of your improved performance.

Conclusion

We know that it's very easy to slip into the traditional mode of lecture, but in our classes we try to follow Wilbert McKeachie's advice on lecturing: "I lecture only when I'm convinced it will do more good than harm." While conducting a workshop on cooperative learning for a combined group of faculty and students at the Norwegian Institute of Technology, one of us (Karl) was convinced that a short lecture on the latest research on learning would be very useful and effective. He asked a focus question at the start, lectured for about 12 minutes, and asked the participants to prepare a summary of the main points and to formulate at least one question. When he finished the short lecture, and asked for a summary, people didn't know what to write. One student jokingly asked, "Karl, what did you say between 'Here's the research' and 'your task is to create a summary?'"

It got a big laugh, but after the lecture several of the faculty came to him and said, "I didn't know what you were talking about. The concepts were somewhat new to me, you were enthusiastic and spoke slowly and clearly, but I really didn't understand what you were talking about." Karl apologized to the group for wasting their time. It was painful for him since he thought he had given an excellent lecture. A couple of faculty came to his defense. They said, "Well, you know, it was a pretty good lecture. It was just kind of new to us." But then a student in the back said, "I understood a little at the beginning, but a lot of lectures are like this for me."

And a student in the front said (with emphasis), "This is what it's like for me every day."

The look on the faces of those faculty! Karl wished he would have taken a photograph. For the first time in a long time, it appeared they understood what it's like to be a student trying to make sense out of these lectures, not understanding, and being frustrated with not understanding.

This is what it's like for many students in college.

Cooperative learning can help you break the pattern. In order to maximize their achievement, especially when studying conceptually complex and content-dense materials, students should not be allowed to be passive while they are learning. One way to get students more actively involved in this process is to structure cooperative interaction into classes so that students have to explain what they are learning to each other, learn each other's point of view, give and receive support from classmates, and help each other dig below the superficial level of understanding of the material they are learning. It is vital for students to have peer support and to be active learners, not only so that more students learn the material, but so that they get to know other students in class and build a sense of community that centers on the academic side of the school.

It is equally important that when seniors graduate they have developed skills in talking through material with peers, listening with real skill, knowing how to build trust in a working relationship, and providing leadership to group efforts. Without developing and practicing the social skills required to work cooperatively with others, how can faculty honestly claim that they have prepared students for a world where they will need to coordinate their efforts with others on the job, skillfully balance personal relationships, and be a contributing member of a community and society?

References

Aronson, E., Blaney, N., Stephan, C., Sikes, J., & Snapp, M. *The Jigsaw Classroom*. Sage, 1978.

Astin, A. *What matters in college: Four critical years revisited*. Jossey-Bass, 1993.

Bruffee, Kenneth A. *Collaborative learning: Higher education, interdependence, and the authority of knowledge*. Johns Hopkins, 1993.

Fullilove, R.E., & Treisman, P.U. "Mathematics Achievement among African-American Undergraduate Students at the University of California, Berkely: An Evaluation of the Mathematics Workshop Program," in *Journal of Negro Education*, 59 (3).

Hestenes, D., & Wells, M. . "A mechanics baseline test," in *The Physics Teacher, 30,* 1992.

Hestenes, D., Wells, M. & Swackhamer, G. "Force concept inventory," in *The Physics Teacher, 30,* 1992.

Johnson, David W., Johnson, Roger T. *Cooperation and competition: Theory and research*. Interaction Book Company, 1989.

Johnson, David W., Johnson, Roger T., & Smith, Karl A. *Active learning: Cooperation in the college classroom*. Interaction, 1991. Also see Johnson, David W., Johnson, Roger T., & Smith, Karl A. *Cooperative learning: Increasing college faculty instructional productivity*. ASHE-ERIC Report on Higher Education 91-4, 1991.

Katzenbach, Jon R. & Smith, Douglas K. *The wisdom of teams: Creating the high-performance organization*. Harvard Business School Press, 1993. Also see, Jon R. Katzenbach & Douglas K. Smith. "The discipline of teams," in *Harvard Business Review, 71*(2), 1993.

Light, Richard J. *The Harvard assessment seminars: Second report*. Harvard University, 1992.

McKeachie, Wilbert; Pintrich, Paul; Yi-Guang, Lin; and Smith, David. *Teaching and Learning in the College Classroom: A Review of the Research Literature.* The Regents of the University of Michigan, 1986.

McKeachie, Wilbert. "Teaching thinking," in *National Center for Research for the Improvement of Postsecondary Teaching and Learning Update,* 1(2), 1988.

Michaelson, Larry K., Jones, Cynthia Firestone, and Watson, Warren E. "Beyond groups and cooperation: Building high performance learning teams," in *To Improve the Academy, 12,* 1993.

Smith, K.A. "Cooperative learning: Making 'groupwork' work," In C. Bonwell & T. Sutherlund, Eds., *Active learning: Lessons from practice and emerging issues,* New Directions for Teaching and Learning, Jossey-Bass, 1996.

_____ "Cooperative Learning: Effective Teamwork for Engineering Classrooms," in *IEEE Education Society/ASEE Electrical Engineering Division Newsletter,* March, 1995.

_____ & Starfield, Anthony M. "Building Models to Solve Problems," in J.H. Clarke & A.W. Biddle (eds), *Teaching Critical Thinking: Reports from Across the Curriculum.* Prentice Hall, 1993.

Starfield, Anthony M., Smith, K.A., & Bleloch, Andrew L. *How to Model It: Problem Solving for the Computer Age.* Burgess International Group, 1994.

Thinking Together: Collaborative Learning in the Sciences. Video. Derek Bok Center for Teaching and Learning. Harvard University, 1991.

Tinto, V. *Leaving college: Rethinking the causes and cures of student attrition.* Second Edition. University of Chicago Press, 1994.

Treisman, U. "Studying Students Studying Calculus: A Look at the Lives of Minority Mathematics Students in College," in *College Mathematics Journal, 23* (5), 1992.

Woods, Donald, R. *Problem-Based Learning: How to Gain the Most from PBL.* Donald R. Woods, 1994.

Academic Controversy: Increase Intellectual Conflict and Increase the Quality of Learning

10

David W. Johnson & Roger T. Johnson

Brothers David and Roger Johnson grew up mainly on a farm in Indiana, parted during their college years, and then joined together at the University of Minnesota in the late 1960s. Roger was a central person in the inquiry science movement in the 1960s and was a great lover of discrepant events and disequilibrium. David focused his research in the 1960s on conflict resolution and the need to demonstrate the positive value of conflict. Together, with important colleagues such as Dean Tjosvold and Karl Smith, they developed a theory of academic controversy and conducted numerous validating studies. As two brothers who had argued and disagreed all their lives (and still do), they had no difficulty in recognizing that you can gain important insights from people you initially believe are misinformed and mistaken.

Together they founded and are co-directors of the Cooperative Learning Center at the University of Minnesota. David is Professor of Educational Psychology, Roger is Professor of Education. David's email address is <johns010@tc.umn.edu>; Roger's is <johns046@tc.umn.edu>.

The Importance Of Intellectual Conflict

Have you learned lessons only of
those who admired you, and were tender
with you, and stood aside for you?

Have you not learned great lessons
from those who braced themselves
against you, and disputed the passage
with you?

Walt Whitman, 1860

In 1859 Horace Greeley and Henry David Thoreau were having a discussion about John Brown's exploits at Harper's Ferry. *"No matter how well intended John Brown was,"* Horace said, *"his methods were completely unacceptable. The man broke the law! Terrorism for a good cause is still terrorism. It does not follow that because slavery is wrong, John Brown's actions were right. No matter how opposed to slavery one is, one cannot condone what John Brown did." "Now Horace,"* Henry replied, *"you are missing the whole point. It does not matter whether John Brown broke the law or not. It only matters what he symbolizes. And he symbolizes eternal justice, glory, and devotion to principle. We should pay homage to the ideas John Brown represents, not get caught in a mundane discussion of legalities."*

Thomas Jefferson would have applauded Greeley and Thoreau's discussion. Jefferson noted, *"Difference of opinion leads to inquiry, and inquiry to truth."* Jefferson had a deep faith in the value and productiveness of conflict. He is not alone. A number of 20th-Century theorists have pointed out the value of conflict. Piaget (1950) proposed that it is disequilibrium within a student's cognitive structure that motivates transitions from one stage of cognitive reasoning to another. He believed that conflict among peers is an essential cause of a shift from egocentrism to accommodation of other's perspectives. Piaget proposed that a person, with an existing way of organizing his or her cognitive structures, enters into cooperative interaction with peers. Conflicts inevitably result that create internal disequilibrium and the inability to assimilate current experiences into existing cognitive structures. The person then searches for a new equilibrium by decentering and accommodating the perspectives of others. This creates the need to organize the person's cognitive structures in a new way. Kohlberg (1969) adopted Piaget's formulation as an explanation for the development of moral reasoning.

Conflict theorists noted that conflict had many positive benefits (Coser, 1956; Johnson & Johnson, 1995a; Simmel, 1955). Berlyne

(1966) emphasized that conceptual conflict creates epistemic curiosity which motivates the search for new information and the reconceptualization of the knowledge one already has. Hoffman and Maier (1972) insisted that higher-quality problem solving depended on conflict among group members. Bruner (1961) proposed that conceptual conflict was necessary for discovery learning and could be created by (a) presenting events that are discrepant with what the student already knows and understands, (b) presenting "mysterious" events that seem inexplicable on the basis of students' present knowledge, and (c) having students argue and disagree with the instructor or with each other. Johnson (1970) posited that since knowledge results from social processes (i.e., "truth" is derived by scholars seeking consensus through discussion), then conflict among ideas, theories, and conclusions becomes an essential part of building a conceptual structure that everyone agrees is valid.

The power of conflict may be clearly seen in the arts. Creating a conflict is an accepted writer's tool for capturing an audience. All drama hinges on conflict. Playwrights and scriptwriters create a conflict whenever they want to gain and hold viewer's attention, create viewer interest and emotional involvement, and excite and surprise viewers. A general rule of modern novels is that if a conflict is not created within the first three pages of the book, the book will not be successful.

Educators, on the other hand, often avoid and suppress any sort of intellectual conflict in the classroom. Despite the (a) daily demonstration of the power of conflict in dramatic productions and (b) the recommendation by theorists that conflict be an essential aspect of learning and teaching, educators have by and large avoided and suppressed intellectual conflict. Far from being a standard instructional procedure, in most colleges creating intellectual conflict is the exception, not the rule. Why do faculty avoid creating intellectual conflict among and within students? The answer to that question is a somewhat of a mystery.

The Avoidance of Inellectual Conflicts

There are a number of hypotheses as to why conflict is so avoided and suppressed in academic situations (Johnson, 1970; Johnson &

F. Johnson, 1975; Johnson, F. Johnson, & Johnson, 1976; Johnson & R. Johnson, 1979, 1989, 1995a).

The first hypothesis is that fear blocks faculty and students from engaging in intellectual conflicts. Since destructively managed conflicts create divisiveness and hostility, when conflicts among students occur, faculty and students may have some anxiety as to whether constructive or destructive outcomes will result. Palmer (1990, 1991), for example, believes that fear of conflict blocks good teaching and learning and recommends that faculty have the courage to promote intellectual conflict among students and between students and faculty despite their apprehensions about doing so.

Hypothesis two is that ignorance of how to engage in intellectual conflict blocks faculty and students from engaging in intellectual conflicts. Until recently there has not been a clear set of instructional procedures that faculty can use in a wide variety of subject areas and with any age student. The development of structured academic controversy gives faculty a clear instructional procedure they can use to structure intellectual conflicts among students in ways that result in increased learning.

The third hypothesis is that lack of training programs to teach faculty how to use intellectual conflict effectively blocks faculty and students from engaging in intellectual conflicts. Most faculty members have not been trained in how to create intellectual conflicts among students and how to use the conflicts to increase students' learning. Such training programs exist only at a few institutions, such as the University of Minnesota. As a consequence, most faculty do not know how to take advantage of the few instructional procedures that are available.

Hypothesis four is that our culture is so anti-conflict that faculty do not see the promotion of intellectual conflicts as a possibility. The view that conflict is a potential positive and powerful force on learning may be culturally unacceptable. A general feeling in our society is that conflicts are bad and should be avoided. Many people, consequently, believe that a well-run classroom is one in which there are no conflicts among students.

The fifth hypothesis is that pedagogical norms may block faculty and students from engaging in intellectual conflicts. Current pedagogy promotes the use of a performer-spectator approach to teaching. Faculty lecture, often in an interesting and entertaining way, and students sit and watch and take notes. In an attempt to cover a whole field in a semester or year, students are often exposed to a blizzard of information within a lecture. Departmental chairs and colleagues may equate telling with teaching. In such a learning climate, the norms of what is acceptable teaching practice may not include creating intellectual conflict among students.

Hypothesis six is that inertia, the power of the status quo, may be so great that faculty just do not try anything new. Faculty may choose to play it safe by only lecturing because it is their personal tradition and the tradition of their college and colleagues.

These six barriers are formidable obstacles to overcome if faculty are to utilize the power of intellectual conflict in their teaching. In order to give faculty the courage to change their teaching practices and to include conflict as a center-piece of instruction, faculty members must know what academic controversy is, the outcomes it promotes, and the procedures that operationalize its use in learning situations.

What Is Academic Controversy?

The best way ever devised for seeking the truth in any given situation is advocacy: presenting the pros and cons from different, informed points of view and digging down deep into the facts.

Harold S. Geneen, Former CEO, ITT

In an English class students are considering the issue of civil disobedience. They learn that in the civil rights movement, individuals broke the law to gain equal rights for minorities. In numerous literary works, such as Huckleberry Finn, individuals wrestle with the issue of breaking the law to redress a social injustice. Huck wrestles with the issue of breaking the law in order to help Jim, the run-away slave. In the 1970s and 1980s prominent public figures from Wall

Street to the White House have felt justified in breaking laws for personal or political gain. In order to study the role of civil disobedience in a democracy, students are placed in a cooperative learning group of four members. The group is then divided into two pairs. One pair is given the assignment of making the best case possible for the constructiveness of civil disobedience in a democracy. The other pair is given the assignment of making the best case possible for the destructiveness of civil disobedience in a democracy. In the resulting conflict, students draw from such sources as the Declaration of Independence by Thomas Jefferson, Civil Disobedience by Henry David Thoreau, Speech at Cooper Union, New York by Abraham Lincoln, and Letter from Birmingham Jail by Martin Luther King, Jr. to challenge each other's reasoning and analyses concerning when civil disobedience is, or is not, constructive.

Academic controversy exists when one student's ideas, information, conclusions, theories, and opinions are incompatible with those of another, and the two seek to reach an agreement. Controversies are resolved by engaging in what Aristotle called *deliberate discourse* (i.e., the discussion of the advantages and disadvantages of proposed actions) aimed at synthesizing novel solutions (i.e., *creative problem solving*). The instructor guides students through the following steps (Johnson, 1970; Johnson & F. Johnson, 1975/1994; Johnson, F. Johnson, & Johnson, 1976; Johnson & R. Johnson, 1979, 1989, 1995a):

1. **Research And Prepare A Position:** Each pair develops the position assigned, learns the relevant information, and plans how to present the best case possible to the other pair. Near the end of the period pairs are encouraged to compare notes with pairs from other groups who represent the same position.

2. **Present And Advocate Their Position:** Each pair makes their presentation to the opposing pair. Each member of the pair has to participate in the presentation. Students are to be as persuasive and convincing as possible. Members of the opposing pair are encouraged to take notes, listen carefully to learn the information being presented, and clarify anything they do not understand.

3. **Engage In An Open Discussion In Which They Refute the Opposing Position And Rebut Attacks On Their Own**

Position: Students argue forcefully and persuasively for their position, presenting as many facts as they can to support their point of view. The group members analyze and critically evaluate the information, rationale, and inductive and deductive reasoning of the opposing pair, asking them for the facts that support their point of view. They refute the arguments of the opposing pair and rebut attacks on their position. They discuss the issue following a set of rules to help them criticize ideas without criticizing people, differentiate the two positions, and assess the degree of evidence and logic supporting each position. They keep in mind that the issue is complex and they need to know both sides to write a good report.

4. **Reverse Perspectives:** The pairs reverse perspectives and present each other's positions. In arguing for the opposing position, students are forceful and persuasive. They add any new information that the opposing pair did not think to present. They strive to see the issue from both perspectives simultaneously.

5. **Synthesize And Integrate The Best Evidence And Reasoning Into A Joint Position:** The four members of the group drop all advocacy and synthesize and integrate what they know into factual and judgmental conclusions that are summarized into a joint position to which all sides can agree. They (a) finalize the report (the instructor evaluates reports on the quality of the writing, the logical presentation of evidence, and the oral presentation of the report to the class), (b) present their conclusions to the class (all four members of the group are required to participate orally in the presentation), (c) individually take the test covering both sides of the issue (if every member of the group achieves up to criterion, they all receive bonus points), and (d) process how well they worked together and how they could be even more effective next time.

Table 1: Controversy, Debate, Concurrence-Seeking, And Individualistic Processes

Controversy	Debate	Concurrence Seeking	Individualistic
Categorizing And Organizing Information To Derive Conclusions	Categorizing And Organizing Information To Derive Conclusions	Categorizing And Organizing Information To Derive Conclusions	Categorizing And Organizing Information To Derive Conclusions
Presenting, Advocating, Elaborating Position And Rationale	Presenting, Advocating, Elaborating Position And Rationale	Active Presentation Of Position	No Oral Statement Of Positions
Being Challenged By Opposing Views	Being Challenged by Opposing Views	Quick Compromise to One View	Presence of Only One View
Conceptual Conflict And Uncertainty About Correctness Of Own Views	Conceptual Conflict And Uncertainty About Correctness Of Own Views	High Certainty About The Correctness Of Own Views	High Certainty About The Correctness Of Own Views
Epistemic Curiosity And Perspective Taking	Epistemic Curiosity	No Epistemic Curiosity	No Epistemic Curiosity
Reconceptualization, Synthesis, Integration	Closed-Minded Adherence To Own Point of View	Closed-Minded Adherence To Own Point of View	Closed-Minded Adherence To Own Point of View
High Achievement, Positive Relationships, Psychological Health and Social Competencies	Moderate Achievement, Relationships, Psychological Health	Low Achievement, Relationships, Psychological Health	Low Achievement, Relationships, Psychological Health

Structured controversies are most commonly contrasted with concurrence seeking, debate, and individualistic learning. *Debate* exists when two or more individuals argue positions that are incompatible with one another and a judge declares a winner on the basis of who presented their position the best. An example of debate is when each member of a group is assigned a position as to whether more or less regulations are needed to control hazardous wastes and an authority declares as the winner the person who makes the best presentation of his or her position to the group. *Concurrence seeking* occurs when members of a group inhibit discussion to avoid any disagreement or arguments, emphasize agreement, and avoid realistic appraisal of alternative ideas and courses of action. Concurrence seeking is close to the *groupthink* concept of Janis (1982) in which members of a decision-making group set aside their doubts and misgivings about whatever policy is favored by the emerging consensus so as to be able to concur with the other members. The underlying motivation of groupthink is the strong desire to preserve the harmonious atmosphere of the group on which each member has become dependent for coping with the stresses of external crises and for maintaining self- esteem. *Individualistic efforts* exist when individuals work alone at their own pace and with their set of materials without interacting with each other, in a situation in which their goals are unrelated and independent from each other (Johnson, Johnson, Smith, 1991).

Table 2: Social Interdependence And Conflict

	Controversy	Debate	Concurrence-Seeking	Individualistic
Positive Goal Interdependence	Yes	No	Yes	No
Resource Interdependence	Yes	Yes	Yes	No
Negative Goal Interdependence	No	Yes	No	No
Conflict	Yes	Yes	No	No

A key to the effectiveness of conflict procedures for promoting learning is the mixture of cooperative and competitive elements within the procedure (see Table 2). The greater the cooperative elements and the less the competitive elements, the more constructive the conflict (Deutsch, 1973). Cooperative elements alone, however, do not ensure maximal productivity. There has to be both cooperation and conflict. Thus, controversy is characterized by both positive goal and resource interdependence as well as by conflict. In a controversy, students are required to advocate opposing positions (conflict) with the intent of learning both sides so all group members can come to consensus about a synthesis of the two positions (positive goal interdependence).

Debate has positive resource interdependence, negative goal interdependence, and conflict. In a debate, students are required to advocate opposing positions (conflict) knowing that a judge will determine who wins (negative goal interdependence) and that they have only one side of the information (resource interdependence). Within concurrence seeking there is positive goal interdependence (students are required to reach consensus about the issue) and resource interdependence (students realize they only have half the information), but no conflict. Within individualistic learning situations there is neither interdependence nor intellectual conflict; students study both sides of the issue without having to advocate either.

How Students Benefit

Whenever faculty want students to be emotionally involved in and committed to learning, controversy is needed. Intellectual "disputed passages" create numerous benefits for students when they (a) occur within cooperative learning groups and (b) are carefully structured to ensure that students manage them constructively. The outcomes of controversy may be grouped into three broad outcomes (Johnson & Johnson, 1989, 1995a):

Effort to achieve. Compared with concurrence-seeking, debate, and individualistic efforts, controversy tends to result in greater motivation to achieve, greater search for more information about the topic being studied, greater mastery and retention of the subject matter being studied, greater ability to generalize the principles learned to a wider variety of situations, more frequent use of higher level reasoning strategies, higher-quality decisions and solutions to complex problems for which different viewpoints can plausibly be developed, more frequent creative insights into the issues being discussed, more frequent syntheses combining more than one perspectives, and greater task involvement reflected in greater emotional commitment to solving the problem, greater enjoyment of the process, and more feelings of stimulation and enjoyment. Controversy tends to be fun, enjoyable, and exciting.

Positive interpersonal relationships: Controversy promotes greater liking and social support among participants than does debate, concurrence-seeking, no controversy, or individualistic efforts.

Psychological health and social competence. Compared with concurrence-seeking, debate, and individualistic efforts, controversy tends to result in higher academic self-esteem and greater perspective-taking accuracy. Being able to manage disagreements and conflicts constructively enables individuals to cope with the stresses involved in interacting with a variety of other people.

==================== **Process of Controversy** ====================

Since the general or prevailing opinion on any subject is rarely or never the whole truth, it is only by the collision of adverse opinion that the remainder of the truth has any chance of being supplied.
John Stuart Mill

Rique Campa, a Professor in the Department of Fisheries and Wildlife at Michigan State University, asked his class, *"Can a marina be developed in an environmentally sensitive area where piping plovers (a shorebird) have a breeding ground?"* He assigns students to groups of four, divides each group into two pairs, and assigns one pair the *"Developer-Position"* and the other pair the *"Department of*

Natural Resources Position." He then follows the structured academic controversy procedure over several class periods and requires students to do extensive research on the issue. Students research the issue, prepare a persuasive case for their position, present their position in a compelling and interesting way, refute the opposing position while rebutting criticisms of their position, take the opposing perspectives, and derive a synthesis or integration of the positions. In conducting the controversy, Professor Campa is operationalizing the theoretical process by which controversy works.

Campa is following the advice of a number of developmental (Hunt, 1964; Kohlberg, 1969; Piaget, 1928, 1950), cognitive (Berlyne, 1966; Hammond, 1973), social (Janis, 1982; Johnson, 1970, 1979, 1980; Johnson & F. Johnson, 1975; Johnson, F. Johnson, & Johnson, 1976; Johnson & R. Johnson, 1979, 1989, 1995a; Johnson, Johnson, & Smith, 1988), and organizational (Maier, 1970) psychologists who theorized about the processes through which conflict leads to the above outcomes. On the basis of their work, we have proposed the following process (Johnson & Johnson, 1989, 1995a):

1. When individuals are presented with a problem or decision, they have an initial conclusion based on categorizing and organizing incomplete information, their limited experiences, and their specific perspectives.

2. When individuals present their conclusion and its rationale to others, they engage in cognitive rehearsal, deepen their understanding of their position, and employ higher-level reasoning strategies.

3. When individuals are confronted by other people with different conclusions based on other people's information, experiences, and perspectives, they become uncertain as to the correctness of their views. A state of conceptual conflict or disequilibrium is aroused.

4. Uncertainty, conceptual conflict, and disequilibrium motivate an active search for more information, new experiences, and a more adequate cognitive perspective and reasoning process (i.e., *epistemic curiosity*) in hopes of resolving the uncertainty. Divergent attention and thought are stimulated.

5. By adapting their cognitive perspective and reasoning through understanding and accommodating the perspective and reasoning of others, a new, reconceptualized, and reorganized conclusion is derived. Novel solutions and decisions that, on balance, are qualitatively better are detected.

Key Elements for Making Controversy Constructive

He that wrestles with us strengthens our nerves, and sharpens our skill. Our antagonist is our helper.

Edmund Burke,
Reflection of the Revolution in France

Although controversies can operate in a beneficial way, they will not do so under all conditions. As with all types of conflicts, the potential for either constructive or destructive outcomes is present in a controversy. Whether there are positive or negative consequences depends on the conditions under which controversy occurs and the way in which it is managed. These key elements are as follows (Johnson & Johnson, 1979, 1989, 1995a):

1. **A cooperative context.** Communication of information is far more complete, accurate, encouraged, and utilized in a cooperative context than in a competitive context. Controversy in a cooperative context promotes open-minded listening to the opposing position, while in a competitive context controversy promotes a closed-minded orientation in which individuals were unwilling to make concessions to the opponent's viewpoint and refused to incorporate any of the opponent's viewpoint into their own position.

2. **Heterogeneous participants.** Heterogeneity among individuals leads to potential controversy, and to more diverse interaction patterns and resources for achievement and problem-solving.

3. **Relevant information distributed among participants.** The more information individuals have about an issue, the more successful their problem solving.

4. **Social skills.** In order for controversies to be managed constructively, individuals need a number of conflict management skills, such as disagreeing with each other's ideas while confirming each other's personal competence, and seeing the issue from a number of perspectives.

5. **Rational argument.** Rational argumentation includes generating ideas, collecting and organizing relevant information, using inductive and deductive logic, and making tentative conclusions based on current understanding.

■■■■ *Structuring Academic Controversies* ■■■

Conflict is the gadfly of thought. It stirs us to observation and memory. It instigates invention. It shocks us out of sheeplike passivity, and sets us at noting and contriving... Conflict is a "sine qua non" of reflection and ingenuity.

John Dewey,
Human Nature and Conduct: Morals Are Human

Over the past 25 years, we have (a) developed and tested a theory of controversy (Johnson, 1970, 1979; Johnson & Johnson, 1979, 1985, 1987, 1989; Johnson, Johnson & Smith, 1986), (b) trained instructors and professors throughout North America and numerous other countries in the use of academic controversy to field-test and implement the controversy procedure, and (c) developed a series of curriculum units on energy and environmental issues structured for academic controversies. The basic format for doing so follows. A more detailed description of conducting academic controversies may be found in Johnson and Johnson (1995a).

In order to use academic controversies in your classes, you should engage in the following steps.

Creating a Cooperative Context ────────────

First, you create a cooperative context for the controversy. The context within which conflicts occur largely determines whether the conflict is managed constructively or destructively (Deutsch, 1973; Johnson & Johnson, 1989; Tjosvold & Johnson, 1983; Watson &

Johnson, 1972). There are two possible contexts for conflict: cooperative and competitive (in individualistic situations individuals do not interact and, therefore, no conflict occurs). When participants are in competition with each other, they will go for victory rather than a constructive resolution of the conflict. It is only when participants focus on their joint goals and strive to maximize mutual benefits that a constructive resolution to conflicts is sought. The easiest way to establish a cooperative context for intellectual conflict is to use cooperative learning. When lessons are structured cooperatively, students work together to accomplish shared learning goals. There is far more to cooperative learning, however, than a seating arrangement. It is only when five basic elements are carefully structured that a group is cooperative. The five essential elements are: Positive interdependence, individual accountability, face-to-face promotive interaction, social skills, and group processing.[1]

Structure the Academic Task

You structure the task (a) cooperatively and (b) so that there are at least two well-documented positions (e.g., pro and con). The choice of topic depends on the interests of the instructor and the purposes of the course. In math courses, controversies may focus on different ways to solve a problem. In science classes, controversies may focus on whether coal (nuclear, wind, solar, geothermal power) should be used as an energy source, whether hazardous wastes should be more regulated, or whether acid rain should be controlled. Since drama is based on conflict, almost any piece of literature may be turned into a controversy, such as having students argue over who is the greatest romantic poet. Since most history is based on conflicts, controversies can be created over any historical event, such as the Federalist papers, the deportation of the Acadians. In any subject area, controversies can be created to promote academic learning and creative group problem solving.

Prepare Instructional Materials

You prepare the instructional materials so that group members know what position they have been assigned and where they

---

[1]See chapter 9 for a more complete description of cooperative learning—eds.

can find supporting information. The following materials are needed for each position:

1. A clear description of the group's task.

2. A description of the controversy procedure.

3. A description of the interpersonal and small group skills to be used during the procedure.

4. A definition of the position to be advocated with a summary of the key arguments supporting the position.

5. Resource materials (including a bibliography) to provide evidence for the elaboration of the arguments supporting the position to be advocated. You create resource interdependence by giving each pair half of the materials.

Make Pre-instructional Decisions and Preparations

You make pre-instructional decisions and preparations. You decide on the objectives for the lesson. You choose a topic that has content manageable by the students and on which at least two well-documented positions (pro and con) can be prepared. You plan how to assign students randomly to groups of four and then divide them into random pairs. You then plan and prepare the instructional materials so that group members know what position they have been assigned and where they can find supporting information. The following materials are helpful for each position:

Explain and Orchestrate the Academic Task, Cooperative Structure, and Controversy Procedure

You explain the academic task so that students are clear about the assignment and understand the objectives of the lesson. Direct teaching of concepts, principles, and strategies may take place at this point. The task must be structured so that there are at least two well-documented positions (pro and con). The choice of topic depends on the interests of the instructor and the purposes of the course.

You structure positive interdependence by assigning two group goals. You tell students to:

1. **Produce a group report detailing the nature of the group's decision and its rationale.** Members are to arrive at a consensus concerning the answer to the question posed. All group members participate in writing a high quality group report. Groups can also be asked to make a presentation of their report to the class.

2. **Individually take a test on both positions.** Group members master all the information relevant to both sides of the issue and help each other score highly on the test.

To supplement the effects of positive goal interdependence, the materials are divided among group members (resource interdependence) and bonus points may be given if all group members score above a preset criterion on the test (reward interdependence).

The purpose of the controversy is to maximize each student's learning. You structure **individual accountability** by ensuring that each student participates in each step of the controversy procedure, by individually testing each student on both sides of the issue, and by randomly selecting students to present their group's report.

You give students the instructions for engaging in an academic controversy. They may be found in Table 1. In addition to explaining the procedure, you may wish to help the students *"get in role"* by presenting the issue to be decided in as interesting and dramatic a way as possible.

▬▬▬ Table Three: Controversy Procedure ▬▬▬

Your overall goals are to learn all information relevant to the issue being studied and ensure that all other group members learn the information, so that (a) your group can write the best report possible on the issue and (b) all group members achieve high scores on the test. The controversy procedure will help you achieve these goals. The procedure is as follows.

1. **Research, Learn, And Prepare Your Position:** Your group of four has been divided into two pairs. One pair has been assigned the pro position and the other pair has been assigned the con position. With your partner, you are to prepare the best case possible for your assigned position by:

a. **Researching your assigned position and learning all relevant information.** Read the materials supporting your position. Find more information in the reference materials to support your position. Give the opposing pair any information you find that supports its ' position.

b. **Organizing the information into a persuasive argument** that contains a thesis statement or claim *("George Washington was the most effective American President")*, the rationale supporting your thesis (*"He accomplished a, b, and c"*), and a logical conclusion that is the same as your thesis (*"Therefore, George Washington was the most effective American President"*).

c. **Planning how to advocate your assigned position** effectively to ensure it receives a fair and complete hearing. Make sure both you and your partner are ready to present your assigned position so persuasively that the opposing pair will comprehend and learn your information and, of course, agree that your position is valid and correct.

2. **Present And Advocate Your Position:** Present the best case for your assigned position to the opposing pair to ensure it gets a fair and complete hearing. Be forceful, persuasive, and convincing in doing so. Use more than one media. Listen carefully to and learn the opposing position. Take notes and clarify anything you do not understand.

3. **Engage In An Open Discussion In Which There is Spirited Disagreement:** Openly discuss the issue by freely exchanging information and ideas. Argue forcefully and persuasively for your position, presenting as many facts as you can to support your point of view. Listen critically to the opposing pair's evidence and reasoning, probe and push the opposing pair's thinking, ask for data to support assertions, and then present counter arguments. Take careful notes on and thoroughly learn the opposing position. Compare the strengths and weaknesses of the two positions. Refute the claims being made by the opposing pair, and rebut the attacks on your position. Give the other position a "trial by fire." Follow the specific rules for constructive controversy. Sometimes a "time-

out" period will be provided so you can caucus with your partner and prepare new arguments. Your teacher may encourage more spirited arguing, take sides when a pair is in trouble, play devil' s advocate, ask one group to observe another group engaging in a spirited argument, and generally stir up the discussion. Remember, this is a complex issue and you need to know both sides to write a good report. Make. sure you understand the facts that support both points of view.

4. **Reverse Perspectives:** Reverse perspectives and present the best case for the opposing position. Change chairs with the other pair. Present the opposing pair's position as if you were they. Use your notes to do so. Be as sincere and forceful as you can. Add any new facts you know of. Elaborate their position by relating it to other information you have previously learned. Strive to see the issue from both perspectives simultaneously. The opposing pair will do the same.

5. **Synthesize:** Drop all advocacy. Find a synthesis on which all members can agree. Summarize the best evidence and reasoning from both sides and integrate it into a joint position that is a new and unique solution. Change your mind only when the facts and rationale clearly indicate that you should do so.

   a. Write a group report on the group's synthesis with the supporting evidence and rationale. All group members sign the report indicating that they agree with it, can explain its content, and consider it ready to be evaluated. Organize your report to present it to your entire class.

   b. Take a test on both positions. If all members score above the preset criteria of excellence, each receives five bonus points.

   c. Process how well the group functioned and how its performance may be improved during the next controversy. The specific conflict management skills required for constructive controversy may be highlighted.

   d. Celebrate your group's success and the hard work of each member to make every step of the controversy procedure effective.

You specify the social skills students are to master and demonstrate during the controversy. The social skills emphasized are those involved in systematically advocating an intellectual position and evaluating and criticizing the position advocated by others, as well as the skills involved in synthesis and consensual decision making. Students should be taught the controversy skills.

━━━━━ *Table Four: Controversy Rules* ━━━━━

1. I am critical of ideas, not people. I challenge and refute the ideas of the opposing pair, while confiming their competence and value as individuals. I do not indicate that I personally reject them.

2. I separate my personal worth from criticism of my ideas.

3. I remember that we are all in this together, sink or swim. I focus on coming to the best decision possible, not on **winning**.

4. I encourage everyone to participate and to master all the relevant information.

5. I listen to everyone's ideas, even if I don't agree.

6. I restate what someone has said if it is not clear.

7. I differentiate before I try to integrate. I first bring out all ideas and facts supporting both sides and clarify how the positions differ. Then I try to identify points of agreement and put them together in a way that makes sense.

8. I try to understand both sides of the issue. I try to see the issue from the opposing perspective in order to understand the opposing position.

9. I change my mind when the evidence clearly indicates that I should do so.

10. I emphasize rationality in seeking the best possible answer, given the available data.

11. I follow the **golden rule of conflict**. The golden rule is, act towards your opponents as you would have them act toward you. I want the opposing pair to listen to me, so I listen to them. I want the opposing pair to include my ideas in their

thinking, so I include their ideas in my thinking. I want the opposing pair to see the issue from my perspective, so I take their perspective.

You structure intergroup cooperation. You explain that when preparing their positions, students can confer with classmates in other groups who are also preparing the same position. Ideas as to how best to present and advocate the position can be shared. If one pair of students finds information that supports its position, members can share that information with other pairs who have the same position. The positive outcomes found in cooperative learning groups can be extended to the whole class by structuring intergroup cooperations. Bonus points may be given if all members of a class reach a preset criteria of excelllence. When a group finishes its work, the teacher should encourage the members to go help other groups complete the assignment.

Monitor the Controversy Groups and Intervention When Needed

While the groups engage in the controversy procedure, you monitor to see what problems they are having completing the assignment and skillfully presenting their positions, refuting the opposing position while rebutting attacks on their own position, reversing perspectives, and synthesizing. Use a formal observation sheet whenever possible and count the number of times you observe appropriate behaviors being used by students. Take notes on specific student actions to illustrate and extend the frequency data. If a group does not understand the academic assignment, you may wish to clarify instructions, review important concepts and strategies, answer questions, and teach academic skills as necessary. If a group is having problems engaging in the controversy procedure (researching their position, presenting it, refuting the opposing position while rebutting attacks on their position, reversing perspectives, or creatively synthesizing), you may wish to provide some clarification, coaching, and encouragement. You may also wish to intervene to improve students' skills in working together and engaging in a controversy. Interpersonal and small group skills (including conflict skills) may be directly taught (Johnson, 1993; Johnson & F. Johnson, 1997). You may also wish to intervene and reinforce particularly effective and skillful behaviors that you notice.

Evaluating Students' Learning and Processing Group Effectiveness

At the end of each instructional unit, students should be able to summarize what they have learned. You may wish to summarize the major points in the lesson, recall ideas, or give examples. You may wish to provide your own summary and answer any final questions students have. You evaluate students' work and give feedback as to how their work compares with the criteria of excellence. Qualitative as well as quantitative aspects of performance may be addressed. Students receive a group grade on the quality of their final report and receive an individual grade on their performance on the test covering both sides of the issue.

You have groups process how well the group functioned. Students should have time to describe what member actions were helpful (and unhelpful) in completing each step of the controversy procedure and make decisions about what behaviors to continue or change. Group processing occurs at two levels—in each learning group and in the class as a whole. In small group processing members discuss how effectively they worked together and what could be improved. In whole-class processing the teacher gives the class feedback and has students share incidents that occurred in their groups.

What Academic Controversy Is Not

There is often misunderstandings about conducting an academic controversy and dealing with controversial issues and controversial subject matter in the classroom. A *controversial issue* is an issue for which society has not found consensus, and is considered so significant that each proposed way of dealing with the issue has ardent supporters and adamant opponents. Controversial issues, by nature, arouse protest from some individual or group, since any position taken will be opposed by those who favor another position. The protest may result from a feeling that a cherished belief, an economic interest or a basic principle is threatened. Academic controversy is aimed at learning, not at resolving political issues within a community.

Second, in many places there are parents who are concerned about certain curriculum materials and topics for study. *Controversial subject matter* varies from college to college and community to community. Any issue or topic has the potential to become controversial at some time or place. Academic controversy is a procedure for learning, not for handling specific subject matter, curriculum materials, or topics.

Academic controversies create interest in subject matter and motivate students to investigate issues and points-of-view they would not ordinarily be interested in. Controversial issues and subject matter are just the opposite. They involve issues that students may be so emotionally involved in and feel so strongly about that a rational discussion is difficult. When unplanned and/or highly emotionally charged issues arise in a class, however, faculty need a procedure and plan for dealing with them.

▬ Learning How to Be a Citizen In a Democracy ▬

The word "democracy" comes from the Greek word *demokratia*, which is a combination of *demos* (the Greek word for people) and *kratos* (the Greek word for "rule"). One admirer of Athenian democracy was Thomas Jefferson. Jefferson believed that free and open discussion should serve as the basis of influence within society, not the social rank within which a person was born. Jefferson was also influenced by one of his professors at William and Mary College, Dr. William Small of Scotland. Small advocated a new method of learning in which students questioned and discussed, examining all sides of a topic, with scant regard for the pronouncements of established authorities. A few years before his death, Thomas Jefferson described his experiences as a student at the College of William and Mary in a letter to Dr. Thomas Cooper (1818): *I was bold in the pursuit of knowledge, never fearing to follow the truth and reason to whatever results they led, and bearding every authority which stood in the way.*

Based on the beliefs of Thomas Jefferson and his fellow revolutionaries, American democracy was founded on the premise that truth will result from free and open discussion in which opposing points of view are advocated and vigorously argued. Every citizen is given the opportunity to advocate for his or her ideas. Once a decision is made, the minority is expected to go along willingly with the majority because they know they have been given a fair and complete hearing. To be a citizen in our democracy, individuals need to master the process of organizing their conclusions, advocating their views, challenging opposing positions, making a decision, and committing themselves to implement the decision made (regardless of whether one initially favored the alternative adopted or not).

Building a Learning Community

Students have to learn how to be contributing members to a learning community in order to achieve the goals of the college and to prepare themselves for most careers where group decision making is an everyday occurrence. For classes and colleges to be learning communities, these steps must be taken.

The first step in creating a learning community is creating positive interdependence among all members of the class or college. The easiest way to create such a cooperative context and a learning community is to use cooperative learning procedures the majority of the day (Johnson, Johnson, & Smith, 1991). From making learning a cooperative effort, faculty may establish the mutual goal of searching for truth and knowledge and build commitment to achieving it. Increasing knowledge and understanding is achieved through cooperative interaction, not isolated thought. Truth and knowledge are consensual, based on intersubjectivity where different individuals reach the same conclusions and make the same inferences after considering theory and facts.

The second step is to make intellectual conflict a way of life. Faculty need to engage students in intellectual conflicts within which they have to prepare intellectual positions, present them, advocate them, criticize opposing intellectual positions, view the issue from a variety of perspectives, and synthesize the various positions into one position. Without intellectual conflict, a learning community in which faculty and students seek truth and knowledge cannot be achieved.

The third step is to make the epistemology and pedagogy used congruent with the need for joint action toward mutual goals and the continued presence of intellectual conflict. The epistemology resulting from (a) a competitive context in which students are ranked from highest to lowest performer and (b) making students passive recipients of lectures and reading mitigates against the formation of a learning community. Developing a learning community requires an epistemology based on the predominant use of cooperative learning and academic controversies. Since cooperative learning increases achievement, committed and caring relationships, increased social competencies, and a number of other important instructional outcomes (Johnson & Johnson, 1989), there will be little objection to making it the dominant mode of learning. In addition to cooperative learning, faculty use academic controversies to create the intellectual conflict and internal disequilibrium needed to increase student critical thinking and use of higher-level reasoning strategies. Finding consensual truth requires mutual commitment to do so and intellectual disagreement and challenge. The combination of cooperative learning and academic controversies makes the epistemology and pedagogy congruent with faculty and students working together to accomplish mutual goals and engaging in continual intellectual conflict. These two instructional procedures thereby promote the creation of a true learning community.

The fourth step is to establish a peer mediation program (see Johnson & Johnson, 1995b). In a learning community, intellectual conflict is not the only type of conflict that arises. A *conflict of interests* exists when the actions of one person attempting to maximize his or her wants and benefits prevents, blocks, or interferes with another person maximizing his or her wants and benefits. When two students both want the same library book or want to use the computer at the same time, a conflict of interests exists. Conflicts among interests deal more with wants, needs, values, and goals than with differences in information and conclusions. Maintaining a learning community requires members to manage their conflicts of interests constructively. Doing so involves training students how to (a) negotiate constructive resolutions to their conflicts-of-interests and (b) mediate the conflicts-of-interests occurring among fellow students. When conflicts among interests occur, settlements must be negotiated. Students, therefore, have to be taught the procedures and skills of negotiating. When students are unable to negotiate an acceptable agreement, they will turn to a mediator for help. *Mediation* exists when a neutral third person—a mediator—intervenes to help resolve a conflict between two or more people in a way that is acceptable to them. A mediator listens carefully to both sides and helps the disputants move effectively through each step of the negotiation sequence in order to reach an agreement that both believe is fair, just, and workable. Many colleges have implemented peer mediation programs. The procedures for doing so are described in Johnson and Johnson (1991). Doing so provides the framework for ensuring that good relationships are maintained among community members.

Summary and Conclusions

Thomas Jefferson based his faith in the future on the power of constructive conflict. There are numerous theorists who have advocated the use of intellectual conflict in instructional situations. There has been a reluctance to do so, perhaps due to a cultural fear of conflict, lack of procedures, and cultural and pedagogical norms discouraging the use of conflict. In order to avoid students engaging in closed-minded attempts to win in answering the academic questions, instructors must structure the learning situation in ways that promote interest, curiosity, inquiry, and open-minded problem solving. To do so instructors must use two interrelated instructional procedures: cooperative learning and academic controversy. Academic controversy provides a clear procedure for faculty to use in promoting intellectual conflicts. There is strong research support indicating that academic controversy results in many positive benefits for students, including higher achievement, more positive relationships with classmates, and increased self-esteem. There is a clear theory as to the process by which controversy works that has been validated by numerous research studies. In well structured controversies, students make an initial judgment, present their conclusions to other group members, are challenged with opposing views, become uncertain about the correctness of their views, actively search for new information and understanding, incorporate others' perspectives and reasoning into their thinking, and reach a new set of conclusions. Controversies tend to be constructive when the situational context is cooperative, group members are heterogeneous, information and expertise is distributed within the group, members have the necessary conflict skills, and the canons of rational argumentation are followed.

While the controversy process sometimes occurs naturally, it may be considerably enhanced when instructors structure academic controversies. This involves dividing a cooperative group into two pairs and assigning them opposing positions. The pairs then develop their position, present it to the other pair, listen to the opposing position, engage in a discussion in which they attempt to refute the other side and rebut attacks on their position, reverse perspectives and present the other position, and then drop all advocacy and seek a synthesis that takes both perspectives and positions into account. More specifically, the instructor's role in conducting an academic controversy involves making a number of pre-instructional decisions and preparations, explaining and orchestrating the task and cooperative structure and the controversy procedure, monitoring students' teamwork and taskwork and engagement in the controversy procedure, and evaluate students' achievement and having the group's process how effectively they functioned.

Academic controversies may be used in any subject area. Yet implementing structured academic controversies is not easy. It can take years to become an expert. Instructors may wish to start small by taking one subject area or one class and using controversy procedures until they feel comfortable, and then expand into other subject areas or other classes. Instructors are well-advised to pick out topics for which they are pretty sure a controversy will work, plan carefully, and do not rush the process. In order to implement academic controversies successfully, instructors will need to teach students the interpersonal and small group skills required to cooperate, engage in intellectual inquiry, intellectually challenge each other, see a situation from several perspective simultaneously, and synthesize a variety of positions into a new and creative decision. Instructors will also want to teach students the academic skills of researching a position, conceptualizing and organizing an intellectual position, using inductive and deductive logic, presenting a scholarly and reasoned position, refuting other's positions, rebutting attacks on one's own position, and integrating information and reasoning from different perspectives and positions.

Walter Savage Landor once said, *"There is no more certain sign of a narrow mind, of stupidity, and of arrogance, than to stand aloof from those who think differently from us."* It is vital for citizens to seek reasoned judgment on the complex problems facing our society. Especially important is educating individuals to solve problems for which different points of view can plausibly be developed. To do so individuals must enter empathetically into the arguments of both sides of the issue and ensure that the strongest possible case is made for each side, and arrive at a synthesis based on rational thought. Structured academic controversies are now being used in numerous elementary, secondary, and college classrooms. From academic units on the relative merits of coal or nuclear power in elementary classrooms to units on hazardous waste management within high school and college classes, individuals are learning how to utilize structured controversy to address the great questions of our (and previous) times and ensure that high quality solutions are found to complex problems.

References

Ames G., & Murray, F. " When two wrongs make a right: Promoting cognitive change by social conflict," in *Developmental Psychology*, 18, 894-897, 1982.

Berlyne, D. "Notes on intrinsic motivation and intrinsic reward in relation to instruction," In J. Bruner (Ed.), *Learning about learning* (Cooperative Research Monograph No. 15). Washington, D. C.: U. S. Department of Health, Education, and Welfare, Office of Education, 1966.

Bruner, J. *The process of education*. Cambridge, MA: Harvard University Press, 1961.

Coser, L. *The function of social conflict*. Glencoe, IL: Free Press, 1956.

Deutsch, M. Cooperation and trust: Some theoretical notes. In M. Jones (Ed.), *Nebraska symposium on motivation*, 275-319. Lincoln, NE: University of Nebraska Press, 1962.

Deutsch, M. *The resolution of conflict*. New Haven, CT: Yale University Press, 1973.

Follet, M. " Constructive conflict," In H. Metcalf & L. Urwick (Eds.), *Dynamic administration: The collected papers of Mary Parker Follet* (pp. 30-49). New York: Harper, 1940.

Hammond, K. "New directions in research on conflict resolution," in *Journal of Social Issues,* 11, 44-66, 1965.

Hoffman, L., & Maier, N. " Sex differences, sex composition, and group problem solving," in *Journal of Abnormal and Social Psychology,* 63, 453-456, 1961.

Hunt, J. "Introduction: Revisiting Montessori," In M. Montessori (Ed.), *The Montessori method*. New York: Shocken Books, 1964.

Janis, I. *Groupthink: Psychological studies of policy decisions and fiascoes*. Boston, MA: Houghton-Mifflin, 1982.

Johnson, D. W. *Social psychology of education*. Edina, MN: Interaction Book Company, 1970.

Johnson, D. W. *Educational psychology*. Englewood Cliffs, NJ: Prentice-Hall, 1979.

Johnson, D. W. "Group processes: Influences of student-student interaction on school outcomes," In J. McMillam (Ed.), *The social psychology of school learning*. New York: Academic Press, 1980.

Johnson, D. W. *Reaching out: Interpersonal effectiveness and self-actualization* (5th ed.). Englewood Cliff, NJ: Prentice-Hal, 1973/1994.

Johnson D. W., & Johnson, F. *Joining together: Group theory and group skills* (5th ed.). Englewood Cliffs, NJ: Prentice-Hall, 1975/1994.

Johnson, D. W., Johnson, F., & Johnson, R. "Promoting constructive conflict in the classroom," in *Notre Dame Journal of Education,* 7, 163-168, 1976.

Johnson, D. W., & Johnson, R. "Conflict in the classroom: Controversy and learning," in *Review of Educational Research,* 49, 51-61, 1979.

Johnson, D. W., & Johnson, R. " Classroom conflict: Controversy versus debate in learning groups," in *American Educational Research Journal,* 22, 237-256, 1985.

Johnson, D. W., & Johnson, R. "Critical thinking through structured controversy," in *Educational Leadership*, 58-64, March, 1988.

Johnson, D. W., & Johnson, R. *Teaching students to manage conflict constructively by involving them in academic controversies.* Paper given at the annual meetings of American Association for the Advancement of Science, February, 1988.

Johnson, D. W., & Johnson, R. *Cooperation and competition: Theory and research.* Edina, MN: Interaction Book Company, 1989.

Johnson, D. W., & Johnson, R. *Creative Controversy: Intellectual challenge in the classroom.* Edina, MN: Interaction Book Company, 1995a.

Johnson, D. W., & Johnson, R. *Teaching students to be peacemakers.* Edina, MN: Interaction Book Company, 1995b.

Johnson, D. W., Johnson, R., & Holubec, E. *Circles of learning: Cooperation in the classroom* (3rd Ed.). Edinā, MN: Interaction Book Company, 1993.

Johnson, D. W., Johnson, R., & Smith, K. " Academic conflict among students: Controversy and Learning," In R. Feldman, (Ed.). *Social psychological applications to education.* Cambridge University Press, 1986.

Johnson, D. W., Johnson, R., & Smith, K. " Controversy within decision-making situations," In M. Rahim (ed.), *Managing conflict: An interdisciplinary approach* (pp. 251-264). New York: Praeger, 1989.

Johnson, D. W., Johnson, R., & Smith, K. *Active learning: cooperation in the college classroom.* Edina, MN: Interaction Book Company, 1991.

Johnson, D. W., Johnson, R., Smith, K., & Tjosvold, D. "Pro, con, and synthesis: Training managers to engage in constructive controversy," In Sheppard, B., Bazerman, M., & Lewicki, R. (eds.), *Research on negotiation in organizations,* 2 (pp. 135-170). Greenwich, CT: JAI Press, 1990.

Kohlberg, L. "Stage and sequence: The cognitive-developmental approach to socialization," In D. Goslin (Ed.), *Handbook of socialization theory and research* (pp. 347- 480). Chicago: Rand McNally, 1969.

Maier, N. *Problem-solving and creativity in individuals and group.* Belmont, CA: Brooks/Cole, 1970.

Palmer, P. "The courage to teach," in *National Teaching and Learning Forum,* 1(2), 1-3, 1991.

Palmer, P. "Divided no more," in *Change,* (Mach/April), 11-17, 1992.

Piaget, J. *The psychology of intelligence.* New York: Harcourt, 1950.

Simmel, G. *Conflict.* New York: Free Press, 1955.

Tjosvold, D. "Flight crew collaboration to manage safety risks," Unpublished manuscript, Simon Frazer University, in press.

Tjosvold, D., & Johnson, D. W. (Eds.). *Productive Conflict Management: Perspectives for Organizations.* New York: Irvington, 1983.

Watson, G., & Johnson, D. W. *Social psychology: issues and insights.* Philadelphia: Lippincott, 1972.

Getting It Together: Learning Communities

Valerie Ann Bystrom

Valerie Bystrom has been experimenting with interdisciplinary studies and student-centered teaching methods since
she began teaching English at Seattle Central Community
College in 1970. In 1984 she was asked to join two other
teachers and 60 students in a learning community at
Evergreen State College; subsequently she launched coordi
nated studies programs at Seattle Central. Since then she
has been heavily involved in the Washington Center for
Improving the Quality of Undergraduate Education, a consortium of two and four year colleges headquartered at
Evergreen State. Today she is Professor of English at Seattle
Central. Her email address is <vbystr@seaccc.sccd.
ctc.edu>.

Jean MacGregor (co-founder, with Barbara Leigh Smith,
of the Washington Center and member of the faculty at
Evergreen State) and Roberta Matthews (formerly of
LaGuardia Community College, now Academic Vice
President of Marymount College, Tarrytown, NY) worked
closely with Valerie in writing this chapter.

I recall an afternoon in the late sixties at the University
of Washington. English faculty and teaching fellows like myself
gathered in the department lounge to hear professors defend their
practice. A senior professor, striking a heroic pose, said he entered
the classroom knowing as much as he possibly could and he conveyed what he knew. Some younger men proposed a more student-centered approach to undergraduate teaching. One said he

no longer lectured but answered questions if students prepared well enough to ask them. Another young teacher, it was reported, held class in a coffee house. The challengers of the old order were advised to find work in a college of education, and we graduate students in English received the clear message: thinking about how to teach was someone else's work and not so important to us as, say, analyzing enjambment in Pope's couplets.

Happily, things have changed since then. Faculty members at all levels and from all disciplines think about how to teach more effectively. But paradigms don't shift neatly. In *The Order of Things*, Michel Foucault says we see "wrinkles traced for the first time upon the enlightened face of knowledge" before we see the "space of order . . . shattered" and new fields of knowledge and intelligibility emerge from the interstices (pp.238-239). Certainly many of us at the University of Washington believed in change. Anti-war groups occupied buildings; we marched and demonstrated. The Black Students' Union made demands for new curriculum, and the Upward Bound program sought to make college a real possibility for at-risk high school seniors. Protesting the Vietnam war and grades, one professor gave an "A" to anyone who came to class consistently. For a time, an alternative college within the College flourished in the Arts and Sciences. In all the conversations and arguments, however, there seemed no satisfactory new philosophy for teaching or a methodology for changing the classroom. Why not lecture? And if you don't lecture, what will you do? We all remembered uncomfortable hours as undergraduates when a professor set aside a day for answering our questions and there were no questions.

In our new jobs, we became competent lecturers and read Paulo Freire. For many of us in literature, finding, reading, and teaching fiction and poetry by women, by African-American, Native-American, Asian-American, Chicano and Chicana writers changed our own and our students' relationship to books, to teaching and learning. Teachers assigned books they had not studied in school, students wanted to talk about the books, and often what we—students and teachers—said about them in class constituted a more elaborate critical response to the texts than any to be found in the scholarly literature. And then we began to approach the canon with new questions. It hardly seemed like school.

While Thomas Kuhn's *The Structure of Scientific Revolutions* had been around since 1962, the implications of it and of the tide of other more non-positivist linguistic and post-Kantian epistemological theories thoroughly unsettled the humanities and social sciences in the seventies. News swept in from various disciplines and from different points in time. We read C. S. Peirce, Ferdinand Saussure, L. S. Vygotsky, and Ludwig Wittgenstein; we grappled with those Frenchmen and Frenchwomen—Roland Barthes, Jacques Derrida, Jacques Lacan, Julia Kristeva, and Michel Foucault; and we appreciated fresh applications and critiques such as Edward Said's *Orientalism*, Richard Rorty's *Philosophy and the Mirror of Nature*, Clifford Geertz's *Local Knowledge*, and Stanley Fish's always lucid elucidations. (The list goes on and on.) It was language, language, everywhere. From a world out there to be known empirically and represented unproblematically in language, we moved to a world conceptualized and made intelligible in language. We are not entirely sure how this world corresponds with the out there. Frederick Jameson fancied it a prison-house of language; others imagined possibilities. That is, if we understand that eternal Truth will not show itself and that human beings decide what counts as true, then we are more rather than less accountable. What people decide is true may change in time and may vary according to context, but this does not mean that any account of the world (or a novel, or basketball game) is as good as any other. Rather, the account is made within a community (a scientific society, a literature class, a group of friends), and communities share standards for making and judging accounts.

For many, the shift in epistemological paradigms gave a more theoretical ground to what we thought should—and did—occur in a classroom. What Freire calls the banking model of teaching and learning seemed even more bankrupt; we no longer supposed our business was to know the world and to make small deposits of that knowledge in our students. To understand knowledge as not simply discovered, stored, conveyed, or analyzed, but made, shared, and evaluated, meant teaching is less about simply conveying information and more about providing the time and space for students to practice making, sharing, and evaluating knowledge. We could envision students talking, as if on the edge of the world as it turns into the morning sun and every moment was a breaking into daylight. Still, new theories, revolutionary intentions, and inspiring metaphors do not guarantee classes that work the way we envision them. We experimented with new pedagogies but rarely came together to discuss practice, and for students, even the best set of engaging classes still added up to a fragmented jumble of unrelated experiences.

In 1984, some fifteen years after the meeting in the UW English lounge, faculty and administrators from many Washington schools met at the University to talk about teaching and learning. We talked about how to improve the quality of undergraduate education—how to make the classes more collaborative, how to make the curriculum more coherent. This was the first meeting of the Washington Center for Improving the Quality of Undergraduate Education. Now, ten years later, state-supported, based at The Evergreen State College, and committed to making learning communities an important part of the college curriculum, the Center is a consortium of forty-six colleges and universities which sponsors planning retreats, workshops, small to very large conferences, faculty exchanges, and manages an enormous supply of books, articles, and pamphlets about collaborative and interdisciplinary teaching, learning, and assessment, many written by the Center staff or members.

Here and across the nation, plenty of alternatives to the banking model of learning have been articulated. Lately, bell hooks, herself inspired by Freire, has reinspired many of us, reminding teachers that classrooms are a "location of possibility," that "education is the practice of freedom." Many books and articles have discussed the connection between the theory of the social construction of knowledge and the practice of collaborative learning. For faculty members unconvinced by social constructionists, there are many reports and studies of successful practice. Math and science faculty have been persuaded to restructure their classes by Uri Treisman's collaborative schemes for promoting academic success among African-American and Hispanic students in the math department at Berkeley and by other models for problem-based collaborative study in medical schools. Hundreds of teachers have developed successful active and collaborative classroom methods. People who want to change the way they teach have excellent resources—books like this one!

Certainly part of our professional satisfaction these days follows from the emphasis on active and collaborative teaching and learning. For a young teacher, abandoning the lecture as the primary teaching tool may mean giving up researching, writing, and rewriting several elaborate, wit-adorned lectures a week. For the older professor, it may mean giving up a trusted series of lectures, typewritten, the paper fading to yellow. No more revving up for and coming down from a performance each hour. Instead, professors now can confidently adopt any number of active and collaborative classroom methods so that rather than simply listening to a lecture, students learn while actively engaged with each other. We consider ways for helping students in an anthropology class to grasp concepts such as anomie, or to comprehend the social world of Jane Austen's *Pride and Prejudice* in an English literature survey, or, in political economy, to distinguish between the Marxian and the Hegelian dialectic. Part of the fun is figuring out what to have the students do, inventing a collaborative process which will help them gain information, skills, and concepts. Our own understanding of the subject often deepens as we think up the collaborative assignment, and, more often than not, when they do the assignment, students exceed our expectations. Their research turns up unexpected facts. Their discussions generate insights we did not anticipate. Their inventiveness bowls us over. People passing in the hall notice the energetic hum of the class. Over the course of a quarter or semester, almost any class engaged in collaborative work may come to feel like a community, and the term "learning community" has been used to refer to several kinds of innovative classrooms.

However, in this chapter, we mean something more when I use the term "learning community." First, we mean, in addition to active and collaborative classroom methods, a curricular structure which includes a collaboration among teachers. (Dreaming up collaborative tasks is fun but dreaming them up with colleagues is really the ticket.) Second, we mean a structure that addresses the issue of curricular coherence by purposeful links among courses in different disciplines. For us, then, a learning community is a course of study designed by two or more faculty which includes work in different disciplines integrated around a particular issue or theme. The Washington Center recently compiled a directory of well over one hundred two- and four-year colleges offering such learning communities.

We argue that even if we change the pedagogy of a course in, say, the English Romantic poets from lecture to a most varied and successful sequence of collaborative activities, and even though students demonstrate their knowledge in brilliant research papers, lively discussion groups, in parodies, in illuminated manuscripts, in staged Meeting of the Minds where they assume the roles of different poets, in student-created exams (usually harder than any we would dare set)—still, it is English 313. There it is, a tidy box-full as noted in the course catalogue and stored in the closet where students put their college experience—Psych 101 top shelf to the right, Japanese Drama second shelf in the back. Learning communities, as we use the term, assume that the human construction of knowledge may be vast and complex, a finally indescribable cathedral with zillions of parts, with vaults, buttresses and dazzling windows, amazing in its aspects but connected, linked, and, if not available to anyone in its totality, still not itself offerable in several hundred, or million, tidy boxes for easy storage.

Interdisciplinary studies lets the knowledge out of the boxes, so that students set to building connections, buttresses, windows. The box of English romantic poets might be integrated with the contents of any number of history boxes: e.g. the industrial revolution, the rise of the working class, or the French revolution. Students in environmental studies could stand to read the romantic poets, too, and so could students in an art class. We can imagine integrating the romantic poets in various ways to explore particular issues: What is a revolution? What is the nature of nature? What the use of the human imagination? Coherent, thematic, interdisciplinary programs of study are more likely to shape how a student lives, how she thinks, how she understands, how she addresses issues. What students take away from such a program cannot be boxed up.

Integrating courses is not a new idea. One of the early proponents was Alexander Meiklejohn, who established a short-lived Experimental College at the University of Wisconsin in 1927.[1] Because he believed liberal education prepares people for participation in a democracy and because he thought delivering knowledge in discrete courses in many disciplines tends to hobble it, he wanted undergraduates to discuss issues rather than take courses. Certainly, a student with a closet full of courses may have only the patchiest way to use them in thinking about real world demands and issues. A

---

[1]Toby Fulwiler, co-author of Chapter 3, began his teaching career as an instructor in the Integrated Studies Program at UW-Madison—the successor to Meiklejohn's Experimental College, itself short-lived.

thematic integration, on the other hand, can show students different ways to analyze the death of marshlands and thus to determine how best to avert it, different ways to approach and interpret Machiavelli's *The Prince* and thus to understand its import, different ways to weigh the effects of drug legislation and thus what to urge. The Meiklejohn education stresses the connection between school learning and "real life" so that long before graduate school, students puts knowledge to work.

During the sixties there was a rush to interdisciplinary team-taught courses, but institutions finally couldn't sustain the cost of two faculty members teaching one course. Experimental colleges with interdisciplinary curricula flourished, then faded. Large, departmentalized institutions driven by the three-course quarter or the five-course semester remain the rule. At such an institution, SUNY Stony Brook, Patrick Hill pioneered learning communities in the 1970's. He explains his motives for restructuring curriculum by telling this story about an undergraduate:

> She was taking a course in behaviorism from 10:00 to 1:00 and a course in existentialism from 1:00 to 4:00. And she was pulling A's in both courses. In the behaviorism course—this was pure Skinner—she was learning about the .67 predictability of human behavior and of the illusory character of consciousness and intentions and certainly of their insignificance in explaining human behavior. In the philosophy course, which was focused on the early Sartre, she was learning that we are ultimately free, even to the point of being able to define the meaning of our pasts.
>
> I asked her which course was right. She said, "What do you mean?"
>
> I said, "If you had to choose between the two courses, which one would you choose?" She said, "I like the psychology teacher better."
>
> I said, "That's not what I'm asking. Which one is correct? Which one is correct about the nature of our human being?" And she said, "I'm getting A's in both courses."
> ("The Rationale for Learning Communities," pp. 3-4)

In response to what he describes as the "atomization of the curriculum" and the "privatization of academic experience," Hill and his colleagues proposed integrated programs which give time for students and teachers to explore not only connections but profound differences in assumptions and methods within and among disciplines. They sought ways to help students to a "common intellectual language" and to exploration of personal values and "life's basic truth."

They developed the Federated Learning Community. Basically, the model included a seminar once a week for a group of students all registered in three courses carefully selected by the planners. The courses would not only link thematically, but would include provocative disciplinary approaches to the issue at hand. The FLC titled "Technology, Values and Society," for instance, included classes in philosophy, history and engineering. Further, a faculty member, freed from his regular teaching responsibilities, traveled to classes along with the students and lead the weekly seminar. There, students could elaborate on the connections they found among the concepts, assumptions, viewpoints, and facts presented in the various courses. The faculty member had the title "Master Learner" and undertook to learn what the students learned, to write papers when the students wrote papers. Sometimes this was a challenge, as when an English teacher studied calculus. She sought help from mathematically more gifted students, which seemed fair exchange for her support in their essay writing. Furthermore, the teacher/master learner relearned the art of being a student, such as the difficulty of sitting through hours of lecture everyday, tuning out but taking notes. Out of this experience, master learners could provide feedback about pedagogy for their colleagues teaching the three courses.

In the current move for reform, schools have adapted this learning community model in ways that faculty at almost any institution could duplicate. One handy structure links a skills course, perhaps English 101, to a content course. That is, students who sign up for the English course are required to sign up for the content course also. To accomplish a link, an English teacher and, say, an anthropology teacher, meet and discuss just how to organize it. They may visit each others classes, and if there are faculty development resources, teachers may get release time to attend each other's classes for a whole quarter. The two teachers then plan their linked courses to make the best fit. Since anthropology classes usually carry a higher enrollment than composition classes, there may be students in the anthropology class that are not enrolled in the linked English class so the anthropology teacher may feel less free to reorganize than the English teacher. The two teachers work it out. Together they plan a new and improved course of study for the students in the link.

Linking makes teaching more collegial. Teaching with someone else gives rise to more talk during the quarter—about the progress of the courses, about what needs changing, about the students we have in common, about how we teach, and about what we teach. For young faculty and for old hands, a great pleasure in learning communities is learning from each other. As one teacher noted, he is now getting an education he missed the first time around. Faculty members who may not otherwise even meet become friends.

The link offers students a coherent program, enhancing learning in both courses. The English class may work as an extraordinary study group for anthropology, and, rather than seeming like a tedious requirement, the critical thinking and writing skills in composition can have a direct application and benefit as students tackle anthropology issues and assignments. Further, talking and writing in the English class gives students occasions to discuss the complementarity, the overlapping, or the friction between the disciplines. Terms taken for granted when writing "My Family" for English may be put into question when used in anthropology class. "Objectivity" may be one thing in English and another in anthro. Students see what can arise at the edges as ways of thinking come in contact; they see wonderment and disagreement and new ideas sprouting in the interstices. Often astounded that teachers don't always agree, students realize they themselves must discern, think critically, and make judgements. They come to see their learning, their knowledge, as their responsibility. All around, there is a keener investment in teaching and learning supported by the sense of community as students and teachers collaborate.

Several schools offer variations on this model. At Centralia Community College, for instance, in an ethics/political science link, one day each week is for seminar. The two teachers and the students meet together for the full two hours. During the week, the teachers include work that prepares students to discuss issues that cut across the courses, but in seminar, they give students the responsibility for the discussion. Taking this responsibility is part of the students' learning, and helping them to take it, part of the teaching. Because both teachers join the seminar, students often observe civil disagreement first hand and sometimes for the first time.

Since 1979, students taking a liberal arts AA degree at LaGuardia Community College take the first quarter of English composition in a three-way link called a cluster. Along with composition, students take a course in the research paper, two other courses from science, social science, or the arts, and an integrating seminar hour. For instance, the cluster "Freedom and Seeing" includes composition, research paper writing, introduction to philosophy and introduction to art. "Work, Labor and Business in American Literature" includes the English courses, an introduction to sociology, and a humanities course. At LaGuardia, the same students enroll in all of the classes. This allows the faculty members to rewrite their syllabi in order to pursue themes, to sequence presentations, and to give assignments that make teaching and learning in the cluster more coherent. The composition class also takes on aspects of an integrating seminar where students discuss and write about the material they cover in the other classes. Further, as the cluster often occurs in a student's first semester of school, a freshman has, at the outset, the support of this small group of students and faculty who come to know each other well.

Some learning communities link courses and students but not necessarily faculty. At the University of Oregon and at the University of Washington, a freshman may sign up for a FIG, a Freshman Interest Group. FIG's are clusters adapted for a university and were invented at Oregon by advisers who appreciate just how alienating the freshman year can be. Rather than leaving entering students to flounder in the huge course catalogue, advisers pre-assemble sensible programs of study and invite students during the summer before their freshman year to select one. A student may choose one of many FIGs, depending on her special interest. For instance, a student with an eye to architecture might enroll in a FIG which includes a survey of the visual arts, landscape, environment and culture, and English composition. A comparative culture link, "Eastern and Western Traditions," offers the literature and culture of ancient and classical China, the history of the ancient world, and English composition. "Ecosystems" includes forest and society, composition and a survey of oceanography.

Although two hundred students may attend some of these classes, the band of twenty-five FIG students moves together through the same schedule of courses and then meets once a week with a peer advisor. These meetings do not proceed as integrating seminars. Rather, peer advisors keep to a fairly strict schedule of projects and assignments ranging from guests or faculty preceptors speaking about work in the field to written reflections on the quarter's work. Writing links tend to make FIG's more integrative, but their primary goal is to help students in their first quarter establish a community in an academic context. Indeed, students love FIG's and so do the peer advisors. Each year more are offered—sixty at UW for fall 1996. The universities do not require extended conversation among the faculty or among the faculty and students. The structure invites it, however, and these conversations do occur.

While Hill pioneered learning communities on the east coast, on the west coast a Meiklejohn-inspired experimental college at Berkeley flourished, and then disappeared in the late sixties. The Evergreen State College in Washington took up the work, accepting its first 1,000 students in 1971. Richard Jones writes that the eighteen founding faculty at Evergreen read Joseph Tussman's *Experiment at Berkeley* and were most influenced by the

> *pedagogical* innovation which [Tussman and Meiklejohn] introduced in order to achieve their curricular objectives: substituting for the traditional format of separate teachers, teaching separate courses, in separated blocks of time, to separate students (who are separately combining different assortments of courses), a format in which *a team of teachers teach the same group of students, who are all studying the same things at the same time, over a prolonged period.* (p. 22)

Evergreen still holds to this model of a learning community. The college does not have typical departments and has few "regular" courses. Instead, professors deliver the curriculum in interdisciplinary programs, called "coordinated studies," taught by faculty teams drawn from different disciplines. Each team plans an organized course of study which constitutes for a large group of students their whole schedule, sometimes for a quarter or two, sometimes for a whole year. In the learning communities described earlier, faculty members may have two or more other teaching commitments, and the time given to the planning and tracking a learning community may seem an addition to a routine teaching load. At Evergreen, the learning community comprises the students' and the teachers' full load.

Faculty have responsibility and latitude in establishing the curriculum. They plan and staff standard programs such as "Molecule to Organism" designed for students who will go on to pre-med or to graduate school in life science. This program includes human physiology, cellular and molecular biology, and organic chemistry and bio-chemistry. "Human Development" usually includes anthropology, psychology, and the biology of human development and is designed for students going on in psychological and social services. Within each of these and other standard programs, a faculty team may further develop an integrating theme. For instance, the upcoming "Molecule to Organism" will focus on the biology and chemistry of food, the "Vital Stuff." Whatever the focus or particular theme, the students get solid disciplinary work.

Faculty teams may also organize programs in response to current issues. For instance, a teaching team is now preparing "The Millennium: On the Brink of the New Age" for 1997. The year-long program will question claims made by Robert D. Kaplan and others (e.g. in the controversial *Atlantic* article, "The Coming Anarchy") that the categories and political structures of the nation state are crumbling while others—ethnic, cultural, and religious—are emerging. Unrest in several parts of the world, Kaplan explains, follows from the tension between the dying nation state and the emerging power structures. The central questions for "The Millennium" include: is the nation state really crumbling? Are we in a time of tension between political structures? Is it accurate to say that emergent forces cause the unrest and hatred?

To address such questions, the learning community will undertake case studies including the Balkans, India, and the Middle East. The traditional frameworks of the disciplines will provide methodology and concepts. Naturally, history will be taught, and to evaluate claims that the unrest is created by centuries old ethnic hatred, it will be important to do ethnography. Further, to evaluate disciplinary answers to the core questions, it will be important to understand discipline based bias. Therefore, students will study not only history but the methods and assumptions of history, not only ethnographies but what it means to do an ethnography. If "culture" is named the culprit, one question will be, What is contained in the category "culture"—anything that could provoke this degree of hatred? Thus, "Millennium" and other strong coordinated studies programs explore the interesting tensions between their organizing core questions and the assumptions, conceptual frameworks, and methodologies of the disciplines. Getting ready for programs like "The Millennium" requires no small amount of preparation. In order to deepen and build on the study she does for it, the anthropology teacher will next year join a program centered on the full range of Mediterranean cultures and histories, and after that, one centered on the Balkans themselves. She spent her sabbatical traveling in the Mediterranean last year and has decided that preparing herself for these programs requires her speaking and reading modern Greek, and so she will study modern Greek. It is she says, read, research and teach, research and teach.

Most faculty at Evergreen hold steady to teaching in the discipline they studied in graduate school, though often their expertise not only expands within their own fields but extends to others. A political scientist may first learn about plays written by Camus in one program, may read more in and about Camus, and may come to value how the dramas express ideas he believes students should explore. When planning programs in the next few years, he may suggest they read Camus and offer to take primary responsibility for presentations on his work. Sometimes a faculty member's major interest changes. An historian of 19th century America has become a competent naturalist; a biologist who once researched the inner ear mechanisms which keep fish swimming upright now researches in two other areas: on the one hand, the mechanism of acupuncture and Jin Shin Jyutsu, a Japanese form of acupressure, and on the other, the geometrical proportions and numerology used by people laying out and constructing Gothic cathedrals.

In the past ten years, colleges connected to the Evergreen-based Washington Center consortium have enthusiastically experimented with several kinds of learning communities. Many have found ways to include even the radical structure of the Evergreen coordinated studies program in institutions organized by traditional courses. The key has been to adapt. Because students who finish a coordinated studies program at Seattle Central Community College, for instance, will receive standard college credits for a set of courses, the responsibility of each teacher is to include within the coordinated studies program an amount and a kind of work which meets the expectations of a course in her discipline. If the learning community offers Anthropology 120, English 102, and History 230, the fundamentals of those courses must be part of the program. Teachers assess what is most important, what is absolutely essential for the students to learn. Some teachers consult those who teach the next course in a sequence. Others, often in conversations with their team, interrogate their disciplinary knowledge: what are the basic assumptions, how do they differ from assumptions in other fields, what fundamental concepts, terms, skills must students at this level learn? Through this process, even science teachers have discovered that "essential" is not the same as everything in a 600-page textbook.

Planning a fully integrated learning community may seem unfamiliar to young faculty and even unsettling for experienced teachers. Experienced teachers enter class on the first day, year after year, with a smile because they come with a tried and true syllabus. It includes a sequence of topics, a selection of texts, the timing of artfully worded assignments (all on disk—at one time on ditto masters), models for the mid-term and final, dates for those delicious points to made in one or another already written lecture, afternoons for specific workshops, research trips, and films. All in all, the subject, whatever it is—politics in ancient Greece, intro to sociology, or the literature of emerging nations—takes the shape of this course, fitted to the teacher's special strengths. (Many of us talk about our educations as a collection of such artifacts: "Howells's Joyce ," "Baenan's cultural anthropology," and "Costigan's English history.") In an integrated learning community, what we teach occurs in a new context, different lights shine on it. We see it differently, often afresh. To prepare for teaching in a learning community, most teachers read more, often much more, within their own fields and outside of it. We venture out from what we know through and through. We may take some treasures from our old Sociology 110 or English 263 and transform them. Moving out of a time-honored syllabus to a fully integrated learning community may feel like space travel—no gravity, some queasiness.

The intrepid team plans on, with confidence in their disciplinary knowledge and pedagogic know-how, to shape a term of study for a group of about seventy-five students. The curriculum for the learning community can include lectures, workshops, lab time, seminars, computer time and training, guest speakers, field trips, films, music, student presentations, peer editing, several kinds of group work and group assignments, exams, papers, portfolios, and self evaluations. This list does not exhaust the possibilities.

For many program activities—lectures, presentations, films, and field trips, for instance—the students and teachers all meet together. At other times students work in smaller groups. A central piece of a program based on the Evergreen model is the book seminar. Twice a week for two hours students divide in groups of twenty to twenty-five and, along with one of the teachers, meet to discuss the book at hand. Meiklejohn considered great books the center of a liberal education, and while not every book we choose is "great," we build coordinated programs around texts, primary texts, significant texts, but not textbooks. Usually the books are chosen because they help develop the theme of the program, but sometimes program themes arise because people want passionately to use certain books. Usually, seminars cover one book a week, and the selection of the books is critical because they carry much of the program content. This routine seems familiar to a literature teacher for whom content often is the great book—Shakespeare's plays, a novel by Eliot, Douglass's autobiography, and so on. It seems less routine for an anthropologist to assign the *Mismeasure of Man,* or *Tristes Tropiques* rather than a textbook. During the quarter, often one of the faculty will give a preparatory lecture before a book is discussed, but the main work of learning from the text and about the text, of making connections between the text and other parts of the program, occurs in the students' seminar discussions. Many faculty find helping students develop rich, productive seminars the hardest work of the program but also the most rewarding.

Michael Oakeshott proposes we think of different fields of endeavor and inquiry as a "variety of distinct languages of understanding." We think of these languages as a variety of voices, he says,

> each the expression of a distinct and conditional understanding of the world and a distinct idiom of human self-under-

standing, and of the culture itself as these voices joined, as such voices could only be joined, in conversation—an endless unrehearsed intellectual adventure in which, in imagination, we enter into a variety of modes of understanding the world and ourselves and are not disconcerted by the differences or dismayed by the inconclusiveness of it all. And perhaps we may recognize liberal learning as, above all else, an education in imagination, an initiation into the art of this conversation in which we learn to recognize the voices; to distinguish their different modes of utterance, to acquire the intellectual and moral habits appropriate to this conversational relationship and thus make our *debut dans la vie humaine.* (p. 39)

While an entire learning community constitutes such a conversation, the seminar, the integrating seminar or the book seminar, offers the time and space for a more intense apprenticeship. In seminar, students sometimes discuss the tough, transcendent, often inflammatory issues, in ways that, frankly, make their occasion the best thing in life and give faculty hope for the human race.

The seminar structure in coordinated studies and in other learning community models also has implications for assessment and evaluation. That is, teachers in stand-alone classes note the progress there of, perhaps, ninety or more students in a quarter or semester. A history teacher may have no idea how a particular student is faring in anthropology or math because students don't bother him about problems in other courses, don't mention dropping calculus halfway through the quarter. The teacher probably thinks an adviser keeps track. Teachers in learning communities do better because they routinely talk a lot about students, and students do report in more.

In learning communities each faculty member gets to know each student in the program, but the closest and richest contact between student and teacher is through the seminar. The twenty-five students in a seminar usually stay together for the quarter or semester, usually with the same teacher who evaluates the students' seminar work and who reads and comments on the students' writing. Further, since she attends the lectures they attend, sees the films, and participates in workshops, she keeps track of their work in the whole program, that is, in all of their school work. She understands how each student is confronting and integrating the material. At the end of a quarter at Evergreen, each teacher writes a lengthy narrative evaluation of each student in the seminar, and each student writes a narrative self-evaluation. Teacher and student discuss these evaluations in conference. At other Washington colleges, we give grades, but we adapt the narrative evaluation process because it has been so powerful for students. Students are sometimes stunned by the attention, by being taken so seriously—as the teacher notes, for instance, the student's curiosity, his ironic approach to the officially significant, his quickness at seeing unlikely connections, his precise and methodical lab work, his particularly lucid explanations during discussion, his trouble with commas, and/or his self-deprecating attitude when making presentations. Ultimately, a student keeps track of himself, but the close contact between students and teachers in learning communities gives the student tremendous support. He gains confidence in reflecting on his own intellectual capabilities, assessing his own accomplishments, and setting himself new goals. Links, clusters, FIGs, and CSP's all help students take responsibility for their own learning.

If these boundary-crossing learning communities seem intriguing and you would like to be involved, find out what is happening on your own campus. Learning communities often appear in honors programs or programs for freshman. General education requirements may be integrated. Certain curricula—women's studies, for instance—may include integrated studies or course-linking structures. Often communication courses, such as writing and speech, are linked to courses in other disciplines.

And remember, it is possible to start from scratch. Talk to someone you would like to teach with. (At Evergreen faculty members are free to "date." They say, "I'd like to teach with you sometime.") Choose your likely colleague or colleagues carefully. Usually, programs arise from shared interests or from friendship, one usually preceding the other. At Seattle Central, all faculty members who want to teach in coordinated studies attend an annual retreat. Approached by a historian to work in a program about the changing lives of women after World War II, a new English teacher might have to make a quick decision: to join or not to join. It depends on her own interest and strength in the period, her information about the historian, and her assessment of the program's possibilities. She may be persuaded when she suggests that students do oral histories and the historian agrees. After initial discussion, they begin planning, along with, say, an art historian or a sociologist. They learn about each others' styles, they see where their work complements, they draw on unexpected resources of experiences and knowledge, and they may build the program nicely.

On the other hand, things can go wrong. For reasons foreseen and unforeseen, some people are not able to work together, and we learn this by trying. There are many ways to start a learning community. Think about your interests, think about likely colleagues, and give yourself time to get ready.

At schools which offer learning communities, the logistics of time, space, and registration have been worked out, but if you are just starting, remember to handle the logistics well before the quarter begins. Assuming you want to schedule a linked course with another teacher, the simplest way is to schedule the two classes in succeeding hours, e.g. composition at nine and oceanography at ten. (We don't advise, though, scheduling all the courses in a cluster one after the other.) The necessary information and instructions for the students must be in the college schedule. You will want to enlist the help of advisers so that students actually enroll. We have found that enthusiastic advising makes a huge difference in successful learning community enrollments. Enlisting the support and administrative savvy of a person with formal administrative authority (a Division Chairperson, an Associate Dean, or the Office of the Vice-Provost for Undergraduate Affairs) can often help you through the administrative maze.

You may propose an even more integrated link, scheduling a two hour block with double the number of students and team teaching both hours. (If the standard enrollment for oceanography, however, exceeds that for English, the faculty/student ratio would drop and incur some added expense.) You would gain tremendous latitude in planning and organizing the program. The two hour stretch may be spent on a single activity. You have options such as a long film, a nicely organized lecture/workshop on a particular topic, a panel of guests, a book seminar, or lab. Note that you will need one larger space for all the students to meet together and two smaller spaces for students to meet in seminar. Basically, this is also how we schedule large coordinated studies programs: in large blocks of time and with room assignments such that students can meet altogether at some times and in separate seminars at others.

We stress that administrative support is essential. If the head of the earth sciences department seems skeptical, for instance, see if the chairperson of English is more sympathetic. A Dean makes an excellent ally. Administrators have been more supportive if the learning community helps address an explicit need or problem on the campus, by helping freshman succeed in their first term, for instance, by enabling students to build coherence in their general education course work, by strengthening writing across the curriculum, or by deepening faculty development.

Learning communities may also address very specific local problems. It may be that nursing students have trouble with the mathematics required in chemistry. By linking mathematics and chemistry, the teachers can work together on how to enable the students to think algebraically. Attaching a study skills class may solve the problem of high attrition in a biology class or in world civilization. If ESL students have difficulty following the specialized terminology of a course, a study skills course may be linked to a content area; working with another teacher, an anthropologist may discover his illustrative examples are simply baffling because culture-bound. Integrating lower division courses can also help students make better career decisions. Rather than simply fulfilling distribution or general education requirements, an integrated program may provide students with a platform, a clearer sense of what it means to be a environmental scientist, a psychologist, or a politician.

In order to confront the high attrition rate among African-American students at Seattle Central, African-American faculty members have developed and teach a coordinated studies program offering basic first-year courses but thematically designed to draw on the experiences and to address the issues that are central for these students. It offers a safe but challenging introduction to academic culture. The spirit of welcome, the high expectations, the collaborative work, and the sense of community help students persist. More of them stay in college, take part in student government, and go on to baccalaureate schools.

It is important to know that links, FIG's, and coordinated studies have all made a difference in student retention. Vincent Tinto, retention guru, reports that students in learning communities not only persist in greater numbers than students in regular classes, but that learning communities make a significant difference in students' motivation and engagement with the academic enterprise. Other studies suggest that learning community alumni have higher GPA's and graduate at a higher rate. Generally, learning communities promote a sense of community that can make all the difference for many urban, commuter students. They provide rich opportunities for the interactions among teachers and students which Alexander A. Astin's studies show make the most difference in a student's learning and development.

The sense of community can make all the difference for teachers, too. For a young faculty member, observing old hands at work can help her find her particular style and voice, can help her build her own collection of effective teaching tools. Even experienced teachers have revolutionized their practice after a quarter in a learning community. Others have refined their practice, picking up subtle things they see their colleagues try: suggesting students set a goal at the beginning of a seminar, placing things in a visual order on the blackboard rather than hither and yon, or having students write about what they do not understand in math class. Unlike the guarded atmosphere generated in competitive scholarly research, within a teaching team, within an institution, and even among institutions nation-wide, learning community faculty have a buoyant sense of shared enterprise.

We caution you that teaching in learning communities means work. At the outset it may seem less work because other people share the responsibility for planning, lecturing, Xeroxing, and so on. You may not need to learn modern Greek, but preparing and planning takes time. Collaborative teaching may be exhilarating, but it can also be frustrating and time consuming. You may lecture less, but lectures in learning communities often entail unexpected research because teachers get big, new ideas, modeling the kind of inquiry and synthesis they expect of students. After years of repeating the same courses, insulated in departments, classrooms, and research, teachers who take up learning communities find themselves exhausted (and excited) by teaching and learning with each other in a multi-disciplinary collaborative environment. Yet, learning communities have revitalized lots of ground-down, demoralized teachers.

Because learning communities are exciting and time-consuming, be careful. If your future depends on your spending time in another way, don't undertake them. Also, do not undertake learning communities if your institution does not reward involvement in new teaching initiatives, especially if you do not have tenure. Be aware of the local politics.

If you can, forge ahead. The venture is worth the risk. You stand to gain—or regain—the freshness and vigor forever the heart of education, of knowledge in the making. And so do your students. They tell about learning communities:

Up until this program, I've been used to getting the answers from the teachers and things on the board. You know, take good notes, pay good attention to what's in front of you. And pretty much feel cut off—you know, the other students are just learning, they don't have the answers. But in this class I've heard some *brilliant* things from other students. I've come to most of my insights through other people. I've really had to look at the way I've been listening to people, and my prejudices in shutting other people's ideas down, and of thinking that I know where the answers spring from.

The integrated studies model . . . is an extraordinary, power-ful, and valuable medium. It was in the context of this model that I began to learn new ways of thinking, rather then simply collecting quanta of information as I had (quite successfully) done at universities I had previously attended. This is the first place I got any *education* at all: where I had the opportunity to integrate bits and chunks of information I was collecting and to synthesize them into a new under-standing of the world I live in, of myself, and of my role as a member of society. It's like the difference between collecting a pile of bricks and building a house.

When I decided to go back to school, I ended up in a coor-dinated studies program where I had an experience I had never had before. The teacher left the lectern and sat beside me. Instead of having teachers just tell me what I should know, they were there learning with us, being exposed to subjects from new perspectives. That way each teacher also became a student. It wasn't such a power structure anymore, but a learning environment, humanized, where everyone was learning. I learned that I have knowledge, that I have what it takes to pursue knowledge, to gain knowledge. I left coordinated studies with the sense that I was free to learn rather than forced to learn.

Learning communities allow us all to be teachers and learners in the deepest sense, to be discovers, explorers, and builders together.

References

Abercrombie, M. L. J. *The Anatomy of Judgement.* Basic Books, 1960.

Astin, Alexander W. *What Matters in College: Four Critical Years Revisited.* Jossey-Bass, 1993.

Avens, C. and R. Zelley. "A Report on the Intellectual Development of Students in the Quanta Learning Community at Daytona Beach Community College 1989-1990." Unpublished report. Daytona Beach (Florida) Community College, 1993.

Barthes, Roland. *Elements of Semiology.* Trans. Annette Lavers and Colin Smith. Hill and Wang, 1968.

Bruffee, Kenneth A. *Collaborative Learning: Higher Education, Interdependence, and the Authority of Knowledge.* Johns Hopkins University Press, 1993.

Derrida, Jacques. *Of Grammatology.* Trans. Gayatri Chakravorty Spivak. Johns Hopkins University Press, 1976.

Fish, Stanley Eugene. *Is There a Text in This Class? The Authority of Interpretive Communities.* Harvard University Press, 1980.

Foucault, Michel. *The Order of Things: An Archaeology of the Human Sciences.* Trans. of Les Mots et les choses. Pantheon, 1971.

Freire, Paulo. *Pedagogy of the Oppressed.* Trans. Myra Bergman Ramos. Herder, 1970.

Gabelnick, Faith, Jean MacGregor, Roberta S. Matthews, and Barbara Leigh Smith. "Learning Communities: Building

Connections Among Disciplines, Students, and Faculty." *New Directions in Teaching and Learning*, No. 41. Jossey-Bass, 1990.

_____ "Learning Communities and General Education." Perspectives, 22(1): 1992.

Geertz, Clifford. *Local Knowledge: Further Essays in Interpretive Anthropology.* Basic Books, 1983.

Gould, Stephen Jay. *The Mismeasure of Man.* Norton, 1981.

Hill, Patrick J. "Communities of Learners: Curriculum as the Infrastructure of Academic Communities." In J. W. Hall and B. L. Kevles (eds.), *In Opposition to the Core Curriculum: Alternative Models of Undergraduate Education.* Greenwood Press, 1985.

_____ "The Rationale for Learning Communities." Paper presented at the Inaugural Conference of the Washington Center for Improving the Quality of Undergraduate Education, Olympia, WA, 1985.

hooks, bell. *Teaching to Transgress: Education as the Practice of Freedom.* Routledge, 1994.

Jameson, Fredric. *The Prison-House of Language: A Critical Account of Structuralism and Russian Formalism.* Princeton University Press, 1972.

Jones, Richard. *Experiment at Evergreen.* Schenkman, 1981.

Kaplan, Robert. "The Coming Anarchy." *The Atlantic Monthly* Feb. 1994: 44-82.

Kristeva, Julia. *Desire in Language: a Semiotic Approach to Literature and Art.* Ed. Leon S. Roudiez. Trans. Thomas Gora, Alice Jardine, Leon S. Roudiez. Columbia University Press, 1980.

Kuhn, Thomas. S. *The Structure of Scientific Revolutions.* University of Chicago Press, 1962.

Lacan, Jacques. *The Language of the Self: The Function of Language in Psychoanalysis.* Trans. with notes by Anthony Wilden. Johns Hopkins UP, 1968.

Levi Strauss, Claude. *Tristes Tropiques.* Trans. John Weightman and Doreen Weightman. Atheneum, 1974.

MacGregor, Jean. "Intellectual Development of Students in Learning Community Programs, 1986-1987." Washington

Center Occasional Paper #1. The Evergreen State College, 1987.

Matthews, Roberta S. "Enriching Teaching and Learning through Learning Communities." In *Teaching and Learning in the Community College*. Ed. T. O'Banion. American Association of Community Colleges, 1994.

Meiklejohn, Alexander. *The Experimental College*. Harper and Row, 1932.

Oakeshott, Michael Joseph. *The Voice of Liberal Learning: Michael Oakeshott on Education*. Ed. Timothy Fuller. Yale University Press, 1989.

Peirce, Charles S. *Collected Papers of Charles Saunders Peirce*. 8 vols. Eds. Charles Hartshorne and Paul Weiss. Harvard University Press, 1931.

Rorty, Richard. *Philosophy and the Mirror of Nature*. Princeton University Press, 1979.

Smith, Barbara Leigh. "Taking Structure Seriously: The Learning Community Model." *Liberal Education* 77 (1991): 42-48.

Said, Edward. W. *Orientalism*. Pantheon, 1978.

Saussure, Ferdinand. *Course in General Linguistics*. Eds. Charles Bally and Albert Reidlinger. Trans. Wade Baskin. Philosophical Library, 1959.

Tinto, Vincent, Anne Goodsell-Love, and Pat Russo. "Building Learning Communities for New College Students: A Summary of Research Finding of the Collaborative Learning Project," Syracuse University, National Center on Postsecondary Teaching, Learning and Assessment.

Tokuno, Kenneth A. and Frederick L. Campbell. "Freshman Interest Groups at the University of Washington: Effects on Retention and Scholarship." *Journal of the Freshman Year Experience* 5 (1992): 7-22.

Treisman, Uri. "A Study of the Mathematics Performance of Black Students at the University of California, Berkeley." Doctoral Dissertation, University of California, Berkeley, 1985.

Tussman, Joseph. *Experiment at Berkeley*. Oxford University Press, 1969.

Vygotsky, L. S. *Thought and Language*. Eds. and trans. Eugenia Hanfmann and Gertrude Vakar. MIT Press, 1962.

Wilkie, Gail. "Learning Communities Enrollment Study, 1986-1990 at North Seattle Community College," North Seattle Community College.

Wittgenstein, Ludwig. *Philosophical Investigations*. Trans. G. E. M. Anscombe. B. Blackwell, 1953.

Afterword: New Paradigms for College Teaching

Karl A. Smith & Alisha A. Waller

Karl Smith and Alisha Waller are authors of Chapter 9, *Cooperative Learning for New College Teachers.* Smith teaches civil engineering at the University of Minnesota; Waller teaches mathematics and computer science at Macalester College, St. Paul, MN.

A paradigm shift is taking place in college teaching, many aspects of which are described by the authors of this book. As each chapter's extent of change illustrates in detail, minor modifications in current teaching practices will not solve the current problems with college instruction. Teaching success in today's world requires a new approach. This chapter starts by summarizing the paradigm we're leaving behind at various rates in colleges and universities across the country. We then present our take on the paradigms we are entering into, explore implications of the changing paradigm for students and faculty, and close by offering some suggestions for fostering change. The aim of this chapter is to stimulate thinking about the changing nature of college teaching and learning and to encourage the reader to engage in reflection and conversation.

The old paradigm of college teaching is based on John Locke's *tabula rasa:* the untrained student mind is like a blank sheet of paper waiting for the instructor to write on it. Student minds are viewed as empty vessels into which teachers pour their wisdom. Because of these and other assumptions, teachers think of teaching in terms of these principal activities and perspectives:

- **Transferring knowledge from teacher to students.** The teacher's job is to give it; the student's job is to get it. Teachers transmit information to students in a one-way interaction.

- **Filling passive, empty vessels with knowledge.** Students are passive recipients of knowledge. Teachers own the knowledge but students are not invited to share that ownership.

- **Students are expected to memorize relevant information.** Tests typically require recall or recognition, e.g., recall memorized formulae and plug in values. Homework assignments are typically pattern matching—see examples in class, do similar problems on homework with the data changed. Although faculty routinely claim that they are interested in promoting critical thinking, course syllabi show that they require memorization, recognition and recall.

- **Classifying students by deciding who gets which grade and sorting students into categories** by deciding who does and does not meet the requirements to be graduated, go on to graduate school, and get a good job. There is constant inspection to weed out any defective students. Teachers classify and sort students into categories under the assumption that ability is fixed, is observable in the current system, and is unaffected by effort and education.

- **Students strive to obtain certification** by checking off requirements, then promptly forgetting much of what occurred in each class that was checked off.

- **Conducting education within a context of impersonal relationships among students and between teachers and students.** Based on the assembly line model of industrial organizations, students and teachers are perceived to be interchangeable and replaceable parts in the educational machine.

- **Maintaining a competitive classroom structure** in which students work to outperform their classmates and faculty work to outperform their colleagues.

- **Cultural uniformity in the classroom is assumed;** students are expected to conform. The same background is assumed for all students through tightly controlled sequences of prerequisites. The goal for each student is the same—one size fits all. "Fairness" means treating each student exactly the same despite their individual differences or needs. The context of knowledge development is ignored or discounted, e.g., math developed by Persians or Mayans.

- **Power is tightly held by faculty.** All topics, assignments, and activities are decided by faculty. An individual student is seen as an independent, self-sufficient unit. Faculty judge student performance, answer questions, explain the correct way of doing or interpreting, etc. Students sit quietly in their seats—eyes front, feet on floor, and mouth shut.

- **Assessment conducted in "objective" mode, often by multiple choice tests.** Minimal assessment formats and infrequent testing (mid-term and final) are common. Student rating of instruction at the end of the course is the only form of faculty/course assessment.

- **A logico-scientific mode of knowing** is assumed. Rational, logical arguments are the only ones accepted. Data must be objective and quantitative. Individual's experiences are averaged together to find the "normal" experience. Logical proof of propositions is required. Empirical evidence must be statistically significant to count.

- How we know is based on the **reductionist,** building-block universe model. Conciseness and elegance are highly valued. The final result is all that matters.

- The use of **instructional technology** is actively resisted by many faculty. "Chalk and talk was good enough for me so it's good enough for them" is a common reaction to the use of instructional technology. Fear of being replaced by a machine is another common (and irrational) reaction to instructional technology.

- **Assuming that anyone with expertise in their field can teach without training to do so.** This is sometimes known as the content premise —if you have a Ph.D. in the field, you can teach. Few college faculty have ever taken a formal course in college teaching; therefore, they typically do not know much about educational research, have not read the literature, and hence do not know the state-of-the-art of college teaching.

Thus, the old paradigm is to transfer faculty's knowledge to passive students as the faculty classify and sort students in a norm-referenced way through competition. Many teachers consider the old paradigm to be the only possibility. Lecturing, while requiring students to be passive, silent, isolated, and in competition with each other, seems the only way to teach. The old paradigm is carried forward by sheer momentum. However, many faculty recognize a growing concern that all is not well.

In many college classrooms, we are dropping the old paradigm of teaching and adopting new paradigms based on theory and research that has clear applications to instruction.

- **Classmates and teachers are seen as collaborators rather than as obstacles to students' own academic and personal success.** Teachers, therefore, structure learning situations so that students work together to maximize each other's achievement. Administrators, likewise, create a cooperative, team-based organizational structure within which faculty work together to ensure each other's success.

- **Students construct, discover, transform, and extend their own knowledge.** Learning is something the learner does, not something that is done to a learner. Students do not passively accept knowledge from the teacher or curriculum. They use new information to activate their existing cognitive structures or construct new ones. The teacher's role in this activity is to create the conditions within which students can construct meaning from new material, study by processing it through existing cognitive structures, and then retain it in long-term memory where it remains open to further processing and possible reconstruction.

- **Students learn by creating connections; by discovering relationships.** Teachers foster thinking about connections among subject matter and across disciplines. Instead of asking students to memorize formulae, they give them a list of formulae and ask them to use them, explain them, justify them, and explore further implications of them.

- **Teachers' efforts are aimed at developing students' competencies and talents.** Colleges and universities add value to graduates by cultivating talent. A 'cultivate and develop' philosophy must replace the 'select and weed out' philosophy. Students' competencies and talents are developed under the assumption that with effort and education, any student can improve.

- **Students approach school as an opportunity to learn and grow.** They work on developing competencies and accomplishing their goals. Students work to build portfolios containing relevant and meaningful experiences.

- **Teachers and students work together, making education a personal transaction.** All education is a social process that can occur only through interpersonal interaction. The more pressure placed on students to achieve and the more difficult the material to be learned, the more important it is to provide social support within the learning situation. Challenge and support are balanced so that students can cope successfully with the stress inherent in learning situations. Learning results when individuals cooperate to construct shared understandings and knowledge. Teachers build positive relationships with students and create the conditions within which students build caring and committed relationships with each other. The school becomes a learning community of committed scholars in the truest sense.

- **A cooperative context is required.** When students interact in a competitive context, communication is minimized, misleading and false information is often communicated, assistance is viewed as cheating, and classmates and faculty tend to dislike and distrust each other. A cooperative learning situation, on the other hand, encourages active construction of knowledge and the development of talent by connecting previously isolated students and creating positive relationships among classmates and teachers.

- **Diversity of life experiences are celebrated and used to enrich all students' experience.** Personal development goals are set by each student. 'Fairness' means meeting each student where they currently are and helping them progress as far as possible. Faculty recognize context and encourage student connection with it.

- **Power is shared between students and faculty.** Students are given choices of project topics and among a variety of evaluation methods. Individuals are part of an interdependent team. Students assess themselves and others. They use primary sources and develop their own ways of learning. Students arrange physical space to their best advantage—working in groups, on board, at computers, etc.

- **Assessment is conducted in a variety of formats.** A rich variety of assessment formats (written, oral, group, personal-portfolio, journal, etc.) and frequent testing (classroom assessment, progress checks, etc. in addition to mid-term and final) are common. Students review instruction at mid-term in addition to the end of the course. Student management teams are commonly used to build quality into the process rather than inspecting it in at the end.

- **Knowing is narrative.** According to the founder of social psychology, Kurt Lewin, "All theory is really autobiography." Context and personal experience are valued. Faculty and students acknowledge the filters people use in gathering and interpreting data. Qualitative data in addition to quantitative data is valued. Each individual's experience is valued on its own. Different experiences are woven together through synthesis. Intuition and initial hypotheses are valued. Even small sample sizes can provide insight.

- **Learning in a constructivist epistemology involves personal self-reflection to resolve internal issues.** The resolution of inner issues occurs through concrete experience, collaborative discourse, and self-reflection. Multiple ways of understanding are sought and valued. The process of developing one's current understanding important.

- **Technology has great potential to enhance the capabilities of the learner and the teacher.** Recent developments in computer-based multimedia, networking, software tools, graphics, etc. indicate that technology can enhance both what students learn and how they learn it. The rapid growth of the Internet and World Wide Web in educational settings are outstanding examples of the positive potential of technology.

- **Teaching is a complex application of theory and research that requires considerable training and continual refinement**

of skills and procedures. Becoming a good teacher is an ongoing commitment that requires a sustained effort.

Major differences between the old and new paradigms of college teaching are summarized in the following table.

Comparison of Old and New Paradigms for College Teaching[1]

	Old Paradigm	New Paradigm
Knowledge	Transferred from Faculty to Students	Jointly Constructed by Students and Faculty
Students	Passive Vessel to be Filled by Faculty's Knowledge	Active Constructor, Discoverer, Transformer of Knowledge
Mode of Learning	Memorizing	Relating
Faculty Purpose	Classify and Sort Students	Develop Students' Competencies and Talents
Student Grow, Goals	Students Strive to Complete Requirements, Achieve Certification within a Discipline	Students Strive to Focus on Continual Lifelong Learning within a Broader System
Relationships	Impersonal Relationship Among Students and Between Faculty and Students	Personal Transaction Among Students and Between Faculty and Students
Context	Competitive/ Individualistic	Cooperative Learning in Classroom and Cooperative Teams Among Faculty

[1]Adapted from Johnson, David W., Johnson, Roger T., & Smith, Karl A. 1991, *Active learning: Cooperation in the college classroom.* Edina, MN: Interaction Book Company.

	Old Paradigm	**New Paradigm**
Climate	Conformity/ Cultural Uniformity	Diversity and Personal Esteem/Cultural Diversity and Commonality
Power	Faculty Holds and Exercises Power, Authority, and Control	Students are Empowered; Power is Shared Among Students and Between Students and Faculty
Assessment	Norm-Referenced (i.e., Graded "On the Curve"); Typically Multiple Choice Items; Student rating of instruction at end of course	Criterion-Referenced; Typically Performances and Portfolios; Continual Assessment of Instruction
Ways of Knowing	Logico-Scientific	Narrative
Epistemology	Reductionist; Facts and Memorization	Constructivist; Inquiry and Invention
Technology Use	Drill and Practice; Textbook Substitute; Chalk and Talk Substitute	Problem Solving, Communication, Collaboration, Information Access, Expression
Teaching Assumption	Any Expert can Teach	Teaching is Complex and Requires Considerable Training

and impersonal character of many college classrooms. [co]operative learning among students in the classroom, and among [facu]lty in departments, colleges and universities is central to achieving positive and constructive change in higher education.

Other contributors to this book suggest different paths to a new [pa]radigm: encouraging students to write to learn (Bishop and [Fu]lwiler), using stories in teaching (Noddings), beginning each [co]urse with complete and inclusive syllabi (Collins), guiding students to learn actively (Nelson), building quality into the learning [p]rocess through student management teams (Nuhfer), forming [l]earning communities (Bystrom), providing electronic means of connecting with students (Creed), drawing knowledge maps (Dansereau and Newbern), and providing a structure for constructively managing controversy on the classroom (Johnson and Johnson). The various proponents of these techniques are convinced that they help students learn.

But don't forget Parker Palmer's admonition: good teaching cannot be reduced to technique. Good teaching, he told us in Chapter 1, is a matter of creating the capacity for connectedness between students, between students and the teacher, between students and the material. Any of the techniques described in this book—and a host of others—can be used to create that capacity for connectedness. What's the right technique for you? It all depends: on you, on your students, on your subject matter, on the goals you and your students bring to the course.

We encourage you to try any or all of the techniques presented in this volume. Take a piece of one, a fragment of another, the philosophical underpinnings of a third, and combine them together to create a new paradigm of college teaching for yourself. Try it, modify it, try something different, modify that, combine it with your first effort, modify it again, and so on. Your students will profit and you'll have much more fun teaching.

References

Barr, Robert B. and Tagg, John. "From Teaching to Learning: A New Paradigm for Undergraduate Education," in *Change*, 27 (6), 1995.

Implications of the New Paradigms and Questions to Ask Self and Students

Just as a fish cannot see the water it lives in, students and faculty often have difficulty seeing the context within which they live. What is your reaction to our list of shifting paradigms? Let's look at some specific aspects. For example, a common fear of beginning faculty is whether they will have enough material to cover during a class period. Bishop and Fulwiler mention this fear in their chapter. Is this a fear of yours? Having enough material to cover is a central tenet of the old paradigm of college teaching. A question faculty would ask under the new paradigms is "How shall I structure the learning environment so that students can explore and discover the important concepts in this course?"

Many beginning faculty assume that students will help each other outside of class, without crossing the line of cheating. However, it is difficult for students to know where that line is if they only work independently in the classroom. The new paradigms ask "How can I help students learn to work cooperatively where each member pulls their own weight?" Practicing teamwork in class will lead to improved teamwork, without cheating, outside of class.

As a final example, consider power negotiation. In the old paradigm, faculty hold power and decision-making with any negotiation being done implicitly. The new paradigm calls for explicit negotiation of power. One way of doing this is to have students write what they like best about the course on one side of an index card and what they would like changed on the other. Then the faculty can sort the change requests into three piles: (1) things that are easy to change, e.g., using bigger chalk that is easier to see from the back of the room; (2) things that the faculty member cannot or will not change, e.g., the temperature of the room or written lab reports; and (3) things that will be explicitly negotiated at the next class meeting, e.g., the dates for exams. One can conduct this assessment and negotiation at two weeks, four weeks, and eight weeks to keep the communication and negotiation explicit and open.

The environment of college teaching is changing rapidly. For example, there are growing pressures in many schools to do more with less and to do a better job. The sense of isolation that many faculty feel, coupled with these mounting pressures, make it very difficult to challenge the status quo and adopt a new paradigm of college teaching. In the next section we will provide some of our thoughts on fostering change.

Fostering Change

Major change, by its nature, is intentionally disruptive and largely unprogrammable. In comparing the management of major versus normal change, one top executive said, "It used to be like I-75. You'd lay it out from Toledo to Tampa. Now it's more like a white-water raft ride. You try to get the right people in the raft and do the best you can to steer it. But you never know what's just around the bend." (Katzenbach & Smith, 1993, p. 208)

Innovation in higher education is contingent on faculty deciding to change the way they work with students and with each other. We suggest establishing or, if already present, strengthening three key conditions for personal and organizational change (Johnson & Johnson, 1989):

1. Promote an attitude of experimentation. Changing the way in which faculty help students learn requires an atmosphere in which there is a willingness to try things and learn from what is attempted.

2. Synthesize common goals, such as "How well are we doing with our students and faculty?". Meaningful change requires everyone pulling together to achieve a common goal.

3. Create collegial support networks of faculty, students, and administrators. Change is hard and typically does not occur without a group of colleagues who care and provide support and encouragement for one another. The research support for cooperation among faculty is just as strong as that for cooperation among students.

One of the best described examples of change in higher education is the restructuring of the MBA program at the Weatherhead School of Management at Case Western Reserve University (Boyatzis, Cowen & Kolb, 1994). They restructu[red] on teaching to a focus on learning. Specifically, focus on how students' organize knowledge by re curriculum in a less discipline-defined and more pro and contextual way. They followed six principles for likelihood of successful organizational change:

1. Adopt an outside-in perspective.

2. Build on the seeds of vision and strategy that lie within.

3. Develop a collaborative attitude.

4. Challenge convention and tradition.

5. Focus on substance rather than form.

6. Provide multifaced leadership.

Further examples of the new paradigm in higher educati include the move to problem-based learning in medicine (se Chapter 1 for a brief description) and veterinary medicine and th extensive changes as a result of the reform calculus movement (including active and interactive learning and the new four prong approach to teaching calculus—symbolic, graphical, numerical and linguistic).

Conclusions

The biggest and most long-lasting reforms of undergraduate education will come when individual faculty or small groups of instructors adopt the view of themselves as reformers within their immediate sphere of influence, the classes they teach every day. (Cross, 1993).

Our favorite means of shifting to the new paradigms of teaching in the college classroom is to use cooperative learning. Cooperative learning provides the means of operationalizing the new paradigm of college teaching and provides the context within which the development of student talent is encouraged. Carefully structured cooperative learning ensures that students are cognitively, physically, emotionally, and psychologically actively involved in constructing their own knowledge and is an important step in changing the pas-

Berquist, William H. *The postmodern organization: Mastering the art of irreversible change.* Jossey-Bass, 1994.

Brooks, J.G. & Brooks, M.G. *In Search of Understanding: The Case for Constructivist Teaching.* ASCD, 1993.

Boyatzis, Richard, Cowen, Scott S., & Kolb, David A. *Innovation in Professional Education: Steps on a journey from teaching to learning.* Jossey-Bass, 1994.

Bruner, Jerome. "Narrative and paradigmatic modes of thought," in Elliot Eisner (Ed.), *Learning and Teaching: The ways of knowing.* Eighty-fourth Yearbook of the National Society for the Study of Education. The University of Chicago Press, 1987.

Cross, K. Patricia. On college teaching. *Journal of Engineering Education.* January, 9-14, 1993.

Dobyns, Lloyd and Crawford-Mason, Clare. *Thinking about quality: Progress, wisdom, and the Deming philosophy.* Times, 1994.

Dywer, David. "Apple classrooms of tomorrow: What we've learned," in *Educational Leadership,* 51(7), 1994.

Johnson, D.W. & Johnson, R. T. *Leading the cooperative school.* Edina, MN: Interaction Book Company, 1989.

Johnson, David W., Johnson, Roger T., & Smith, Karl A. *Active learning: Cooperation in the college classroom.* Interaction, 1991. Also see Johnson, David W., Johnson, Roger T., & Smith, Karl A. *Cooperative learning: Increasing college faculty instructional productivity.* ASHE-ERIC Report on Higher Education 91-4, 1991.

Katzenbach, Jon R. & Smith, Douglas K. *The wisdom of teams: Creating the high-performance organization.* Harvard Business School Press, 1993.

Norman, Donald A. *Things that make us smart: Defending human attributes in the age of the machine.* Addison-Wesley, 1993.

Date Due

Implications of the New Paradigms and Questions to Ask Self and Students

Just as a fish cannot see the water it lives in, students and faculty often have difficulty seeing the context within which they live. What is your reaction to our list of shifting paradigms? Let's look at some specific aspects. For example, a common fear of beginning faculty is whether they will have enough material to cover during a class period. Bishop and Fulwiler mention this fear in their chapter. Is this a fear of yours? Having enough material to cover is a central tenet of the old paradigm of college teaching. A question faculty would ask under the new paradigms is "How shall I structure the learning environment so that students can explore and discover the important concepts in this course?"

Many beginning faculty assume that students will help each other outside of class, without crossing the line of cheating. However, it is difficult for students to know where that line is if they only work independently in the classroom. The new paradigms ask "How can I help students learn to work cooperatively where each member pulls their own weight?" Practicing teamwork in class will lead to improved teamwork, without cheating, outside of class.

As a final example, consider power negotiation. In the old paradigm, faculty hold power and decision-making with any negotiation being done implicitly. The new paradigm calls for explicit negotiation of power. One way of doing this is to have students write what they like best about the course on one side of an index card and what they would like changed on the other. Then the faculty can sort the change requests into three piles: (1) things that are easy to change, e.g., using bigger chalk that is easier to see from the back of the room; (2) things that the faculty member cannot or will not change, e.g., the temperature of the room or written lab reports; and (3) things that will be explicitly negotiated at the next class meeting, e.g., the dates for exams. One can conduct this assessment and negotiation at two weeks, four weeks, and eight weeks to keep the communication and negotiation explicit and open.

The environment of college teaching is changing rapidly. For example, there are growing pressures in many schools to do more with less and to do a better job. The sense of isolation that many faculty feel, coupled with these mounting pressures, make it very difficult to challenge the status quo and adopt a new paradigm of college teaching. In the next section we will provide some of our thoughts on fostering change.

Fostering Change

Major change, by its nature, is intentionally disruptive and largely unprogrammable. In comparing the management of major versus normal change, one top executive said, "It used to be like I-75. You'd lay it out from Toledo to Tampa. Now it's more like a whitewater raft ride. You try to get the right people in the raft and do the best you can to steer it. But you never know what's just around the bend." (Katzenbach & Smith, 1993, p. 208)

Innovation in higher education is contingent on faculty deciding to change the way they work with students and with each other. We suggest establishing or, if already present, strengthening three key conditions for personal and organizational change (Johnson & Johnson, 1989):

1. Promote an attitude of experimentation. Changing the way in which faculty help students learn requires an atmosphere in which there is a willingness to try things and learn from what is attempted.

2. Synthesize common goals, such as "How well are we doing with our students and faculty?". Meaningful change requires everyone pulling together to achieve a common goal.

3. Create collegial support networks of faculty, students, and administrators. Change is hard and typically does not occur without a group of colleagues who care and provide support and encouragement for one another. The research support for cooperation among faculty is just as strong as that for cooperation among students.

One of the best described examples of change in higher education is the restructuring of the MBA program at the Weatherhead School of Management at Case Western Reserve University

(Boyatzis, Cowen & Kolb, 1994). They restructured from a focus on teaching to a focus on learning. Specifically, they decided to focus on how students' organize knowledge by reorganizing the curriculum in a less discipline-defined and more problem-centered and contextual way. They followed six principles for increasing the likelihood of successful organizational change:

1. Adopt an outside-in perspective.
2. Build on the seeds of vision and strategy that lie within.
3. Develop a collaborative attitude.
4. Challenge convention and tradition.
5. Focus on substance rather than form.
6. Provide multifaced leadership.

Further examples of the new paradigm in higher education include the move to problem-based learning in medicine (see Chapter 1 for a brief description) and veterinary medicine and the extensive changes as a result of the reform calculus movement (including active and interactive learning and the new four prong approach to teaching calculus—symbolic, graphical, numerical and linguistic).

Conclusions

The biggest and most long-lasting reforms of undergraduate education will come when individual faculty or small groups of instructors adopt the view of themselves as reformers within their immediate sphere of influence, the classes they teach every day. (Cross, 1993).

Our favorite means of shifting to the new paradigms of teaching in the college classroom is to use cooperative learning. Cooperative learning provides the means of operationalizing the new paradigm of college teaching and provides the context within which the development of student talent is encouraged. Carefully structured cooperative learning ensures that students are cognitively, physically, emotionally, and psychologically actively involved in constructing their own knowledge and is an important step in changing the passive and impersonal character of many college classrooms. Cooperative learning among students in the classroom, and among faculty in departments, colleges and universities is central to achieving positive and constructive change in higher education.

Other contributors to this book suggest different paths to a new paradigm: encouraging students to write to learn (Bishop and Fulwiler), using stories in teaching (Noddings), beginning each course with complete and inclusive syllabi (Collins), guiding students to learn actively (Nelson), building quality into the learning process through student management teams (Nuhfer), forming learning communities (Bystrom), providing electronic means of connecting with students (Creed), drawing knowledge maps (Dansereau and Newbern), and providing a structure for constructively managing controversy on the classroom (Johnson and Johnson). The various proponents of these techniques are convinced that they help students learn.

But don't forget Parker Palmer's admonition: good teaching cannot be reduced to technique. Good teaching, he told us in Chapter 1, is a matter of creating the capacity for connectedness between students, between students and the teacher, between students and the material. Any of the techniques described in this book—and a host of others—can be used to create that capacity for connectedness. What's the right technique for you? It all depends: on you, on your students, on your subject matter, on the goals you and your students bring to the course.

We encourage you to try any or all of the techniques presented in this volume. Take a piece of one, a fragment of another, the philosophical underpinnings of a third, and combine them together to create a new paradigm of college teaching for yourself. Try it, modify it, try something different, modify that, combine it with your first effort, modify it again, and so on. Your students will profit and you'll have much more fun teaching.

References

Barr, Robert B. and Tagg, John. "From Teaching to Learning: A New Paradigm for Undergraduate Education," in *Change, 27* (6), 1995.

Berquist, William H. *The postmodern organization: Mastering the art of irreversible change.* Jossey-Bass, 1994.

Brooks, J.G. & Brooks, M.G. *In Search of Understanding: The Case for Constructivist Teaching.* ASCD, 1993.

Boyatzis, Richard, Cowen, Scott S., & Kolb, David A. *Innovation in Professional Education: Steps on a journey from teaching to learning.* Jossey-Bass, 1994.

Bruner, Jerome. "Narrative and paradigmatic modes of thought," in Elliot Eisner (Ed.), *Learning and Teaching: The ways of knowing.* Eighty-fourth Yearbook of the National Society for the Study of Education. The University of Chicago Press, 1987.

Cross, K. Patricia. On college teaching. *Journal of Engineering Education.* January, 9-14, 1993.

Dobyns, Lloyd and Crawford-Mason, Clare. *Thinking about quality: Progress, wisdom, and the Deming philosophy.* Times, 1994.

Dywer, David. "Apple classrooms of tomorrow: What we've learned," in *Educational Leadership,* 51(7), 1994.

Johnson, D.W. & Johnson, R. T. *Leading the cooperative school.* Edina, MN: Interaction Book Company, 1989.

Johnson, David W., Johnson, Roger T., & Smith, Karl A. *Active learning: Cooperation in the college classroom.* Interaction, 1991. Also see Johnson, David W., Johnson, Roger T., & Smith, Karl A. *Cooperative learning: Increasing college faculty instructional productivity.* ASHE-ERIC Report on Higher Education 91-4, 1991.

Katzenbach, Jon R. & Smith, Douglas K. *The wisdom of teams: Creating the high-performance organization.* Harvard Business School Press, 1993.

Norman, Donald A. *Things that make us smart: Defending human attributes in the age of the machine.* Addison-Wesley, 1993.

Date Due